The Globalisation of School Choice?

Edited by
Martin Forsey,
Scott Davies & Geoffrey Walford

Oxford Studies in Comparative Education
Series Editor: David Phillips

SYMPOSIUM
BOOKS

Symposium Books
PO Box 204 Didcot Oxford OX11 9ZQ United Kingdom
the book publishing division of wwwords Ltd
www.symposium-books.co.uk

Published in the United Kingdom, 2008

ISBN 978-1-873927-12-0

This publication is also available on a subscription basis
as Volume 19 Number 2 of *Oxford Studies in Comparative Education*
(ISSN 0961-2149)

Typeset by wwwords Ltd
Printed and bound in the United Kingdom by Cambridge University Press

Contents

Acknowledgements

This collection results from a stimulating and very well organised two-day symposium that was sponsored by the Institute of Advanced Studies at the University of Western Australia. The editors wish to acknowledge and thank Terri-Ann White, the Director of the Institute, who facilitated the organisation of the School Choice symposium; Susan Takao, the IAS Manager who did so much of the work leading up to the meeting, and Milka Bukilic, whose administrative skills helped keep the event on track. We are also very grateful to the symposium delegates, many of whom endured long flights to Perth and, despite the jetlag, participated so enthusiastically in the meeting.

CHAPTER 1

The Globalisation of School Choice? An Introduction to Key Issues and Concerns

MARTIN FORSEY, SCOTT DAVIES & GEOFFREY WALFORD

SUMMARY As one would expect of any complex reform process, the results of recent neo-liberal reform to Australian schooling are at best unpredictable. While choice has always been part of Australian schooling, governments of all political hues have been enhancing their commitment to educational choice by increasing funding to the non-government sector. There is now no choice but to choose and parents, students, teachers, politicians and bureaucrats have been drawn further into reproducing a social system that exacerbates social inequality. However, they are not simply dominated by a new freedom of choice or by naïve consumerism. Keynesian-style welfarism remains influential enough in the political machinations accompanying the reformation of Australian schooling and, as some parents have found, the private sector does not necessarily generate greater levels of efficiency and accountability, nor are its standards automatically higher than those found in the public sector. Not only that, far from being the great source of openness, freedom and democracy that some would have us believe we will find in private enterprise, it is quite capable of squashing individual freedoms.

Choice is one of the key economic and social slogans of our time, or at least in the more economically developed nations of the globe. In a world marked by apparently infinite abundance, the logic of choice is compelling. Pushed along by desire for, and experience of, variety, profusion, richness and the possibility of reformation, people living in a variety of places are encountering a consumerist ethic that is difficult to resist. The *idea* of choice offers alluring promises of equality, freedom, democracy and pleasure that traverses political and social boundaries. It reflects and evokes deep desires for autonomy, control and self-expression. In societies built upon the liberal commitment to freedom of thought and action a commitment to the expansion of choice simultaneously reflects and helps create a common-sense understanding of how the world should be organised.

Taking a lead from Hayakawa's (1974, pp. 40-41) analysis of language in action, scrutinising words in terms of what they reveal about a person's 'state of mind' rather than what they might have to say about the facts of the matter at hand, choice is what he calls a 'purr-word'. It does not 'snarl' at us in the ways that its apparent antonyms, the concepts it is mobilised against, can do. When, in political discourse and everyday speech, 'choice' is lined up against concepts such as 'compulsion', 'regulation', 'homogeneity' and 'bureaucracy', it is clear what we are meant to like and to dislike. If it is a politician extolling the virtues of school choice, she or he can be fairly confident that the intended audience will share some degree of antipathy for the sorts of bureaucratic compulsion and homogenising regularity that the right to choose is meant to liberate us from. And as Boulton & Coldron (1996, p. 299) have shown in the British context, parents are strongly attracted to the promise of control over important decision making that the idea of educational choice is thought to bring to them.

While this volume is not arguing for the curtailing of choices being made available to people, the various authors do question and complicate the persuasive logic of consumption underpinning a commitment to choice as it is applied to various forms of education. In a radically unequal world, where some are clearly born with more choice than others, it seems imperative that we do so. But we are not simply responding out of the equally compelling logic of equality that also underpins a commitment to freedom and democracy, we are interested in the *practice* of choice in a wide variety of educational settings, as well as in the consequences and outcomes of the uneven flow around the globe of the ideas and ideals that underpin this practice.

According to Duesenberry's (1960) popular distinction between economic and sociological analysis, 'economics is all about how people make choices', while 'sociology is all about how they don't have any choices to make'. Determinism is not an issue in this collection. Despite the obvious sociological/anthropological training evident through all of the papers in this collection, there is no appetite for portraying people as dupes of the system. Nor for that matter are we interested in the economic determinism underpinning the beliefs associated with the so-called rational choices from which human action is said to be derived. Rather, we are interested in interrogating the dynamic interplay between culture, structure and agency evident in the real-world choices made by flesh and blood human beings, the constraining factors, the enabling opportunities and the more prosaic moves towards 'getting by' and 'making do' that mark the everyday activities of human subjects. The vast majority of the papers in this collection draw on a rich array of empirical data emerging from the 'local level'. They help illustrate the ways in which global ideals are always inflected through local realities and the importance of comprehending the geographic specificity of globalisation. However, before considering the implications of what is revealed through the volume, it is useful to consider some of the broader theoretical and ideological issues surrounding the question that many parents perceive to be one of the most important of their lives – at which school should I enrol my child? And as this volume shows, the dilemmas of this decision are not confined to the more economically developed world.

Economic Imperatives

Those of us born into this more economically developed world, and who are old enough to remember, can probably recall a time when business and stock market reports were not part of the daily news broadcasts on radio or television. This helps highlight how in the past three decades or so we have witnessed and experienced a dramatic increase in the influence of economic theory on social action and political practice, a movement that Henig (1990) attributes to Milton Friedman's enormously influential book *Capitalism and Freedom* (1962). Pusey (1991, p. 3) argues that since the late 1970s most nations have been driven by a conservative political agenda that has aimed at shifting the coordinating functions of society away from nation states and bureaucracies towards economies and markets. This 'hegemony of economic theory' has helped ensure that political action is now perceived and experienced as a subset of economic behaviour (Henig, 1990, pp. 653-654).

A commitment to the expansion of consumer choice is undoubtedly one of the key driving forces behind the changes we have witnessed in the relatively recent past, but as early as 1881 one of the pioneers of the discipline, Francis Edgeworth, asserted that 'the first principle of Economics is that every agent is actuated only by self-interest'. Despite the obvious oversimplification at play here, a point that Edgeworth readily acknowledged, this sort of representation of humanity persists in contemporary economic models (Sen, 1982, p. 84). It continues to exert a powerful influence on economic thinking. Rational choice theory, which assumes that all agents within a given political sphere maximise their own individual welfare by acting out of narrow self-interest, is a dominant assumption of the neoclassical economic enterprise (Johnston et al, 2000). This influential idea has generated two broad theoretical streams, that of public choice theory and social choice theory. The former emphasises the politics behind the selection of goods in the public arena, and the latter focuses on the strategies evident when groups of social agents make their mythical rational choices (see Audi, 1999; Black, 2003).

The literature on these broad topics is enormous and we are not going to replay the vexed and strikingly abstract ideas contained in this body of literature. We do, however, wish to align ourselves with scholars who see individual persons as more than *Homo economicus*. The unnecessarily impoverished nature of a theoretical base that conceives of human action as motivated exclusively by strategies aimed at maximising economic benefits is clearly challenged through this volume. Humans are not atomistic beings; they are deeply connected to the social structure in which they are embedded (Granovetter, 1985; Shepsle, 1989, p. 134). The economist Amartya Sen (1982) is correct in asserting that traditional economic theory pays insufficient attention to social structures and contexts, mainly because the *realism* of the chosen conception of humanity is usually not an object of economic inquiry (pp. 88, 99). The single-preference ordering of classical, and neoclassical, economic theory does not offer enough scope to comprehend the various interests and ideas of what should be done that underlie the actual choices and behaviours made by individual persons. Sen describes 'the *purely* economic man' as a 'social moron' and astutely observes that 'economic theory has been much preoccupied with this rational fool decked in the glory of his *one* all-purpose preference ordering' (1982, p. 99).

More than twenty years ago the sociologist Granovetter (1985, p. 484) observed that 'the idealized markets of perfect competition have survived intellectual attack in part because self-regulating economic structures are politically attractive to many'. Granovetter's proclamation remains apposite to the current era. In the wake of the reforms initiated in the mid 1980s by the Thatcher and Reagan regimes of the United Kingdom and the USA respectively, that have long since washed up onto many a shore around the globe, the convenient fiction of self-regulating economic structures remains politically attractive. These waves of reform, which emphasised the classically liberal ideals of the private over the public, individuals over collectivities, self-reliance rather than welfare, and self-discipline rather than bureaucracy, are now often situated by scholars of various political hues under the umbrella term of neo-liberalism. The political consensus has shifted in many parts of the world to the point where the so-called 'big government' of the welfare state has become the enemy of efficient and free markets, where citizens are portrayed as clients of the state or consumers of government products, and individuals are construed as the basis of community (rather than the other way round). As part of the emergent neo-liberal logic the expansion of consumer choice has trumped equity as a major political goal.

Choice as a Neo-liberal Imperative

According to one of the leading scholars of globalisation, neo-liberalism comprises a set of political economic practices based on the proposition that human well-being is best advanced by 'liberating individual entrepreneurial freedoms and skills within an institutional framework characterised by strong private property rights, free markets and free trade' (Harvey, 2005, p. 2). The state's role, one that is often not acknowledged, is to provide the basic infrastructure and institutions necessary to secure private property rights and the functioning of the market. If necessary, this is achieved by force. Current forms of neo-liberalism are closely associated with the push for a globally unified economy. The growing power and influence of transnational corporations and the organisations that protect their interests is significant. In terms of the latter, by far the three most significant are the World Trade Organisation, the World Bank, and the International Monetary Fund. The practices associated with the development of so-called free markets on this global scale, such as structural adjustment and debt repayments, are so varied and massive in scale that it can be difficult to trace their many impacts, intended or otherwise (Forsey & Lockhart, 2004).

According to Harvey (2005, p. 65), neo-liberals aim to generate competition by fusing privatisation and deregulation together. The advocates of this philosophical approach to human organisation advocate a competitive environment because of its ability to eliminate red tape and to increase efficiency and productivity. Additionally, competition is also said to mitigate overt and covert consumer costs through the production of cheaper commodities and services and by reducing the tax burden. While Kipnis in his discussion of Chinese education systems in this volume challenges assertions that a commitment to privatised, deregulated state institutions is a necessary condition for the production of hugely competitive and seemingly efficient and productive systems of human enterprise, the broader point we wish to make here is that the real-world consequences of economic and institutional reform are never as straightforward as neo-liberal advocates posit them to be. Granovetter (1985) has pointed out that in classical and neoclassical economics the social relations of human subjects, if they are acknowledged at all, are treated as 'a frictional drag that impedes competitive markets' (Granovetter, 1985, p. 484). While economists may be disinclined to pay attention to the messiness of actual practice, the gaps between the rhetoric that justifies the reform and its actual practice are not only striking, but are important because they can, and should, inform future policy developments.

As already indicated, choice is a difficult concept to argue against, but looking at it as an example of language in action, the effects of choice policies are not necessarily as benign as their stated intentions suggest. A number of researchers in different parts of the world have commented on the ways in which the neo-liberal emphasis on choice has reshaped earlier concerns with equity and social welfare (Jenson & Sineau, 2001, p. 241; Daune-Richard & Mahon, 2001; Kershaw, 2004, p. 928; Forsey, 2004, Walford, 2006). Writing about child care in Canada, Kershaw (2004, p. 928) draws an explicit link between the language of choice and the articulation of neo-liberal principles. He argues that this has happened within a politically neutral rhetorical framework that shifts the responsibility for social inequality to individual citizens (Kershaw, 2004, p. 928). In Sweden, according to Daune-Richard & Mahon (2001, p. 161), market choice has been posited as the means for truly respecting difference and variety in the light of the apparent failure to do so within standardised solutions offered by the paternalistic welfare state. And the rhetoric is seductive; as Boulton & Coldron (1996, p. 299) show out of their research among British parents, even those who have not been particularly concerned about choosing a particular school for their child still place high value on the availability of choice. For these researchers the conclusion is clear: 'educational discourse has shifted to embrace the ideology of competition and market forces'.

Institutional Imperatives

But today's calls for choice are being voiced in a particular institutional context that preceded the spread of contemporary neo-liberal thought. The twentieth century, particularly in the post-World War II era, ushered in a revolution of mass education enrolments, and constructed public school systems even in the poorest of nations. A multitude of 'one-best-systems' have been established around the world, most rooted in a global template of mass education. Choice policies are very much an aftermath of this worldwide institutionalisation of schooling. Neo-liberal and other forces are taking existing organisational templates and are variously reshaping them in unique ways across and within different nations. Further, choice agendas are being influenced by other broad policy currents, particularly those that aim to promote quality assurance and academic standards. Many states are implementing standardised test score regimens to gauge levels of learning among students and compare them across jurisdictions. Indeed, comparisons of these scores are increasingly international. These 'quality' reforms are also often paired with 'choice' reforms in wide-ranging reform agendas that attempt to harness schooling to strategies for wealth creation (e.g. Finn, 2002). But quality reforms sometimes stand in tension with choice; whereas choice programmes are premised on the necessity of decentralising power by stimulating market forces in ways that presumably empower parents and teachers, quality assurance frameworks often serve to centralise governance over education, and redirect much decision-making power to the hands of bureaucrats. The different ways in which these broad reform agendas interact in each country provides another source of international variation.

School Choice as Global Policy

The worldwide institutionalising of education over the twentieth century occurred largely through bureaucratic methods of organisation. Bureaucracy used to enjoy higher levels of communal agreement in the industrialised world, and was seen to deliver fairness and efficiency to national populations; a consensus that has been undermined in recent years (Connell et al, 1982, p. 19). In response to a perceived crisis in national economic competitiveness felt in a range of nation-states, the last twenty-five years or so has seen a new global education policy consensus emerge. Not surprisingly, given the current ascendancy of neo-liberalism, this new programme advocates the flattening of bureaucratic structures, a greater focus on excellence ahead of equity, and shifting the emphasis of national governance from citizenship and service towards clientship and consumerism (Adnett & Davies, 1999, p. 221; Lingard, 2000, p. 84). The belief is that greater levels of equality are only achievable through the sorts of excellence promoted by 'market devolution' and the privatisation of public institutions (Lingard et al, 2002, p. 12).

Chubb & Moe (1990), two political scientists who have been particularly influential on education policy in the USA and beyond, were among the first scholar-activists to clearly articulate a programme of market-based reform of schooling. Readily borrowing ideas from Thatcher's Britain (Chubb & Moe, 1992), they count themselves among the many who believe that 'centralization and bureaucratization are substantially at odds with the effective organisation of schools and the successful provision of education' (1990, p. 142). They assert that for government schools to become substantially more effective, the institutions managing them must cede control to individual schools (pp. 183-184). Indeed, they argue elsewhere (Chubb & Moe, 1988) that private schools provide the die upon which public schools should be shaped, a view that has become politically orthodox in many different polities (Edwards et al, 1985; Tooley, 2000; Brown, 2002; Forsey, 2007). In developing countries, where educational equity is usually even more problematic than it is in the industrial nations, structural adjustment policies have been imposed largely as a means of ensuring stability for foreign capital (Morrow & Torres, 2000, pp. 43, 52). These policies, which are normally associated with correcting imbalances between foreign accounts and domestic consumption and the ameliorative remedies of deregulation and privatisation of the economy, are often correlated with public sector austerity (Carnoy, 1995, p. 653). Some of the consequences for education systems in these developing nations have included reductions in public funding for education programmes, an increased emphasis on private education initiatives, and a concomitant reduction in the amounts of household income available for the education of children (Reimers & Tiburcio, 1993, p. 14). In other instances, equity concerns are increasingly embedded within choice and quality frameworks. One prominent example is the US *No Child Left Behind Act*, which attempts to join quality and equity goals by extending choice to students in schools deemed to be low performing. Another example is provided by voucher programmes that are targeted to disadvantaged populations. Neo-liberal thinking has reshaped the policy landscape in many countries not by entirely eliminating equity concerns but rather by re-embedding them within choice and accountability frameworks.

In warning against seeing the new political configurations of our time as 'monolithic projects imposed upon passive victims', Larner (2005, p. 12), a social geographer, urges researchers to pay attention to the specificities of neo-liberal political economies, and to be sensitive to the complex, hybrid 'political imaginaries these new spaces, socialities and subjects are likely to embody'. This was certainly a significant part of the rationale for the symposium that brought these papers together. The anthropologist Appadurai (1996) urges us to think of globalisation as a current, a tide, as a flow of ideas, of capital and people, of material goods, of policies and practices. As already suggested, the flow of ideas and policies is uneven, and as Appadurai has argued, it is important to acknowledge the uneven ways in which they embed themselves into local cultural-political landscapes. The implementation of national and regional educational policies cannot be understood separately from the specific sociocultural settings in which they become embedded (Phillips, 1992; Walford, 2001). Inevitably, the ideals and ideas lose at least some of their internal coherence as they are incorporated into the local political systems. Showing this complexity is part of the point of this collection.

Outlining the Chapters

The chapters gathered together here emerged from a symposium held at the University of Western Australia (UWA) in late 2006. Convened by the authors of this introduction, our aim was to develop a range of empirically-based research profiles from a wide variety of nation-states to explore a significant global trend. With the generous support and sponsorship of the Institute of Advanced Studies at UWA we were able to realise this aim. The collection of chapters shows that while some nations have managed to resist the neo-liberal imperative to diversify and privatise school systems, the vast majority have embraced the ideology of competition and market forces at least to some degree, although it is important to acknowledge straight away that some nations have been cajoled and bullied into opening their arms as part of a structural adjustment of the body politic.

The first substantive chapter by Christopher Lubienski examines the choice movement in the United States. While the USA has not been the prime world leader in the actual use of market mechanisms in schooling, it does have a disproportionate presence on the global educational scene, serving as an aggressive exporter of neo-liberal, market-driven educational policies. Lubienski describes the growth of different forms of choice reforms, and summarises the growing body of research (including his own) of charter schools and voucher programmes. This comprehensive review leads Lubienski to be sceptical about the ability of choice mechanisms to consistently produce school outcomes that are more efficient, equitable, or effective. Yet Lubienski finds that this paucity of supporting evidence has not deterred choice advocates. Some are simply avoiding independent, peer-review processes in favour of writing 'op-eds' or publishing for in-house think-tank outlets. Others are replacing their original empirical claims about the performance-enhancing power of markets with more normative arguments about the harmlessness of choice. Lubienski concludes that despite the accessibility of technically-refined research on school choice, American policy making is increasingly reverting to an ideological mandate, and may be increasingly disconnected from empirical findings. Using some illustrative cases, Lubienski links this trend to a changing policy-making arena that is increasingly politicised, and a new political economy of research production in which partisan advocates can bypass traditional scholarly processes that were designed to instil an element of quality control. In this new 'marketplace' of research, he notes, rigour is often less important than talking points, rapid response, and institutional branding, and calls for free markets are heavily subsidised by well-resourced advocacy groups.

Scott Davies & Janice Aurini argue that Canada's school choice movement has imported and adapted American understandings of choice in ways that underplay market rationales. Rather than hailing choice as a mechanism to boost test scores or desegregate minority students, Canadian choice-seekers appear to be energised by emerging middle-class parenting cultures. Davies & Aurini connect school choice to 'concerted cultivation', an intensive form of parenting in which middle-class parents increasingly structure their children's lives and treat them as projects-in-the-making. Sociologists typically invoke this concept to link the varying strategies that parents use to align their child-rearing practices with school requirements, such as providing their children with extra lessons, assisting with them homework, or lobbying educators for prized spots in special school programmes, and to emphasise how such parental resources are unequally distributed by class and race. Davies & Aurini extend the concept of concerted cultivation by linking this parental agency to school choice, noting that choice-seeking alters parental relations with public educators from mere supportive roles to more directing and even adversarial roles. To substantiate their argument, Davies & Aurini first present survey data showing that wealthier and more educated parents are more likely to engage in choice seeking, and that choosers are more likely to embrace contentious notions of parental authority. They next present focus group data that illustrate how choice proponents rationalise their actions. Davies & Aurini find that choice advocates acknowledge concerns about the potential threat of choice policies to equity, but then redraw moral boundaries by portraying choice as a responsible and necessary form of parental involvement in schooling. They interpret these findings as illustrating new forms of parental agency and expressive cultural ideals in processes of class reproduction.

Focusing on his home town of Perth, the capital of Western Australia, Martin Forsey reports on research conducted among parents and their children regarding their educational choices. The people targeted for this research all chose to change systems, either from so-called 'private' schools to the government education system, or vice versa. While choice has always been part of Australia's schooling systems, governments of all political hues have been busily enhancing their commitment to opening up educational choices for parents and students through increasing funding to the non-government sector. There is no choice but to choose argues Forsey, but he notes that the attempts to 'de-governmentalise the state' in education is not the source of unbridled joy and satisfaction among the Australian population. Parents, students, teachers, politicians and bureaucrats have been drawn further into reproducing a social system that exacerbates social inequality but they are not simply dominated by a new freedom of choice or by naïve consumerism. As Forsey shows, Keynesian style welfarism remains an influential enough element in the political machinations accompanying the reformation of Australian schooling. The free market is rarely ever free, and, as some of the parents interviewed found, the private sector does not necessarily generate greater levels of efficiency and accountability, nor are their standards automatically higher than those found in the public sector. Not only that, far from being the great source of openness, freedom and democracy that some would have us believe we will find in private enterprise, they are quite capable of squashing individual freedoms. As one would expect of any complex reform process, the results of recent neo-liberal reform to Australian schooling are at best unpredictable.

Geoffrey Walford's chapter reviews the history of school choice in England, focusing particularly on the motivations for changes in 1988 and in subsequent years. It argues that, rather than being a case of 'policy borrowing' from Australia, the changes that occurred in England were more a case of 'policy corruption'. England now has a well-established choice system in the state sector and there has been a considerable amount of research conducted on it. This chapter describes and evaluates several of these studies and discusses the relationship between greater choice of school and increased standards of attainment. It then examines the research work that has been conducted on the effects of choice on social segregation and finds mixed results.

The next chapter, by Izhar Oplatka, focuses on controlled choice within the city of Tel Aviv, Israel. Tel Aviv can be divided into three large socio-economic areas with large differences between the three. During the late 1960s attempts were made to ensure greater integration between different ethnic and social groups by bussing children from one area to another. In the 1990s, however, this system has gradually been replaced by one of controlled choice where parents are given a list of schools in different areas to choose from. The schools were encouraged to differentiate themselves from one another in terms of curriculum, extracurricular activities and teaching methods, and to establish clear criteria for admission. The education authority uses these choices to give as many people as possible their first choice while ensuring that all schools have a demographic make-up that is a fair representation of the population of the city as a whole. Oplatka argues that the reform was a result of a combination of integrative, egalitarian values with liberal, pluralist ones. He then examines how schools and parents have reacted to these changes. First, he investigates the marketing messages to be found in school prospectuses and through interviews with principals. Then he reports on interviews with parents. Oplatka finds that both the schools' and parents' responses were more closely linked to individualistic, liberal and competitive values than to collective and egalitarian ones.

Mariano Narodowski's chapter examines the escalating provision of private schooling in Argentina. After a half century of steady growth, 25% of all student enrolments are now in the private sector, with wealthier families having practically exited the public system. In 2003, 92% of households in the highest income quintile sent their children to private schools, compared to only 8% of the poorest quintile. Searching for conceptual tools to understand this trend, Narodowski reasons that the Argentine Government can no longer be said to wield a 'state monopoly' on education, to borrow Milton Friedman's phrase. Instead, the public and private sectors co-exist in equilibrium between a 'quasi-monopoly' and a 'quasi-market'. Since most parents who can afford private schools have now opted out of the public system, that system can spend more money per pupil than it could previously. The private system consists of hybrid institutions that partly compete according to market rules, and yet also draw some state funds for teachers' wages, which lower their operation costs. Yet, Narodowski is struck by the continual thriving of private schools in Argentina, despite their lack of larger subsidies, and despite the absence of choice programmes or voucher experiments that might further stimulate their growth. Why then are private schools increasingly popular among Argentina's upper and middle classes? According to Narodowski, higher income families are seeking private schools as part of a broader process of social self-segregation. In a Bourdieuian process of distinction, these families are using private schools to differentiate themselves culturally from lower socio-economic status groups, and to construct exclusive identities based on notions of needing to protect their children from increasingly violent and dangerous public spaces. Yet, despite this rising inequality, both school segments are relatively stable, Narodowski contends, since the public system can now spend more per capita funds on needy students, while the private sector can attract an ample clientele and enjoy much governing leeway.

Educational opportunity in Tanzania, according to Kristin Phillips & Amy Stambach, is characterised more by 'being chosen' than it is by consumerist principles. In one of the poorest nations in the world, wealth is to be found in people, and poverty simultaneously refers to both destitution and not having enough children to support parents in old age. Cultivating educational opportunities for at least one child offers the promise of a safer future for parents, a process that involves a delicate balance of building social relationships. Drawing on intensive field research conducted in two socio-economically contrasting areas of Tanzania, Phillips & Stambach argue that the notion of school choice is peripheral to everyday social contexts of Tanzania. Reflecting on the history and contexts of formal schooling in the two research sites, they reveal the various 'hands' at work in Tanzania's educational systems. Phillips & Stambach uncover the mythical status of the free-standing subject exercising a right to educational choice from a free-floating range of educational options that is so fondly propounded by marketeers. There is little that is 'free' about educational opportunities in Tanzania; not only are fees prohibitive, the opportunities for secondary schooling are rarely 'open' chances for enrolment. Opportunities surface only in the context of social relations, and Phillips & Stambach's ethnography shows very clearly how people cultivate horizontal relationships of reciprocity at the same time as they place themselves at the debt and the mercy of richer benefactors. Unlike other types of political jurisdictions, in Tanzania choice does not offer a means of mobilising sympathy or support for access to education, much less access to a specific quality of education. Rather, it is the cultivation of relationships – with neighbours, extended family, patrons, and God – that provides the means for accessing the all too scarce opportunities for educational advancement.

Andrew Kipnis offers a richly detailed description of the policies of one county in rural China that are aimed mostly at preventing school choice. At the same time they promote intensive competition between students as individuals, classes of students, teachers, schools, principals and school districts, as well as 'quality' audits that are often absurd in their scientistic nature. The county government does not encourage school choice, but occasionally allows it to happen when it feels a need to raise revenues and can identify a means of earning money by allowing a minority of wealthy parents to exercise some rather limited choices. The opportunity for choice is neither valued in itself nor linked to an ideology of freedom. The county government's combination of governing techniques can be said to have a coherent logic of sorts, but this logic cannot be explained by the type of analysis that sees the promotion of competition and audit as going together with school choice as forms of neo-liberalism. Rather, what is happening in rural China is that competition is valued as a tool for disciplining students and teachers, and this discipline is valued in and of itself, for a wide variety of reasons.

Prachi Srivastava's chapter explores the tremendous growth of low-fee private (LFP) schools in India by outlining and explaining the school choice processes of one group of disadvantaged households accessing the LFP sector in the Lucknow district of Uttar Pradesh. Rejecting notions of 'false consciousness' and 'dependency' among the poorer parents in economically developing countries choosing private educational options for their children, Srivastava shows very clearly that the parents in Uttar Pradesh are very actively engaged in the choice process. There are problems with this of course, not least because of the deleterious effects the movement to the LFP sector can have on the state education sector in India. Contrary to India's official policy of Education for All, schools were conceptualised by Srivastava's informants as operating in highly marketised, privatised and hierarchical schooling arenas, a reality that challenges official Indian visions of a 'common school system' aimed at providing a universally available and equitable education system. The research participants in the study placed much greater value on the LFP sector than the state, and chose it for almost all of their children, even if the sector did not provide 'good' quality in any objective sense. Unless the state sector can convince parents that it can provide meaningful education opportunities for all, it is sowing the seeds for its own demise. If the state sector is as bad as it is perceived and documented to be, argues Srivastava, the resultant cream-skimming of clients even from among disadvantaged groups does not augur well for the future of schooling for the most disadvantaged peoples of India. While greater school choice through the LFP sector seems desirable to some disadvantaged groups, it may also be highly inequitable if it does not allow the state system to recuperate in any way.

The chapter by Lesley Vidovich & Yap Meen Sheng explores the development of school choice in Singapore through private international schools. From independence in 1965, the Singaporean Government invested heavily in education, and schooling was characterised by a high degree of centralised control. School diversity and choice were minimal until the late 1980s saw cautious steps towards enhanced school autonomy and limited privatisation. In the early 2000s the Government's renewed, yet restricted, moves to enhance school privatisation and choice were embedded in a broader economic goal to turn Singapore into a 'global schoolhouse' which sought to offer a diverse and distinctive mix of quality education services to the world. It was believed that international full-fee customers would be attracted to Singapore's new privately-funded, international schools. Concurrently, the outflow of local students purchasing education in other countries would be slowed because the Government would allow them to choose to enrol in Singapore-based international schools for the first time. Thus, school choice in Singapore has a strong international dimension, consistent with Singapore's active engagement with globalisation and its attempts to forge lucrative international education markets in a knowledge-based economy.

Their chapter examines two new privately-funded, international schools that opened in Singapore in 2005 and argues that, although restricted in scale, the policy shift was symbolically significant. Although the Government does not directly fund these new schools, they must comply with key national education policies. The configuration of school choice in Singapore suggests a confluence of deregulatory and regulatory policies, with all of the inherent tensions. Using the results of parental surveys and other material, the authors show how the Singaporean Government is strongly steering school choice, and simultaneously navigating both local and global education markets.

Finally, the chapter by Julian Dierkes examines two related aspects of choice in Japan. First, the chapter gives an overview of the recent introduction of choice within the public primary and secondary sectors. There, the moves towards choice that have occurred in the late twentieth and early twenty-first centuries have been designed mainly to diversify the system in order to promote a more individualistic and potentially creative workforce and to encourage poorly performing schools to reform themselves through competitive pressures. But the number of municipalities with choice programmes is still very limited, and it is too early to be able to assess the effects of the change.

In contrast, the second part of Dierkes's chapter examines an area where there has long been freedom of choice – the private 'shadow education' system of the for-profit afternoon and evening *juku*. Within metropolitan areas, in particular, a whole system of supplementary 'cram schools' has flourished for more than thirty years. Drawing on his current research into the nature of these *juku*, Dierkes describes some of the diversity of the sector. He shows that the free market has not produced diversity of teaching approaches, but a minute differentiation of education offerings to target populations that remains wedded to the overall educational philosophy of the Japanese curriculum and examination system.

The Globalisation of School Choice?

So, what do the essays gathered in this volume show? Offering a thorough engagement with empirical realities in a range of geographical and socio-economic areas, they suggest that calls for choice in education are indeed global, but their spread has been uneven and assume forms and emphases that depend upon the local social, political, economic and historical contexts. While there is a general concern about increasing inequality in the wake of the reforms to the organisation of educational systems that have taken place across the globe in the past three decades or so, the book's wide range of nations reveals differences and similarities in school choice reform and its effects on the organisation and practice of schooling. The collections suggest that globalisation is best understood through the prism of the local, and challenge any grand generalisations about the effects of the significant raft of policy developments that emerged from the Thatcher/Reagan reorganisation of public institutions. School choice reforms assume a wide variety of incarnations from country to country. The vocabulary of 'choice' provides a loose and malleable language for a variety of actors to pursue widely ranging goals. Importantly, choice frameworks can incorporate the interests of even those actors who otherwise have little affinity with market thinking in education (Davies & Quirke, 2005; Aurini & Davies, 2005). Beyond its neo-liberal advocates, religious, ethnic and linguistic minorities in many countries are adapting the phrasing of 'choice' to suit their assorted interests. The strength of this collection lies in the close attention it pays to the ways in which choice ideals have to be adapted to fit more comfortably to local political landscapes. It also shows that choice is often not the most appropriate term to use when describing what has happened in recent reformation of schooling systems. While the movement towards private educational options can in theory open up educational opportunities in state sectors that always operate in a limited financial environment, in practice it often results in further diminution of state-run schools. In other words, the options available to people have all too often become more limited in the new choice environments produced across the globe.

References

Adnett, Nick & Davies, Peter (1999) Schooling Quasi-Markets: reconciling economic and sociological analyses, *British Journal of Educational Studies*, 47(3), 221-234. http://dx.doi.org/10.1111/1467-8527.00115

Appadurai, Arjun (1996) *Modernity at Large: cultural dimensions of globalization.* Minneapolis: University of Minnesota Press.

Audi, Robert (1999) Social Choice Theory, in *The Cambridge Dictionary of Philosophy.* Cambridge: Cambridge University Press.

Aurini, Janice & Davies, Scott (2005) Choice without Markets: homeschooling in the context of private education, *British Journal of Sociology of Education*, 26(4), 461-474. http://dx.doi.org/10.1080/01425690500199834

Black, John (2003) Public Choice, in *A Dictionary of Economics.* Oxford: Oxford University Press.

Boulton, Pam & Coldron, John (1996) Does the Rhetoric Work? Parental Responses to New Right Policy Assumptions, *British Journal of Educational Studies*, 44(3), 296-306. http://dx.doi.org/10.2307/3122457

Brown, Frank (2002) Privatization of Public Elementary and Secondary Education in the United States of America, *Education and the Law*, 14(1), 99-115. http://dx.doi.org/10.1080/09539960220149218

Carnoy, Martin (1995) Structural Adjustment and the Changing Face of Education, *International Labour Review*, 134(6), 653-673.

Chubb, J. & Moe, T. (1988) Politics, Markets and the Organization of Schools, *American Political Science Review*, 82(4), 1065-1087.

Chubb, J. & Moe, T. (1990) *Politics, Markets and America's Schools.* Washington, DC: The Brookings Institution. http://dx.doi.org/10.2307/1961750

Chubb, J. & Moe, T. (1992) *A Lesson in School Reform from Great Britain.* Washington, DC: The Brookings Institution.

Connell, R., Ashenden, D., Kessler, S. & Dowsett, G. (1982) *Making the Difference: schools, families and social division.* Sydney: George Allen & Unwin.

Daune-Richard, Anne-Marie & Mahon, Rianne (2001) Sweden: model in crisis, in *Who Cares? Women's Work, Childcare and Welfare State Redesigns.* Toronto: Toronto University Press.

Davies, Scott & Quirke, Linda (2005) Providing for the Priceless Student: ideologies of choice in an emerging educational market, *American Journal of Education*, 111(4), 523-547. http://dx.doi.org/10.1086/431182

Duesenberry, James (1960) Comment on an Economic Analysis of Fertility, in *Demographic and Economic Change in Developed Countries: a conference of the Universities-National Bureau Committee for Economic Research.* Princeton: Princeton University Press.

Edgeworth, Francis (1881) *Mathematical Psychics: an essay on the application of mathematics to the moral sciences*. London: Kegan Paul.

Edwards, Tony, Fitz, John & Whitty, Geoff (1985) Private Schools and Public Funding: a comparison of recent policies in England and Australia, *Comparative Education*, 21(1), 29-45. http://dx.doi.org/10.1080/0305006850210104

Finn, Chester E. (2002) Real Accountability in K-12 Education: the marriage of Ted and Alice, in M.E. Williamson & H.J. Walberg (Eds) *School Accountability*. Stanford: Hoover Institution Press.

Forsey, Martin (2004) Equity versus Excellence: responses to neo-liberal ideals in a government high school, *Anthropological Forum*, 14(3), 283-296. http://dx.doi.org/10.1080/0066467042000269530

Forsey, Martin (2007) *Challenging the System? A Dramatic Tale of Neo-liberal Reform in an Australian High School*. Charlotte: Information Age Publishing.

Forsey, Martin & Lockhart, Chris (2004) Guest Editors' Introduction: Neo-liberalism in Australia, *Anthropological Forum*, 14(3), 227-235.

Friedman, Milton (1962) *Capitalism and Freedom*. Chicago: University of Chicago Press.

Granovetter, Mark (1985) Economic Action and Social Structure: the problem of embeddedness, *American Journal of Sociology*, 91(3), 481-510. http://dx.doi.org/10.1086/228311

Harvey, D. (2005) *A Brief History of Neoliberalism*. Oxford: Oxford University Press.

Hayakawa. S.I. (1974) *Language in Thought and Action*. London: George Allen & Unwin.

Henig, Jeffrey (1990) Privatization in the United States: theory and practice, *Political Science Quarterly*, 104(4), 649-670. http://dx.doi.org/10.2307/2151103

Jenson, Jane & Sineau, Mariette (2001) *Who Cares? Women's Work, Childcare and Welfare State Redesigns*. Toronto: Toronto University Press.

Johnston, R.J., Gregory, Derek, Pratt, Geraldine & Watts, Michael (2000) Public Choice Theory, in *The Dictionary of Human Geography*. London: Blackwell.

Kershaw, Paul (2004) Choice Discourse in BC Child Care: distancing policy from research, *Canadian Journal of Political Science*, 37(4), 927-950. http://dx.doi.org/10.1017/S0008423904990142

Larner, W. (2005) Neoliberalism in (Regional) Theory and Practice: the Stronger Communities Action Fund in New Zealand, *Geographical Research*, 43(1), 9-18. http://dx.doi.org/10.1111/j.1745-5871.2005.00294.x

Lingard, Bob (2000) It Is and It Isn't: vernacular globalization, education policy, and restructuring, in N. Burbules & C. Torres (Eds) *Globalization and Education: critical perspectives*, 79-108. New York and London: Routledge.

Lingard, Bob, Hayes, D. & Mills, M. (2002) Developments in School-based Management: the specific case of Queensland, Australia, *Journal of Educational Administration*, 40(1), 6-30. http://dx.doi.org/10.1108/09578230210415625

Morrow, R. & Torres, C. (2000) The State, Globalization and Educational Policy, in N. Burbules & C. Torres (Eds) *Globalization and Education: critical perspectives*, 27-56. London and New York: Routledge.

Phillips, D. (1992) Borrowing Educational Policy, *Oxford Studies in Comparative Education*, 2(2), 49-55.

Pusey, M. (1991) *Economic Rationalism in Canberra: a nation building state changes its mind.* Cambridge: Cambridge University Press.

Reimers, Frenand & Tiburcio, Luis (1993) *Education, Adjustment and Reconstruction: options for change.* Paris: UNESCO.

Sen, Amartya (1982) *Choice, Welfare and Measurement.* Oxford: Blackwell.

Shepsle, Kenneth A. (1989) Studying Institutions: some lessons from the rational choice approach, *Journal of Theoretical Politics*, 1(2), 131-147. http://dx.doi.org/10.1177/0951692889001002002

Tooley, James (2000) *Reclaiming Education.* London: Cassell.

Walford, G. (2001) Privatization in Industrial Countries, in H Levin (Ed.) *Privatizing Education: can the marketplace deliver choice, efficiency, equity and social cohesion?* 178-199. Boulder: Westview Press.

Walford, Geoffrey (2006) *Markets and Equity in Education.* London: Continuum.

CHAPTER 2

School Choice Research in the United States and Why It Doesn't Matter: the evolving economy of knowledge production in a contested policy domain

CHRISTOPHER LUBIENSKI

SUMMARY School choice has flourished in recent years in the United States, expanding in a number of forms across almost all areas of the country. Yet even as policy makers enthusiastically embrace charter schools, voucher plans for private schools, and other school choice programs, the research basis for these programs appears to be tenuous, at best. This chapter offers a brief overview of the growth of various forms of school choice, and then examines the research for two of the most prominent models: charter schools and vouchers for private schools. The review indicates that these programs are not performing as market-based reformers claim in terms of academic achievement – the most anticipated outcome for school choice programs. However, the disjuncture between the rapid expansion of these programs and their weak empirical record illustrates the influence of a coalition of policy advocates/researchers, media, and think tanks in asserting a consensus not necessarily supported by research, and the power of these coalitions in producing the 'information' needed to justify ideologically-driven policy decisions. The concluding discussion considers the new political economy of education research in the USA, noting the changing roles of researchers in universities and advocacy groups, and pointing to the further politicization and commercialization of research.

School choice as a reform movement has blossomed and matured in the USA over the past two decades. In that time, research on school choice policies has also developed, apparently advancing beyond its early incarnation as little more than an ideological commentary on the appropriateness or rejection of market forces in public education. However, there is a growing distance between school choice policies in the USA and an evidentiary basis for those policies. Even as the research around school choice has developed, policy making increasingly reverts back to an ideological, not empirical mandate. This disjuncture on this issue epitomizes a new policy-making arena characterized by the continued politicization, and emerging commercialization, of research.

The US case is instructive for understanding the changing relationship between outcomes and policy making around this issue, not only regarding more marketized school reforms, but in a more marketized policy-making environment as well. The USA represents a presence on the global scale disproportionate to its actual size, and, in many ways, it also serves as the intellectual center of the global movement for using market models in education. Thus, while the ideas promoted by US policy elites are often further developed in other nations, it is useful to consider the rapid expansion of choice programs in the USA over the last decade, particularly in light of research on outcomes of those programs.

As school choice plans have grown in the USA, we now have a relatively extensive empirical basis from which to evaluate outcomes of school choice policies, in light of the goals set out for them. However, despite the rhetoric that predominates in policy arenas, the overall results reflected in this research do not provide the compelling evidence that many expected and wish to find emerging from choice programs. Indeed, a comprehensive review of the research indicates that the initial, optimistic expectations for outcomes such as more efficient and effective school organizational behaviors, more equitable educational opportunities, and (especially) improved academic outcomes are not supported by the growing body of research on these questions. Instead, we are seeing significant shifts in the discourse supporting school choice – from claims about the empirically demonstrable power of markets in enhancing performance to more values-based arguments about the appropriateness and harmlessness of choice.

Still, the popularity of choice programs among policy makers continues to grow in the USA, both at the state and national levels. This is largely due to the political and media savvy of influential advocacy coalitions that have coalesced around the choice issue. Concerted groups of think tanks, issue organizations, and policy advocates in academia have demonstrated a notable ability to shape policy discourse and action around this issue primarily by shaping public and policy maker perceptions through engagement with the media regarding research on the issue. Using a few illustrative cases, this chapter highlights the role of school choice advocacy coalitions in creating a new political economy of research production and dissemination around US policy making. A key component of this effort is the strategy of bypassing and thus marginalizing traditional scholarly processes that were designed to instill an element of quality control on knowledge production. In this new 'marketplace' of ideas, research rigor is often less important than talking points, rapid response, and institutional branding, all driven by a well-resourced coalition of advocacy groups. In the new 'marketplace' of ideas, ideas calling for free markets are heavily subsidized.

The chapter begins with a brief overview of the growth of different forms of school choice reforms in the USA in recent decades. Next is a summary of the research on the two most prominent forms of choice, charter schools and voucher programs for students to attend private schools. While noting several of the promises made to advance these policies, the focus here is on the most prominent argument for choice in the USA: gains in academic achievement. The last half of the chapter examines the rising role of advocacy coalitions in asserting a consensus not necessarily supported by research, and the power of these coalitions in producing the evidence needed to justify ideologically-driven policy decisions. The concluding discussion considers the new political economy of education research in the USA, noting the changing roles of researchers in universities and advocacy groups, and pointing to the further politicization and commercialization of research.

School Choice Programs in the USA[1]

Of course, US education has not necessarily been in the forefront of the global movement toward market mechanisms for the production and distribution of schooling. Other nations, such as Chile and New Zealand, have gone further and faster in developing comprehensive, nation-wide school choice systems. But examining school choice in the USA is an interesting endeavor, if only because of America's prominent role in the global arena as an aggressive exporter of neo-liberal, market-driven social policies. Moreover, it serves as an instructive case regarding the production and use of research to inform such policy. Indeed, choice has become more pervasive in US education in recent years, and represents one of the most celebrated and contested examples of the use of market mechanisms for organizing public services. Charter schools, voucher programs, open-enrollment plans, home schooling, private schooling, and the federal No Child Left Behind (NCLB) Act all illustrate the increasing popularity of choice.

In general, students in the USA are assigned to particular public schools according to their home address. Nearly three-quarters of students attend their assigned schools, but many parents have a range of choices in selecting schools for their children. These choices include an increasing number of options in both the (tax-funded) public and (tuition-based) private sectors. According to one estimate, the percentage of students attending 'schools of choice' has increased from 20% in 1993 to 26% in 2003 (US Department of Education, 2006).

Of course, in a residence-based scheme, parents with the means can 'choose' a school through Tiebout-style sorting by deciding to locate to a particular neighborhood (Tiebout, 1956). In 2003, 24% of parents reported that they moved to their current location for the school, and presumably a greater percentage have this option, even if they do not actively exercise it. Middle and upper class parents and urban parents were more likely to report moving for a particular school (US Department of Education, 2006). However, 'school choice' in the USA is generally understood to refer to particular programs, typically provided through government policies (or, in some instances, through privately sponsored programs). These programs range from plans that reflect a stronger government role in providing and regulating school services, to more laissez-faire arrangements in which the state plays little or no role.

Public School Choice

Parents in many school districts can send their children to the assigned public school, or choose another public school within the district – an option that is provided for in cases of 'failing' neighborhood schools through the federal NCLB legislation. In some cases, parents can also choose public schools in other school districts, but this policy is usually voluntary by district, meaning that districts cannot keep students from leaving, but may exclude students from outside their boundaries, or students from certain districts (Lubienski, 2005).

In 2003, 15% of all students attended a 'chosen' public school, while 51% of students' parents reported having the opportunity to send them to a chosen public school. A significantly higher percentage of African American students (42%) than white students (22%) attended a chosen public school when they had the opportunity (US Department of Education, 2006). Parents can sometimes choose specialized public schools to which they were not assigned by location. In the 1960s and 1970s, many urban centers attempted to desegregate their schools while stemming 'white flight' to suburban districts through well-resourced specialty schools called 'magnet schools'. These schools are managed by districts, but are often selective in admissions, and established around a certain curricular theme or specialty. In the 2001-02 school year, there were 1736 magnet schools serving 3% of all students. The prevalence of magnet schools varies widely between states, and two states account for more than half of all magnet schools (Hoffman, 2003).

Charter Schools

Charter schools are publicly funded schools managed independently of direct state administration – representing a public–private hybrid approach to provision. Charter schools are the most rapidly growing form of public school choice. Since they were first authorized through the efforts of progressive educators and lawmakers in Minnesota in 1991, they have proliferated quite rapidly across 40 states (and the District of Columbia). They are technically 'public schools' in the USA, typically authorized by a public governing body, and receive funding on a per-pupil basis. However, most charter schools have at least some degree of exemption from conventional public school regulations. They tend to be smaller schools, and often utilize specialized instructional approaches (Snyder & Hoffman, 2003).[2] Charter schools are usually managed by non-profit organizations, but charters can be granted to for-profit businesses in some states. Students are generally admitted on a 'first come, first served' basis or by lottery. There are estimated to be 3977 charter schools operating in 2006-07, serving over 1.1 million students, or 2.3% of total public school enrollment (Center for Education Reform, 2006). This represents approximately 400% growth in the last eight years. Charter schools, which are frequently located in urban areas, are more likely than conventional public schools overall to have a higher percentage of minority students, but the degree to which they serve more disadvantaged students is disputed (Snyder & Hoffman, 2003; Carnoy et al, 2005).

Private Schools

Many parents choose to send their children to private schools, which are usually run by religious organizations, and recent legislation has made this option somewhat more feasible for poor and working-class families in some areas. The percentage of all students attending private schools has hovered around 10% for the last 20 years, but recent declines in overall enrollment could generate more political pressure for public subsidies. Roman Catholic schools constitute the largest category of private schools, but their overall share of the market has declined as Conservative Christian and non-sectarian private schools have grown significantly (Broughman & Swalm, 2006).[3] Secular and for-profit private schools are less common, and tend to serve specific market segments, and be more concentrated in some regions of the country. The vast majority of private schools are in urban and suburban settings, and white students constitute 76% of total enrollment, as opposed to 58% of public school enrollment (US Department of Education, 2006).

Because they are outside the traditional publicly funded sector, private schools need to charge tuition to generate revenues. In recent years, many states (and the US Congress) have directed funding to help support the cost of tuition and other related expenses. In the past, the USA assumed a 'wall of separation' between Church and State, but for the past 50 years this wall has been steadily eroded through litigation. In a major federal constitutional ruling in 2002, the US Supreme Court allowed state governments to support religious schools as long as the governments themselves do not preferentially support one religion or sect over another (*Mitchell v. Helms*, 2000; *Zelman v. Simmons-Harris*, 2002). Many state constitutions, however, have more specific and constraining language preventing tax-funded support of religious organizations. Current legal theory has opened the door in some states for a variety of means of direct and indirect public support of private schools:

Vouchers: Vouchers are certificates with a particular financial value that can be applied to tuition costs at private schools (Friedman, 1955). Many school reformers believe this is the best method for channeling public funds to private schools, but the issue has been extremely controversial in the USA. Publicly funded vouchers are currently available across two states [4], as well as in Milwaukee, Cleveland, and Washington, DC. Many states and cities also have privately funded voucher programs, funded by philanthropic groups or political activists.

Tax credits and savings accounts: Six states have tax policies in which parents and others (including corporations in some states) can claim deductions for tuition and other educational expenses. Federal tax codes also allow parents to put some money for future education expenses in tax-sheltered savings accounts. These accounts are most commonly used for higher education expenses but can also be used for primary and secondary education.

Home Schooling

Although all states have mandatory school attendance laws, parents are also permitted to instruct their children at home. The degree of home-schooling regulation varies quite widely. Some states require parents to be certified teachers and use approved curricula, or to report activities to local school authorities, while other states have very minimal regulations and limited enforcement. A few states allow 'cherry picking', in which students can receive instruction in some subjects at public schools and be taught other subjects at home, or participate in public school extra-curricular activities like organized sports and student clubs. Estimating total home schooling enrollment is problematic because of non-reporting, but virtually all data indicate that this form of school choice is rapidly growing in popularity. For instance, by one estimate, in 1994 there were approximately 345,000 children schooled at home across the USA (Henke & Kaufman, 2000). By 2003, an estimated 1.1 million students were home schooled, representing 2.2% of total school enrollment (Princiotta & Bieleck, 2006).

So, in view of these trends, it appears that school choice is likely to be a permanent fixture on the education landscape in the USA. Indeed, with regard to the elements typically associated with longevity in education reforms – considerations such as constituencies, compatibility and the support of social movements (Cuban, 1992; Tyack & Cuban, 1995) – it would appear that school choice may well be integrated into the core institutions of education. Furthermore, activity in the legislative, legal, community organizing and advocacy arenas suggests there is little reason to think that school choice is likely to retreat from its prominent position at the cutting edge of social policy in the USA. However, this remarkable momentum begs the questions around the effects of school choice. That is, in view of the notable growth of these different types of school choice options in the USA, we might expect to see compelling evidence on the impact of these programs. But what does the research indicate?

Research on School Choice Outcomes

As school choice has developed in the USA, so too has the research around school choice programs – with data and methods that allow us now to move well beyond the early debates around ideology and market theory. And yet there are competing claims for conflicting areas of consensus emerging from the research on this topic. To address these questions, it is useful to consider the initial policy justifications for advancing school choice programs. In the USA, different forms of choice were advanced largely on three lines.[5] First, early arguments for choice were made largely on equity grounds, most notably by liberals and progressives (e.g. Jencks, 1972; Coons & Sugarman, 1978), but more recently by conservatives and their allies, arguing that choice is the 'new civil right' (e.g. King, 1997; Holt, 1999; Will, 2003). Under this line of thought, combining both normative claims and economic logic, choice affords opportunities for students financially excluded from more desirable schools, and the competitive effects of choice can lead to overall improvements in the quality of education, even for those who do not choose. Second, choice was advanced largely as a means of changing the organizational behavior of schools. In this reasoning, choice can create competitive incentives that (in combination with associated policies such as autonomy and per-pupil funding) force schools to change their productive processes – evident in areas such as innovation, responsiveness, and entrepreneurialism (Kolderie, 1994; Nathan, 1996; Rebarber, 1997; Brandl, 1998; Manno et al, 1998). Finally, the ultimate outcome anticipated from school choice reforms has been increases in academic achievement. Since parents are afforded the opportunity to seek better (presumably, more effective) schools, and since schools will compete to ratchet up quality in order to attract and retain students, many reformers and market theorists anticipated measurable gains in test scores for both individual students as well as for students in choice systems in general (Chubb & Moe, 1990; Clune, 1990; Peterson, 1999).

While there is accumulating evidence on the first two arguments [6], this last consideration is the most widely predicted outcome for school choice policies in the USA. This is not surprising, given the nature of the research enterprise in the USA. Indeed, there is a relatively comprehensive research community focused on education issues in the USA, where most universities and many other research organizations include education research components, and large organizations such as the American Educational Research Association and the American Educational Studies Association reflect multidisciplinary perspectives on myriad educational issues in North America and around the globe. While there is a substantial element of qualitative and interpretive research, much of this research infrastructure has its roots in psychometric analysis. Furthermore, the recent interest of researchers from economic and political science in education issues, as well as the increasingly prominent role of federal funding through the 'Institute of Education Sciences', with its emphasis on experimental studies, has directed inquiry toward quantifiable indicators of reforms' success. And since academic achievement is now the predominant consideration in the era of NCLB, it is the one that has attracted the most interest from researchers. Studies of academic achievement resulting from school choice programs in the USA have tended to focus on two of the most prominent and controversial reforms: charter schools and voucher programs.[7]

Achievement in Charter Schools

In the USA, charter schools are shaped largely by state-level policies, and academic achievement in these schools varies substantially by state, apparently depending on particulars of legislation and local policy context.[8] However, charter schools are also a national phenomenon, present now in most states, and virtually all charter schools share the same essential characteristics of (1) being schools of choice, (2) receiving funding on a per-pupil basis, and (3) enjoying some operational autonomy from local educational authorities. Consequently, they are expected to capitalize on the opportunities and incentives to adopt more innovative and effective educational processes. A number of recent studies have appeared, most using national-level data to investigate the effects of charter schools on academic achievement.

Since issues of selection bias can cripple attempts to study schools of choice such as charter schools, researchers must account for potentially confounding variables such as background characteristics of students in different schools. In the USA, the largest data set available that allows researchers to implement those controls is the National Assessment of Educational Progress (NAEP), containing student achievement data, student background data and information on school characteristics from nationally representative samples of schools. In 2003, NAEP also included for the first time data on a special, representative sample of charter schools. In an analysis released in 2004, the American Federation of Teachers (AFT) – the nation's second largest teachers' union and a known critic of charter expansion – found charter school students performing at a level beneath their public school counterparts in grades 4 and 8 (the only grades for which data were collected in 2003). The researchers noted that students in charter schools were about a half-year behind in mathematics and reading, and were less likely to reach 'proficiency' levels (Nelson et al, 2004). Because of limitations of the web-based data format, the analysis included only some crude controls for single background factors, and was harshly criticized by charter school advocates (see Carnoy et al, 2005). In response to the AFT report, Harvard economist Caroline Hoxby released on her website two studies of charter school achievement. In the first, Hoxby (2004a, b) matched almost all charter schools in the USA to their nearest neighborhood public schools (and to the nearest schools with similar student populations). She reported that students in charter schools were more likely to reach proficiency levels on state mathematics and reading assessments than they otherwise would have. The methodology in this study was claimed to be an improvement over the sampled (but representative) NAEP data used in the AFT study, but was fraught with errors in school matching and test comparisons (Carnoy et al, 2005; Roy & Mishel, 2005). In a second, much more rigorous study, Hoxby & Rockoff (2004) found a positive school effect on academic achievement for three charter schools in Chicago.

In the wake of the controversy about the AFT report, two separate research teams concluded multilevel analysis of the raw NAEP data, allowing them the indispensable advantage of simultaneously controlling for multiple background factors known to impact student achievement. Using hierarchical linear modeling to examine mathematics achievement, Lubienski & Lubienski (2006a, b, c) found charter school students to be performing at a level significantly beneath their public school counterparts in grade 4, both before and after controlling for differences in demographics and location. For grade 8, the authors found differences to be statistically insignificant. In a similar study commissioned by the federal government, Braun et al (2006a) largely replicated those findings in mathematics, and came to similar results in reading as well.[9]

While the debates about academic outcomes will undoubtedly continue, it is hard to make an argument that charter schools in general are boosting academic achievement in any significant or sustained manner; in fact, it may be that they have a negative impact on academic achievement in too many instances (Miron & Nelson, 2002; Bettinger, 2005). Indeed, over a decade into this reform, some advocates are moving away from optimistic claims about charter school achievement, and many are instead now highlighting parent satisfaction as evidence of success (Greene, 2000; Solomon, 2003; Robinson, 2005).

Achievement in Voucher Programs

While charter schools have sparked some controversy, publicly funded voucher plans are a lightning rod for policy and advocacy battles. The older programs in the industrial cities of Milwaukee, Wisconsin and Cleveland, Ohio have attracted the most attention from researchers. Milwaukee's program was started by the state legislature as an experiment in providing access for disadvantaged students to secular private [10] schools at state expense, and an evaluation component was included in the program. However, when official evaluations found no significant private school advantage for voucher students in mathematics and reading achievement

(Witte & Thorn, 1995), the state ended the evaluation, and has continued to expand the experiment. Meanwhile, Paul Peterson and colleagues from Harvard's Program on Education Policy and Governance (PEPG) conducted a secondary analysis of the data using different control groups in a randomized model, demonstrating significant private school effects for voucher students in mathematics and reading (Greene, Peterson et al, 1996, 1998). While these studies were criticized for issues of sample size, attrition, and reporting [11], a third analysis was conducted by Princeton economist Cecelia Rouse (1998a, b). In that study, she found no gains in reading, and significant gains in mathematics, but indicated that greater academic gains were evident for public school students in smaller classes (Rouse, 1998a, b). A similar debate unfolded around Cleveland's voucher program, where official evaluations initially found little or no advantages for students using vouchers (Metcalf et al, 1998, 2003). Subsequent re-analyses by PEPG found significant gains for voucher students, but were contested on methodological grounds (Greene, Howell et al, 1997, 1998; Metcalf, 1998; Metcalf & Tait, 1999). Most recent studies find little advantage, or indicate the possibility of a *negative* effect of using a voucher (Belfield, 2006).

So, as with charter schools, no clear consensus has emerged on compelling evidence of gains (or losses) due to the use of vouchers to attend private schools. If any general finding is available, it is that advantages to academic outcomes stemming from voucher programs are at most notably modest, and almost certainly do not rise to the level anticipated by the early optimistic assumptions advancing such programs.

Advocacy Coalitions and Research

Although research on school choice outcomes has been mixed, at best, policy makers are actively promoting and expanding these programs in the USA as if there were compelling and overwhelming evidence of their effectiveness. This apparent disconnect between research and policy can be explained largely by the fact that influential coalitions are actively advocating for school choice programs on the grounds that they are effective (e.g. Ladner, 2006). These advocacy coalitions represent alliances of advocacy organizations, journalists, researchers, and policy makers that work in concert to formulate, advance, and implement policy initiatives in policy subsystems such as school choice. They (1) form around policy issues such as school choice, (2) find areas of common ground, even when they are otherwise somewhat disparate advocacy groups, (3) strategically fund research and publicize arguments supporting their common agendas, and (4) engage targeted media forums to shape public debates, perceptions and policy making (on advocacy coalitions in education policy, see Kirst, 2006; DeBray-Pelot et al, 2007). Indeed, one of the primary roles that these coalitions play is to marshal and promote evidence to support policy positions, even when actual research on such positions lends only weak (or no) support.[12] When advocacy coalitions hold substantial sway over public debates and perceptions on an issue, they are in a position to actively neglect (and thereby peripheralize) research that challenges their agendas, or, in cases where such evidence is difficult to ignore, they can neutralize such research by producing their own experts.

In this section, I take a second look at the research basis for school choice, as seen through the lens of the advocacy coalitions supporting school choice. These coalitions have been wildly successful in getting 'airtime' to promote their message (see below). (Indeed, many of these organizations and individual researchers measure their success through the number of op-ed pieces or media citations they generate.) By looking at the research highlighted in the advocacy literature, we can see what is likely to be the strongest case that can be made for school choice, and then consider the underlying evidence. I outline here a few prominent examples of how research is used by advocacy/research organizations around the school choice issue, and then consider how this is changing the production of research in the USA.

1. In a recent report for the National Alliance for Public Charter Schools, Bryan Hassel (2005) reviewed 38 studies on achievement in charter schools, concluding that the 'existence of high quality charter schools and high growth rates for charter schools, at least in many states and studies, suggests that chartering holds promise as an approach to getting better schools' (p. 8). This synthesis is often held up to demonstrate that charter schools boost achievement. Hassel [13] bases this recommendation on a process of categorizing the research reports by data and methods, noting that value-added studies are more likely to show improvement for charter schools than are cross-sectional studies. However, this process neglects the fact that the studies more likely to find negative effects for charter schools are the larger scale, national studies (see also Betts, 2006). This is probably due to the fact that some of the smaller studies focus on local areas where charter schools are performing quite well.[14] (That is, Hassel's unit of analysis is studies, instead of states or schools.) Perhaps more interesting, of the nine studies lauded for more rigorous methods, six are unpublished/working papers or reports published by think tanks with known advocacy positions on school choice. Notably, only one of the 38 studies cited (one with relatively rigorous methods, according to Hassel) has gone through a formal peer-review process, and its findings are at odds with the thesis of the Hassel report (see Bettinger, 2005).

2. Another review of the research on school choice was held up as 'one of the most comprehensive reviews available on the research on recent school voucher programs in the United States' (Fuller, 2006, p. 7). The synthesis, posted by Marquette University's Institute for the Transformation of Learning [15], indicates 'an emerging consensus that school choice programs ... can lead to improved academic achievement [and] positive results in

public schools' (Robinson, 2005, p. 1).[16] The review, focusing on voucher programs, is based on 27 studies 'which mainly involve peer-reviewed research, by recognized scholars, that has appeared in prestigious journals' (Fuller, 2006, p. 7). In fact, only three of the 27 studies appeared in any peer-reviewed journals [17], and two of those showed little or no positive effect for using vouchers, or an effect similar to that of other public schools.[18] Of the 27 studies cited to show positive effects for choice, 24 were produced by researchers associated with the PEPG program at Harvard.

3. Manhattan Institute and University of Arkansas researcher Jay Greene (2000) reviewed studies on school choice outcomes in a paper that has been published in different forums (see also Greene, 2001a, b, c). Greene examined 19 studies of school choice outcomes in areas such as parental satisfaction, integration and civic values. In focusing on academic achievement, he highlighted eight reports, identifying

> a positive consensus among all eight studies, of five existing choice programs, conducted by four different groups of researchers. To be sure differences exist among these studies, but all have found important benefits of choice for the families that participate in them. (2000, p. 12)

Of the eight studies cited, five found clear evidence that vouchers enhance academic achievement. Those five were produced by Greene or his colleagues at PEPG, and none was published in peer-reviewed journals. However, they are often cited as compelling evidence that vouchers work (e.g. Ladner 2006). The other three studies, two of which were peer-reviewed, were much more measured in their conclusions: one – authored by John Witte (1998), who has 'endorsed school choice', according to Greene (2000, p. 4) – actually finds essentially no academic benefits to vouchers. The second, by Cecelia Rouse (1998a, b), found positive effects of vouchers comparable to (and slightly less than) those of public school programs, such as smaller class size. The third study, the official evaluation of the Cleveland voucher program, is reported by Greene to show a gain of six 'national percentile points' in language, and four national percentile points 'benefit in science after two years for existing schools' (2000, p. 19). This evaluation project – led by Kim Metcalf, a person Greene also characterizes as a supporter of school choice (p. 5) – actually concluded that there were no significant advantages in academic outcomes for students using vouchers.[19] Nevertheless, Greene points out that 'perhaps the most striking finding from the review of school choice research is the absence of evidence about how school choice harms students or society' (p. 13).[20]

4. In a recent debate on the relative academic performance of public and private schools [21], a number of advocacy organizations weighed in on the debate, without offering any new evidence on the topic. Several pointed to

previous working papers from Harvard's PEPG on *voucher* programs as proof that private schools are inherently superior.[22] For instance, writing for the conservative Heritage Foundation, Shanea Watkins highlights seven studies of school voucher programs, concluding, 'They all reached the same conclusion: students who received vouchers experienced greater math and/or reading achievement gains than did the students who remained in the public school system' (p. 4). In fact, of the seven studies cited, four are non-peer-reviewed and heavily criticized reports from PEPG authors. Of the other three also cited as proof of voucher effectiveness, one actually comes to the opposite conclusion (Krueger & Zhu, 2004a). The second attempted to create a model for overcoming attrition and missing data, and concluded: 'Results from our model in the school choice study do not indicate strong treatment effects for most of the subgroups examined', finding 'no advantages in reading, but some mathematics gains for some students from certain schools' (Barnard et al, 2003, p. 308). The third study suggested that advantages to vouchers could be understood as resulting from smaller class sizes in private schools (Rouse, 1998a, b).

5. A report published by the Center for Education Reform in Washington, DC purports to show 'what the research reveals about charter schools' (Center for Education Reform, 2001). Of 65 'objective, research-based studies' reviewed for this report [23], the 'conclusion of the overwhelming majority (61) of these papers is that charter schools have been innovative, accountable, and successful' (p. 1). In fact, at least 13 of the studies were produced by think tanks or advocacy organizations with known agendas regarding charter schools. Not one of the 65 was peer-reviewed. Furthermore, this advocacy group has earned a reputation for misinterpreting or mischaracterizing research in ways that support its agenda. In this case, for instance, the report includes a number of studies as proof that charter schools are having a positive impact, when, in fact, these studies made no claims about academic achievement, and found many more concerns regarding charter schools (e.g. Horn & Miron, 1999, 2000).

These few examples are but a handful of what is increasingly becoming a cottage industry of advocacy-based research reporting (Deparle, 2006). Many other examples of advocacy-driven research from national, state-level, and even university-affiliated think tanks are available, but too numerous to cite. In fact, these emerging sources of research serve as a type of echo chamber. As evidenced above, many of the researchers/advocates active in the area of school choice are likely to cite mostly one another in their reports, or to include each other's work in their edited volumes published by think tanks that endorse school choice. Sponsoring organizations such as think tanks are quite successful at getting attention for these reports, but too often pay little or no attention to counter-evidence, research standards, or to peer-reviewed research in advancing their own studies. Consequently, we see research that is becoming quite prominent in policy debates, but is left wanting in the area of intellectual rigor and standards, and even more so in terms of diversity of intellectual perspectives.

The question of intellectual rigor has traditionally been addressed in scholarly circles through the process of peer review. Indeed, even enthusiasts such as Peterson, Greene, Hoxby and other school choice researchers and advocates have argued that we must 'assess carefully any research sponsored by interest groups engaged in policy debates. Such studies need to be vetted by independent scholars, as is commonly done in coverage of research on the biological and physical sciences'.[24]

However, as indicated above, if we use this standard, the research supporting school choice in the USA based on academic outcomes is rather thin indeed. In reviewing the claims made by school choice advocates regarding the empirical basis for school choice – highlighting studies presumably most favorable to that agenda – precious few studies on academic outcomes meet this standard, and the few that do tend to be much more mixed in their assessments than is indicated in the advocacy literature. In reviewing that literature, only two commonly cited studies have actually been published in scholarly peer-reviewed research journals. John Witte (who, indeed, has tepidly endorsed choice) found no advantages for students using vouchers to attend private schools. In the other study, Cecelia Rouse (1998a, b) found some advantages for students using vouchers, but noted that these gains were similar to (or outpaced by) public school students in classes similar in size to those in private schools. She has since endorsed class size as a more effective route to academic gains (Rouse & Barrow, 2006).

There are also a few other peer-reviewed studies on school choice and academic achievement, less frequently cited in the advocacy research. But these also fail to offer compelling evidence for school choice. In a rigorous longitudinal study of academic gains in Michigan charter schools (cited by Hassel, see above), Bettinger (2005) found that gain scores for students in charter schools are no better than for students in public schools, and charter schools may actually have a relative *negative* impact on scores.[25] Greene and his PEPG colleagues succeeded in publishing one of their reports on academic achievement in a peer-reviewed journal, but in a special issue, so review standards are unclear (Greene et al, 1999). In a study highly acclaimed for its innovative methodology, Hoxby (2000) found academic advantages for students in regions believed to have more competition – however, other researchers have not been able to replicate the findings, and have shown serious inconsistencies in the use of data in that study (Rothstein, 2004).[26] Similarly, Paul Peterson reported significant academic gains for students using vouchers in a study of privately funded programs in Washington, Ohio, and New York (Howell et al, 2000; Mayer et al, 2002; Peterson & Howell, 2003). However, other researchers (as well as members of Peterson's own research team) noted that gains were evident when reported as averages, were restricted to one group in one grade in one city (suggestive of a statistical fluke), and are dependent on highly questionable classifications and treatment of data (Zernike, 2000; General Accounting Office, 2002; Krueger & Zhu, 2004a, b). Thus, even when examining research that has met the highest standards of academic review, the research basis for academic effectiveness stemming from school choice is still tenuous, at best.[27] While doing 'no harm' might be the new mantra of school choice advocates/researchers, it may very well be that the integrity of research in this area is suffering substantial harm due to such advocacy research.

Nevertheless, even questionable contributions to this shallow research basis receive substantial attention in policy discussions – and not simply by accident. Supported by a strong and active institutional infrastructure, advocacy scholars are easily able to bypass professional norms and checks such as the traditional academic peer-review process by going directly to the media. For instance, Jay Greene, supported by millions in funding from the pro-choice Walton family, lists on his curriculum vitae at least 145 op-ed articles that he has written, including for newspapers such as the *Wall Street Journal* and the *New York Post*. Paul Peterson, whose activities on school choice have been funded by the conservative Scaife, Bradley, Smith Richardson, Friedman, and Olin Foundations, as well as the Bush federal government, also lists impact in areas such as op-eds in national publications.[28] A LexisNexis search of major newspapers since the publication of the Bettinger charter school study shows nine citations on the school choice issue for Peterson, 19 for Hoxby, 29 for Center for Education Reform leader Jeanne Allen [29], and 62 for Greene – while none for the Bettinger study, which was published in a prestigious peer-reviewed journal. Moreover, advocacy coalitions have the institutional resources to petition policy makers regarding their agenda. For example, in the landmark ruling legalizing publicly funded vouchers, the US Supreme Court entertained amicus briefs from groups such as the American Education Reform Council (2002) and Howard Fuller's Black Alliance for Educational Options (BAEO) (2002) [30], citing research in support of vouchers.[31] Of the 55 articles cited in these briefs, over half are authored by researchers associated with Harvard's PEPG. Again, only three studies were published in peer-reviewed journals, and their findings were often selectively represented. Data from PEPG researchers were also cited in the court's main ruling and a justice's concurring opinion (*Zelman v. Simmons-Harris*, 2002).

Toward a New Political Economy of Education Research?

While data and methods for education research issues have advanced notably since Milton Friedman (1955) first proposed vouchers in the 1950s, the research on school choice is still quite mixed, without the compelling story anticipated by its advocates. While Friedman saw school choice as the epitome of freedom in education, now major debates on the efficacy of choice in the USA hinge on one's definition of a 'stream', or on whether classifications of a child's minority status should depend on the race of one parent or both parents (e.g. Peterson & Howell, 2003, 2004; Krueger & Zhu, 2004a; Howell & Peterson, 2004; Hoxby, 2005; Rothstein, 2004). Although Chubb & Moe famously pushed choice as 'a panacea' for schools, we are now asked to accept that, at the very least, choice does 'no harm' (Greene, 2000). While the promise of the Hippocratic Oath is a worthy goal in both medicine and education, it is hardly a sufficient justification in itself for unproven experiments involving children – experiments that have raised reasonable concerns about individual and social harm.

And yet, in fact, such debates on research are largely beside the point. As the review of research provided here suggests, school choice in the USA is growing rapidly regardless of what the research 'says'. Partly this is due to an increasingly powerful constituency – nurtured in part by think tanks – that is becoming quite accustomed to publicly funded school choice. Indeed, evidence of the relative merits of national samples of charter schools is not of particular concern to a local parent with a child in a failing public school, and research suggests that the simple power to choose may increase satisfaction regardless of – or even in spite of – actual outcomes (Botti & McGill, 2006). But the other reason that these debates are largely 'academic' (in the sense of being irrelevant) is because they reflect tension over the changing nature of increasingly marginalized academic scholarship.

What we are witnessing may well be the emergence of a new political economy of research production and consumption in the USA, with school choice issues at the forefront of that shift. In the new political economy, privately funded think tanks are rapidly eclipsing independent university researchers in shaping the thinking around this issue, providing slick websites, expensive conferences and glossy publications designed for the media and policy makers. Here, the quality of research may matter less than the strength of the 'brand' of its institutional source, or the efficacy of the promotional campaign designed to market that research.

In that regard, strong evidence on the effectiveness of school choice in producing the anticipated academic outcomes is a relatively minor concern. Although, as noted above, much advocacy research does not rise to the peer-review standard publicly embraced by many school choice researchers/advocates, the resources available through school choice advocacy coalitions allow advocacy researchers to bypass traditional peer-reviewed venues – going straight to the press with their research, or setting up their own 'peer-reviewed' outlets. For instance, PEPG has a strong media component, actively engaging the press through press releases around PEPG reports (in lieu of the imprimatur of the peer-review process). Furthermore, PEPG researchers have set up 'peer-reviewed' outlets such as Peterson's magazine at the conservative Hoover Institute, *Education Next* ('a journal of opinion and research' [32])and Greene's *Education Working Paper Archive* (a 'refereed, scholarly' source of 'research that meets professional academic standards' [33]). Together, the editorial boards for these publications read like a who's who of school choice advocacy, and include no known skeptics or critics of that advocacy agenda.

Indeed, this tactic of setting up alternative 'peer-reviewed' publication outlets is consistent with the overall strategy since the 1970s for the right to set up parallel institutions to rival the institutional hegemony of universities, which were believed to be controlled by the left (Smith, 1991). The increasing dominance of conservative think tanks in research and policy discussions is the direct result of concerted conservative efforts to fund an alternative research infrastructure. Furthermore, although the think tank sector is the most notable area of this new political economy, universities are also playing a substantial (and perhaps expanding) role. As Slaughter & Rhoades (2004) have pointed out, since 1980, American academia has been moving toward a new model where knowledge production is profit-driven, and traditional boundaries between public and private sectors have been blurred. In this environment, advocacy-oriented think tanks have played a more central role than before. Noticing this success, universities have followed suit by hosting the creation of largely independent research outfits fashioned on the think tank model, where entrepreneurial-minded scholars can pursue externally-funded research contracts and grants, in response to the availability of research funds. This sets up a situation where, not only are prestigious university names essentially for hire, but, in fact, the more prestigious the institutional 'brand' of the university, the more attractive it is for private interests wishing to advance their policy agenda by funding researchers at 'independent' institutions of higher learning.

The problem with this political economy of advocacy-driven research is that many forms of public and professional accountability, instituted to promote high-quality research, are rapidly eroding. Accountability for research through public research funding boards or to scholarly peer-reviewers is undermined. Instead, research is oriented to the vast amounts of money becoming available through private foundations and through an increasingly politicized federal bureaucracy surrounding education reform in the USA. Thus, in a sense, we are seeing the privatization and further politicization of research agendas, with fewer formal regulations on the quality of research. Of course, many of the researchers/advocates capitalizing in this new political economy are well intentioned, and many have a deep concern for the equitable opportunities of disadvantaged children and communities. However, this new political economy appears to establish and subsidize a market-driven research apparatus to support a market-oriented agenda for schools. This new climate appears designed to privilege desire over data.

Notes

[1] Peter Weitzel contributed substantially in drafting this section.

[2] 72.3% of charter schools have enrollments of less than 300 students (Snyder & Hoffman, 2003).

[3] Between 1990 and 2002, total private school enrollment increased from 4.8 to 5.3 million students. However, from 2002 to 2004, enrollment declined from 5.3 to 5.1 million. Roman Catholic schools constituted 54.5% of private schools in 1990 but had declined to 46.2% in 2004. Over the same time period, Conservative Christian schools increased from 10.9% of the total to 15.1%. Non-sectarian schools increased from 13.2% to 18% of the total.

[4] A recent state Supreme Court ruling in Florida held that the state's voucher program was unconstitutional – not on religious, but on governance grounds. A similar ruling struck down a proposed program in Colorado. On the other hand, Utah lawmakers passed a voucher program, which was subsequently rejected in a referendum in 2007.

[5] Actually, a fourth line on which choice was advanced – and a very prominent one – has been around the argument of cost-effectiveness. However, it is not reviewed here for the following reasons. Most cost-effectiveness arguments hinge on presumptions of a critical mass of competing schools that would create an environment in which competitive incentives would drive down the extraneous costs of schooling (Hoxby, 1994, 2002; Merrifield, 2002). Now, many charter school advocates, for instance, are abandoning their earlier hopes for cost efficiencies, and are instead claiming that outcomes in charter schools are inhibited in cases where charter schools receive less funding than other public schools. Some weak attempts have been made recently to research this question (see Aud & Michos, 2006; and response by Lubienski, 2006a), but it is only very recently that a comprehensive choice system has been established in which competitive pressures might be reasonably expected to have an impact on costs. For instance, while the District of Columbia now sees about one-quarter of public school students in charter schools, many local administrators still report no direct competitive pressures on public schools, despite the recent addition of a voucher program (Lubienski, in preparation). On the other hand, charter schools have been the preferred model for rebuilding the New Orleans school system in the wake of Hurricane Katrina, and now make up approximately 70% of the market share (Ziebarth, 2006). However, it is too early to evaluate this emerging market. Finally, questions of costs typically focus on financial costs, and researchers are less able to account for social costs of education programs in areas, such as loss of social cohesion or democratic accountability.

[6] On the equity issue, see, for instance, see Campbell et al (2005), or Carnoy et al (2005); on organizational issues, see, for instance, Lubienski (2003a, 2006b).

[7] Claims have also been made for other practices, such as home schooling (Rudner, 1999), but methodological issues hamper efforts to understand the effects of such practices on achievement (Lubienski, 2003b).

[8] The study of differences between different states is fascinating, and a number of state-level evaluations may provide some insights into the impact of different charter school policies on achievement (e.g. Miron & Nelson, 2000,

2002). However, researchers must account for other local and regional factors, and such a discussion falls beyond the scope of this current analysis.

[9] Paul Peterson and Elena Llaudet (Peterson & Llaudet, 2006) of Harvard University's Program on Education Policy and Governance posted an analysis of the data using 'alternative models' (see below). In attempting to upend the earlier findings, they noted (in a footnote) only that, after their re-analysis, 'one finds few significant differences between the performance of charter schools and traditional public schools' (p. 35, n. 14).

[10] Later the program was expanded to include religious schools.

[11] Virtually all studies conducted by PEPG on school choice issues have been heavily criticized by other scholars for issues with data, methods, and/or reporting. Furthermore, Peterson is a public proponent of vouchers.

[12] Prominent examples in the USA include the 'debates' around global warming, evolution, abstinence education, the purported link between abortion and breast cancer, the efficacy of faith-based social programs, and the lead-up to the war in Iraq. Several researchers and writers have documented the role of these networks in the misuse and politicization of evidence, anti-intellectualism, and the importance of ideological loyalty with both the Bush administration and US conservative movements in general (Union of Concerned Scientists, 2004; Mooney, 2005; Goldberg, 2006).

[13] Hassel is a former student of Paul Peterson's, who went on to found a research and consulting firm active in charter school advocacy (Mezzacappa, 2006).

[14] Moreover, the process for selecting studies for inclusion in the synthesis does not appear to be rigorous. For instance, the study of three Chicago charter schools by Hoxby & Rockoff (2004) was included because of its methodology, even though it violated the standard of examining 'a significant segment of the charter sector' (Hassel, 2005, p. 4).

[15] The Institute is directed by Howard Fuller. The site lists as its banner: 'accurate information about school choice' (see http://schoolchoicewi.org/).

[16] Fuller goes on to add that 'their high quality suggests a *causal* link between parental choice and improved test scores' (Fuller, 2006, p. 7; emphasis in original).

[17] One of the studies cited does not appear in Robinson's reference list, so it is difficult to determine where it was published (see the reference to Howell, 2004, as cited in Robinson, 2005, p. 10).

[18] In fact, some of the studies cited showed little or no impact for vouchers, which is not mentioned in the Robinson synthesis. Instead, they were included apparently because they indicate higher levels of parental satisfaction.

[19] In fact, the evaluator was upset with the mischaracterization of his research findings, and noted that 'it is possible that they [Greene and fellow PEPG researchers] are engaged in a deliberate effort to misrepresent the Cleveland data in order to influence educational policy' (Metcalf, 1998, p. 39).

[20] Caroline Hoxby has backpedaled into similar claims (Stossel, 2006).

[21] See (Braun et al, 2006b; Lubienski & Lubienski, 2006a; Peterson & Llaudet, 2006).

[22] The use of voucher studies to address the question of academic performance in public and private schools overall is inappropriate. Voucher studies tend to be smaller-scale, localized projects that suffer from organization-level selection bias – based on students leaving (presumably failing) public schools for the private schools that have elected to participate in voucher programs (and studies). Such samples of schools are hardly representative. On the other hand, public–private school studies can offer some insights into voucher programs in general because such programs are premised on assumptions of inherent private school superiority.

[23] Apparently, as opposed to '[o]ther analyses with credible, positive findings but not research per se' (p. 17).

[24] This statement was signed by these scholars in a full-page advertisement placed by the Center for Education Reform in the *New York Times*, in response to the charter school report released by the AFT (Various Scholars & Center for Education Reform, 2004). Peterson has suggested elsewhere that such standards should be at play, (inaccurately) insinuating that my own work fails to meet peer-review standards (Peterson & Llaudet, 2006, p. 35, and note 14; Lubienski & Lubienski, 2006b, c).

[25] Other studies in other areas of school choice also hint at the possibility of a detrimental impact of choice schools. See, for example, Figlio & Stone (1997), Lubienski et al (2008).

[26] Similar methodological errors were noted in another of Hoxby's (2004a, b) research papers on charter schools (Roy & Mishel, 2005). However, this one was not peer-reviewed.

[27] Other studies on choice have been published in peer-reviewed journals, but do not examine academic achievement as an outcome (see note 8, above).

[28] See http://mediatransparency.org/

[29] The Center for Education Reform receives funding from the Walton family as well as the ultra-conservative Bradley Foundation, which funded the infamous *Bell Curve*.

[30] BAEO founder Howard Fuller is also director of the Institute for the Transformation of Learning at Marquette University (see Robinson, 2005), and is married to a vice-president at Christopher Whittle's Edison Schools. The BAEO receives funding from the Bradley Foundation, and now the Bush administration (Scott, in press).

[31] It should be noted that, according to a clerk on the court at the time of that ruling, members of the high court only consider research put before them (A. Saiger, personal communication, October 19, 2006).

[32] http://www.hoover.org/publications/ednext/about

[33] http://www.uark.edu/ua/der/EWPA/index.htm

References

American Education Reform Council (2002) Brief as Amici Curiae Supporting Petitioners. *Zelman v. Simmons-Harris*, 536 U.S. 639; 122 S. Ct. 2460; 153 L. Ed. 2d 604.

Aud, S.L. & Michos, L. (2006) *Spreading Freedom and Saving Money: the fiscal impact of the D.C. Voucher program*. Washington, DC: Cato Institute and the Friedman Foundation.

Barnard, J., Frangakis, C.E., Hill, J.L. & Rubin, D.B. (2003) Principal Stratification Approach to Broken Randomized Experiments: a case study of school choice vouchers in New York City, *Journal of the American Statistical Association*, 98(462), 299-324. http://dx.doi.org/10.1198/016214503000071

Belfield, C.R. (2006) *The Evidence on Education Vouchers: an application to the Cleveland scholarship and tutoring program*. Occasional Paper No. 112. New York: National Center for the Study of Privatization in Education.

Bettinger, E.P. (2005) The Effect of Charter Schools on Charter Students and Public Schools, *Economics of Education Review*, 24(2), 133-147. http://dx.doi.org/10.1016/j.econedurev.2004.04.009

Betts, J.R. (2006) School Choice as a Remedy for America's Public Schools: promising theories sail into the empirical fog. Paper presented at the Spencer Foundation Conference on 'Values and Evidence in Education Reform', 24-25 October, Chicago.

Black Alliance for Educational Options (2002) Brief as Amici Curiae Supporting Petitioners. *Zelman v. Simmons-Harris*, 536 U.S. 639; 122 S. Ct. 2460; 153 L. Ed. 2d 604.

Botti, S. & McGill, A.L. (2006) When Choosing is Not Deciding: the effect of perceived responsibility on satisfaction, *Journal of Consumer Research*, 33, 211-219. http://dx.doi.org/10.1086/506302

Brandl, J.E. (1998) Governance and Educational Quality, in P.E. Peterson & B.C. Hassel (Eds) *Learning from School Choice*, 55-81. Washington, DC: Brookings Institution.

Braun, H., Jenkins, F. & Grigg, W. (2006a) *A Closer Look at Charter Schools Using Hierarchical Linear Modeling*. No. NCES 2006-460. Washington, DC: National Center for Education Statistics.

Braun, H., Jenkins, F. & Grigg, W. (2006b) *Comparing Private Schools and Public Schools Using Hierarchical Linear Modeling*. No. 2006-461. Washington, DC: National Center for Education Statistics.

Broughman, S.P. & Swalm, N.L. (2006) *Characteristics of Private Schools in the United States: results from the 2003-2004 private school universe survey*. Washington, DC: National Center for Education Statistics.

Campbell, D.E., West, M.R. & Peterson, P.E. (2005) Participation in a National, Means-Tested Voucher Program, *Journal of Policy Analysis and Management*, 24(3), 523-541. http://dx.doi.org/10.1002/pam.20113

Carnoy, M., Jacobsen, R., Mishel, L. & Rothstein, R. (2005) *The Charter School Dust-Up: examining the evidence on enrollment and achievement*. Washington, DC: Economic Policy Institute.

Center for Education Reform (2001) *What the Research Reveals about Charter Schools*. Washington, DC: Center for Education Reform.

Center for Education Reform (2006) *National Charter School Data: new school estimates 2006-2007*. http://www.edreform.com/index.cfm?fuseAction=stateStats&pSectionID=15&cSectionID=44 on 10/16/06

Chubb, J.E. & Moe, T.M. (1990) *Politics, Markets, and America's Schools*. Washington, DC: Brookings Institution.

Clune, W.H. (1990) Educational Governance and Student Achievement, in W.H. Clune & J.F. Witte (Eds) *Choice and Control in American Education, volume 2: The Practice of Choice, Decentralization and School Restructuring*, 391-424. London: Falmer Press.

Coons, J.E. & Sugarman, S.D. (1978) *Education by Choice: the case for family control*. Berkeley: University of California Press.

Cuban, L. (1992) Why Some Reforms Last: the case of the kindergarten, *American Journal of Education*, 100(2), 166-194. http://dx.doi.org/10.1086/444013

DeBray-Pelot, E., Lubienski, C. & Scott, J.T. (2007) The Institutional Landscape of Interest Group Politics and School Choice, *Peabody Journal of Education*, 82(2-3), 204-230.

Deparle, J. (2006) Preaching the Gospel of Small Government, *New York Times*, 17 November.

Figlio, D.N. & Stone, J.A. (1997) *School Choice and School Performance: are private schools really better?* Discussion Paper no. 1141-97. Madison: Institute for Research on Poverty.

Friedman, M. (1955) The Role of Government in Education, in R.A. Solo (Ed.) *Economics and the Public Interest*, 127-134. New Brunswick: Rutgers University Press.

Fuller, H. (2006) Parental Choice: scarce and widespread. Paper presented at the Spencer Foundation Conference on 'Values and Evidence in Education Reform', 24-25 October, Chicago.

General Accounting Office (2002) *School Vouchers: characteristics of privately funded programs*. Report to the Honorable Judd Gregg, U.S. Senate no. GAO-02-752. Washington, DC: General Accounting Office.

Goldberg, M. (2006) *Kingdom Coming: the rise of Christian nationalism*. New York: W.W. Norton.

Greene, J.P. (2000) *A Survey of Results from Voucher Experiments: where we are and what we know*. Civic Report no. 11. New York: Center for Civic Innovation, Manhattan Institute.

Greene, J.P. (2001a) The Hidden Research Consensus for School Choice, in P.E. Peterson & D.E. Campbell (Eds) *Charters, Vouchers, and Public Education*. Washington, DC: Brookings Institution.

Greene, J.P. (2001b) The Surprising Consensus on School Choice, *The Public Interest*, 144, 19-35.

Greene, J.P. (2001c) A Survey of Results from Voucher Experiments: where we are and what we know, in C.R. Hepburn (Ed.) *Can the Market Save Our Schools?* Vancouver, BC: The Fraser Institute.

Greene, J.P., Howell, W.G. & Peterson, P.E. (1997) *An Evaluation of the Cleveland Scholarship Program*. Occasional Papers. Cambridge, MA: Program on Education Policy and Governance, Harvard University.

Greene, J.P., Howell, W.G. & Peterson, P.E. (1998) Lessons from the Cleveland Scholarship Program, in P.E. Peterson & B.C. Hassel (Eds) *Learning from School Choice*, 357-392. Washington, DC: Brookings Institution.

Greene, J.P., Peterson, P.E. & Du, J. (1996) *The Effectiveness of School Choice in Milwaukee: a secondary analysis of data from the program's evaluation*. Research Papers Series. Cambridge, MA: Harvard Program on Education Policy and Governance, Harvard University.

Greene, J.P., Peterson, P.E. & Du, J. (1998) School Choice in Milwaukee: a randomized experiment, in P.E. Peterson & B.C. Hassel (Eds) *Learning from School Choice*, 335-356. Washington, DC: Brookings Institution.

Greene, J.P., Peterson, P.E. & Du, J. (1999) Effectiveness of School Choice: the Milwaukee experiment, *Education and Urban Society*, 31(2), 190-213. http://dx.doi.org/10.1177/0013124599031002005

Hassel, B.C. (2005) *Studying Achievement in Charter Schools: what do we know?* Washington, DC: National Alliance for Public Charter Schools.

Henke, R. & Kaufman, P. (2000) *Issues Related to Estimating the Home-Schooled Population in the United States with National Household Survey Data*. US Department of Education, National Center for Education Statistics. NCES 2000-311. Washington, DC: US Government Printing Office.

Hoffman, L. (2003) *Overview of Public Elementary and Secondary Schools and Districts: school year 2001-02*. US Department of Education, National Center for Education Statistics. NCES 2003-411. Washington, DC: US Government Printing Office.

Holt, M. (1999) *Not Yet 'Free at Last': the unfinished business of the civil rights movement: our battle for school choice*. Oakland: Institute for Contemporary Studies.

Horn, J. & Miron, G. (1999) *Evaluation of the Michigan Public School Academy Initiative*. Final Report. Kalamazoo: The Evaluation Center, Western Michigan University.

Horn, J. & Miron, G. (2000) *An Evaluation of the Michigan Charter School Initiative: performance, accountability, and impact*. Final Report. Kalamazoo: The Evaluation Center, Western Michigan University.

Howell, W.G. & Peterson, P.E. (2004) Uses of Theory in Randomized Field Trials: lessons from school voucher research on disaggregation, missing data, and the generalization of findings, *American Behavioral Scientist*, 47(5), 634-657. http://dx.doi.org/10.1177/0002764203260153

Howell, W.G., Wolf, P.J., Peterson, P.E. & Campbell, D.E. (2000) *Test-Score Effects of School Vouchers in Dayton, Ohio, New York City, and Washington, D.C.: evidence from randomized field trials*. Cambridge, MA: Harvard Program on Education Policy and Governance, Harvard University.

Hoxby, C.M. (1994) *Do Private Schools Provide Competition for Public Schools?* Working Paper no. 4978. Cambridge, MA: National Bureau of Economic Research.

Hoxby, C.M. (2000) Does Competition among Public Schools Benefit Students and Taxpayers? *American Economic Review*, 90(5), 1209.

Hoxby, C.M. (2002) *School Choice and School Productivity (or Could School Choice Be a Tide that Lifts All Boats?* Working Paper no. w8873. Cambridge, MA: National Bureau of Economic Research.

Hoxby, C.M. (2004a) *Achievement in Charter School and Regular Public Schools in the United States: understanding the differences*. Cambridge, MA: Harvard University and National Bureau of Economic Research.

Hoxby, C.M. (2004b) *A Straightforward Comparison of Charter Schools and Regular Public Schools in the United States*. Cambridge, MA: Department of Economics, Harvard University.

Hoxby, C.M. (2005) *Competition among Public Schools: a reply to Rothstein (2004)*. NBER Working Paper no. 11216. Cambridge, MA: National Bureau of Economic Research.

Hoxby, C.M. & Rockoff, J. (2004) *The Impact of Charter Schools on Student Achievement: a study of students who attend schools chartered by the Chicago charter school foundation*. Cambridge, MA: Department of Economics, Harvard University.

Jencks, C. (1972) *Inequality: a reassessment of the effect of family and schooling in America*. New York: Basic Books.

King, A.C. (1997) Fighting for School Choice: it's a civil right, *The Wall Street Journal*, 11 September.

Kirst, M. (2006) *Politics of Charter Schools: competing national advocacy coalitions meet local politics*. New York: National Center for the Study of Privatization in Education.

Kolderie, T. (1994) Charters: an invitation to change, *Educational Leadership*, 52(1), 36.

Krueger, A.B. & Zhu, P. (2004a) Another Look at the New York City School Voucher Experiment, *American Behavioral Scientist*, 47(5), 658-698. http://dx.doi.org/10.1177/0002764203260152

Krueger, A.B. & Zhu, P. (2004b) Inefficiency, Subsample Selection Bias, and Nonrobustness: a response to Paul E. Peterson and William G. Howell, *American Behavioral Scientist*, 47(5), 718-728. http://dx.doi.org/10.1177/0002764203260150

Ladner, M. (2006) The Moynihan Challenge, *National Review Online*, 23 March. http://www.nationalreview.com/comment/ladner200603230738.asp

Lubienski, C. (2003a) Innovation in Education Markets: theory and evidence on the impact of competition and choice in charter schools, *American Educational Research Journal*, 40(2), 395-443. http://dx.doi.org/10.3102/00028312040002395

Lubienski, C. (2003b) A Critical View of Home Education, *Evaluation and Research in Education*, 17(2/3), 167-178.

Lubienski, C. (2005) School Choice as a Civil Right: district responses to competition and equal educational opportunity, *Equity and Excellence in Education*, 38(4), 331-341. http://dx.doi.org/10.1080/10665680500299809

Lubienski, C. (2006a) *Report on 'Spreading Freedom and Saving Money: the fiscal impact of the D.C. Voucher Program' from the Cato Institute and Milton & Rose D. Friedman Foundation*. No. EPSL-0602-118-EPRU. Tempe: Educational Policy Research Unit, Education Policy Studies Laboratory, Arizona State University.

Lubienski, C. (2006b) School Diversification in Second-Best Education Markets: international evidence and conflicting theories of change, *Educational Policy*, 20(2), 323-344. http://dx.doi.org/10.1177/0895904805284049

Lubienski, C. (in preparation) Do Voucher Programs Increase Competitive or Cooperative Strategies between Public, Private, and Charter Schools? University of Illinois.

Lubienski, C. & Lubienski, S.T. (2006a) *Charter, Private, Public Schools and Academic Achievement: new evidence from NAEP mathematics data*. Occasional Paper no. 111. New York: National Center for the Study of Privatization in Education.

Lubienski, S.T. & Lubienski, C. (2006b) School Sector and Academic Achievement: a multi-level analysis of NAEP mathematics data, *American Educational Research Journal*, 43(4), 651-698. http://dx.doi.org/10.3102/00028312043004651

Lubienski, C. & Lubienski, S.T. (2006c) Charter Schools, Academic Achievement and NCLB, *Journal of School Choice*, 1(3), 55-62.

Lubienski, C., Crane, C.C. & Lubienski, S.T. (2008) What Do We Know about School Effectiveness? Academic Gains in Value-Added Analysis of Public and Private Schools, *Phi Delta Kappan*, 89(9), 689-695.

Manno, B.V., Finn, C.E., Bierlein, L.A. & Vanourek, G. (1998) How Charter Schools are Different: lessons and implications for a national study, *Phi Delta Kappan*, 79, 489-498.

Mayer, D.P., Peterson, P.E., Myers, D.E., Tuttle, C.C. & William, H.G. (2002) *School Choice in New York City after Three Years: an evaluation of the school choice scholarships program*. Final Report. Princeton, NJ: Mathematica Policy Research.

Merrifield, J. (2002) *The School Choices: true and false*. Oakland: The Independent Institute.

Metcalf, K. (1998) Commentary – Advocacy in the Guise of Science: how preliminary research on the Cleveland voucher program was 'reanalyzed' to fit a preconception, *Education Week*, 18(34), 39.

Metcalf, K. & Tait, P. A. (1999) Free Market Policies and Public Education: what is the cost of choice? *Phi Delta Kappan*, 81, 65-75.

Metcalf, K., Boone, W., Stage, F., Tait, P., Stacey, N. & Mueller, P. (1998) *Evaluation of the Cleveland Scholarship Program: second year report*. Bloomington: Indiana Center for Evaluation, Indiana University.

Metcalf, K., West, S.D., Legan, N.A., Paul, K.M. & Boone, W.J. (2003) *Evaluation of the Cleveland Scholarship and Tutoring Program: summary report 1998-2002*. Bloomington: Indiana University.

Mezzacappa, D. (2006) Market Forces: Professor Paul Peterson's influential protégés, *Education Sector: Analysis and Perspectives*, 2 May.

Miron, G. & Nelson, C. (2000) *Autonomy in Exchange for Accountability: an initial study of Pennsylvania charter schools*. Kalamazoo: The Evaluation Center, Western Michigan University.

Miron, G. & Nelson, C. (2002) *What's Public about Charter Schools? Lessons Learned about Choice and Accountability*. Thousand Oaks: Corwin Press.

Mitchell v. Helms (2000) Supreme Court of the United States, 2000. 530 U.S. 793, 120 S. Ct. 2530.

Mooney, C. (2005) *The Republican War on Science*. New York: Basic Books.

Nathan, J. (1996) *Charter Schools: creating hope and opportunity for American education*. San Francisco: Jossey-Bass.

Nelson, F.H., Rosenberg, B. & Van Meter, N. (2004) *Charter School Achievement on the 2003 National Assessment of Educational Progress*. Washington, DC: American Federation of Teachers.

Peterson, P.E. (1999) Vouchers and Test Scores, *Policy Review*, Jan/Feb.

Peterson, P.E. & Howell, W.G. (2003) *Efficiency, Bias, and Classification Schemes: estimating private-school impacts on test scores in the New York City voucher experiment*. Cambridge, MA: Program on Education Policy and Governance, Harvard University.

Peterson, P.E. & Howell, W.G. (2004) Efficiency, Bias, and Classification Schemes: a response to Alan B. Krueger and Pei Zhu, *American Behavioral Scientist*, 47(5), 699-717. http://dx.doi.org/10.1177/0002764203260158

Peterson, P.E. & Llaudet, E. (2006) *On the Public–Private School Achievement Debate*. No. PEPG 06-02. Cambridge, MA: Program on Education Policy and Governance, Harvard University.

Princiotta, D. & Bieleck, S. (2006) *Homeschooling in the United States: 2003*. U.S. Department of Education. National Center for Education Statistics. NCES 2006-042. Washington, DC: US Government Printing Office.

Rebarber, T. (1997) *Charter School Innovations: keys to effective charter reform*. Policy Study no. 228. Los Angeles: Reason Public Policy Institute.

Robinson, G. (2005) *Survey of School Choice Research*. Milwaukee: Institute for the Transformation of Learning, Marquette University.

Rothstein, J. (2004) *Does Competition among Public Schools Benefit Students and Taxpayers? A Comment on Hoxby (2000)*. Working Paper no. 10. Princeton: Princeton University.

Rouse, C. (1998a) *Schools and Student Achievement: more evidence from the Milwaukee parental choice program*. Princeton: Princeton University and the National Bureau of Economic Research.

Rouse, C.E. (1998b) Private School Vouchers and Student Achievement: an evaluation of the Milwaukee parental choice program, *Quarterly Journal of Economics*, 113(2), 553-603. http://dx.doi.org/10.1162/003355398555685

Rouse, C.E. & Barrow, L. (2006) U.S. Elementary and Secondary Schools: equalizing opportunity or replicating the status quo? in S. McLanahan & I. Sawhill (Eds) *The Future of Children: fall 2006*. Washington, DC: Brookings

Institution Press and the Woodrow Wilson School of Public and International Affairs at Princeton University.

Roy, J. & Mishel, L. (2005) *Advantage None: re-examining Hoxby's finding of charter school benefits*. Briefing Paper no. 158. Washington, DC: Economic Policy Institute.

Rudner, L.M. (1999) Scholastic Achievement and Demographic Characteristics of Home School Students in 1998, *Education Policy Analysis Archives*, 7(8). http://epaa.asu.edu/epaa/v1997n1998/ (accessed April 24, 1999).

Scott, J.T. (in press) Managers of Choice: race, gender, and the political ideology of the 'new' urban school leadership, in W. Feinberg & C. Lubienski (Eds) *School Choice Policies and Outcomes: philosophical and empirical perspectives on limits to choice in liberal democracies*. Albany, NY: State University of New York Press.

Slaughter, S. & Rhoades, G. (2004) *Academic Capitalism and the New Economy: markets, state, and higher education*. Baltimore: Johns Hopkins University Press.

Smith, J.A. (1991) *The Idea Brokers: think tanks and the rise of the new policy elite*. New York: Free Press.

Snyder, T.D. & Hoffman, C.M. (2003) *Digest of Education Statistics, 2002.* U.S. Department of Education, National Center for Education Statistics. NCES 2003-060. Washington DC: US Government Printing Office.

Solomon, L.C. (2003) *Findings from the 2002 Survey of Parents with Children in Arizona Charter Schools: how parents grade their charter schools*. Santa Monica: Human Resources Policy Corporation.

Stossel, J. (2006) Stupid in America: how lack of choice cheats our kids out of a good education, *20/20*, 13 January.

Tiebout, C.M. (1956) A Pure Theory of Local Expenditures, *Journal of Political Economy*, 64(4), 416-424. http://dx.doi.org/10.1086/257839

Tyack, D.B. & Cuban, L. (1995) *Tinkering toward Utopia: a century of public school reform*. Cambridge, MA: Harvard University Press.

Union of Concerned Scientists (2004) *Scientific Integrity in Policymaking: an investigation into the Bush administration's misuse of science*. Cambridge, MA: Union of Concerned Scientists.

US Department of Education, National Center for Education Statistics (2006) *The Condition of Education 2006*. NCES 2006-071, Washington, DC: US Government Printing Office.

Various Scholars & Center for Education Reform (2004) Charter School Evaluation Reported by the *New York Times*, Fails to Meet Professional Standards, *New York Times*, 25 August. http://www.edreform.com/_upload/NewYorkTimesAd.pdf

Will, G. (2003) School Choice is a Civil Right. http://www.townhall.com/, 14 September (accessed September 15, 2003).

Witte, J.F. (1998) The Milwaukee Voucher Experiment, *Educational Evaluation and Policy Analysis*, 20(4), 229-251. http://dx.doi.org/10.2307/1164323

Witte, J.F. & Thorn, C. (1995) *The Milwaukee Parental Choice Program, 1990/1991-1994/1995* (computer file): Madison: Data and Program Library Service [distributor].

Zelman v. Simmons-Harris (2002) Supreme Court of the United States. 536 U.S. 639, 122 S. Ct. 2460; 536 U.S. 659; 122 S. Ct. 2471; 153 L. Ed. 2d 621 (2002); 536 U.S. 675-676; 122 S. Ct. 2479-2480; 153 L. Ed. 2d 631-632 (2002.

Zernike, K. (2000) New Doubt is Cast on Study that Backs Voucher Efforts, *New York Times*, 15 September.

Ziebarth, T. (2006) *Top 10 Charter Communities by Market Share*. Washington, DC: National Alliance for Public Charter Schools.

CHAPTER 3

School Choice as Concerted Cultivation: the case of Canada

SCOTT DAVIES & JANICE D. AURINI

SUMMARY Canada's school choice movement has imported and adapted American understandings of choice in ways that underplay market rationales. Rather than hailing choice as a mechanism to boost test scores or desegregate minority students, Canadian choice-seekers are energized by emerging middle-class parenting cultures. School choice is connected to 'concerted cultivation', an intensive form of parenting in which middle-class parents increasingly structure their children's lives and treat them as projects-in-the-making. Sociologists typically invoke this concept to link the varying strategies that parents use to align their child-rearing practices with school requirements, and to emphasize how such parental resources are unequally distributed by class and race. Here the concept of concerted cultivation is extended by linking this parental agency to school choice, noting that choice-seeking alters parental relations with public educators from mere supportive roles to more directing and even adversarial roles. Survey data is presented showing that wealthier and more educated parents are more likely to engage in choice-seeking, and that choosers are more likely to embrace contentious notions of parental authority. Focus group data illustrates how choice proponents rationalize their actions. It is shown that choice advocates acknowledge concerns about the potential threat of choice policies to equity, but then redraw moral boundaries by portraying choice as a responsible and necessary form of parental involvement in schooling. These findings illustrate new forms of parental agency and expressive cultural ideals in processes of class reproduction.

Introduction: Canada in international context

Canada is an interesting site to examine the globalization of school choice. Canadians are increasingly pursuing an array of educational options. In 2005, 8% of all enrolments were in independent or private schools, up from

5% in 1998 (Guppy et al, 2005). In Ontario, Canada's largest province, both private enrolments and the number of private schools have risen 50% over the past decade, and other educational preferences such as home schooling and private tutoring are growing sharply as well (Davies et al, 2006).[1] Several provinces have expanded their menus of special themed schools in major urban centres, and have extended funds to independent schools. This activity has sparked a two-pronged debate: whether authorities should expand choice options within public school systems (e.g. more themed schools or open enrolment policies), and whether they should further extend public funds to independent schools (e.g. charter schools, tuition tax credits, or funds for private schools).

While Canada's choice debates echo those elsewhere, they manifest a particular type of globalization. Canadian advocates draw on (largely) American policy options and meanings of choice, but adapt them to their own peculiar landscape. Think tanks such as the Fraser Institute routinely import American referents when calling for charter schools or vouchers, pointing to policy experiments in US cities and states, or citing luminaries such as Chubb & Moe, Milton Friedman, or Caroline Hoxby to buttress their claims. They draw on a similar vocabulary that associates school choice with parental rights, equity, and educational quality, but then recast these issues to accord with their own institutional setting. That setting has a number of noteworthy traits. First, Canada does not have a national education authority like each of the three British nations, or a federal government that is increasingly involved in schooling, as in the United States. Since responsibility for schooling lies with each of the 10 provinces, Canada lacks a coherent national-level discourse about school choice. Debates and policy over choice have evolved separately and somewhat uniquely in each province. They are a low priority in rural politics, and have higher profiles in more populous areas. Some provinces fund a variety of religious schools, while others fund only Catholic schools. Some provide grants for independent schools, while others do not. Only Alberta has charter schools and vouchers for home schoolers.[2] Provinces like Ontario do not have any charter schools, vouchers or private tuition tax credits whatsoever. While all provinces offer some choice within their publicly-funded systems, none fully funds private schools.

Beyond the decentralized nature of Canadian education, several factors serve to infuse Canadian choice debates with an individualized quality. As virtually all provinces have historically funded religious schools, Canadian debates do not invoke American principles of separating Church and State (or challenges to those principles). Since most provinces fully fund Catholic schools, Catholics are not part of Canada's choice movement. Further, the pervasive American image of failing inner-city schools resonates far less north of the border. Provincial equalization policies serve to lessen school disparities across neighbourhoods. Few Canadians tout choice as a lever for racial desegregation, as per many US cities, since Canada has somewhat lower levels of segregation, and its rising immigrant population has widely varying levels of school success. The largely rural-based Native population is by far the most disadvantaged in the federation, but Natives have partial sovereignty over their own schools, and do not seek choice per se. Popular debate over education is probably less divisive and intense in Canada than in either the United States or Britain. Anti-state rhetoric, so popular in the United States, is seldom voiced in Canada, which is home to stronger 'Red Tory' and social democratic traditions. Canadians generally rate their public schools more favourably, and with fewer politicians decrying the failings of provincial schools, there is no policy equivalent to America's No Child Left Behind Act. Finally, Canadian debates are not fuelled by a 'high-stakes' educational culture. While choice movements often take root in countries with highly stratified markets for post-secondary credentials and policy cultures that use test scores to evaluate schools, Canada lacks a steep hierarchy of post-secondary institutions and standardized entrance tests for university (Davies & Hammack 2005). Since few provincial tests are used to evaluate students, at least for now, choice is rarely hailed as a tool to boost test scores.

Given this absence of comparable legal doctrines, constitutional principles, anti-state sentiments, or warnings of a looming crisis of quality, what is fuelling Canada's growing private education market and its debates about choice? Below we argue that school choice advocacy in Canada assumes a more individualistic hue, one that prizes the wants of parents.

School Choice as Concerted Cultivation

Annette Lareau (2002, 2003) has coined the term 'concerted cultivation' to capture how today's middle-class parents are increasingly structuring their children's lives. An emerging literature is documenting how today's parents – the most educated generation of caregivers ever – are expanding their repertoire of education-oriented practices, and are intensifying their child rearing (e.g. Adler & Adler, 1994; Frones, 1994; Arendell, 2001; Stevens, 2001). A concerted cultivator believes that 'good' parents not only provide food and shelter but also nurture a stimulating environment in the name of child development. For instance, studies show that despite women's longer hours of employment, recent cohorts of parents are investing even more time in their children's development, much devoted to structured and educational activities (Sayer et al, 2004). Parents increasingly use summer vacations, formal art and music lessons, and private tutors to augment their children's education (Chin & Phillips, 2004; Dumais, 2005; Baker & LeTendre, 2005; Aurini, 2006). More parents than ever are assisting with homework, enrolling their children in prized programmes, and are strategically interacting with teachers. Lareau emphasizes how this trend offers well-educated parents a consequential advantage: they are more likely to become intimately knowledgeable of schools' inner workings, and learn to successfully navigate through its options and requirements. By being involved in education, these parents are better positioned to align their child-rearing practices with schools' expectations and reward structures.

We argue that school choice is a species of concerted cultivation. Choosing requires that parents actively search for school alternatives, thus necessitating a level of agency beyond standard forms of involvement such as helping with homework or volunteering at school. We emphasize that its wilful character – no one *forces* Canadian parents to engage in choice – can alter parents' relations with educators. Choice is premised on a philosophy that encourages parents to assert their authority and challenge institutional experts such as teachers and principals. Choice-seekers are rarely content to merely complement existing school arrangements, and strive instead to manage their children's education. Educators readily approve of supportive forms of parental involvement such as assisting with homework and helping with fund-raising, but choice-seeking is far less consensual. Professional teachers rarely initiate choice programmes. Instead, those reforms are typically endorsed by politicians and parents who want educators to comply with *their* wants for a particular school philosophy, not vice versa. Choosing parents sometimes take defiant and adversarial stances toward school officials, and in extreme forms such as home schooling, they appropriate the role of 'educator' altogether. Choice-seeking is thus a form of concerted cultivation that can alter conventional home–school relationships.

In this chapter we investigate which kinds of Canadians seek school choice, and the nature of public opinion and discourse about choice. For the former task we use survey data to examine the demographics and educational attitudes of parents who engage in various types of choice. We document some striking attitudinal similarities between choosers and non-choosers, but also those stances that polarize parents (which we refer to as 'wedge issues').[3] For the latter task, we bolster the survey data with focus group material to explore how Canadians understand choice. We use this qualitative material to unpack the wedge issues and examine how choice advocates and supporters construe their own motives. While some researchers reduce choice-seeking to a parental strategy for class advantage, and/or an expression of neo-liberal ideology, we seek to capture *public* discourse and understandings, particularly the meaning-making of choice-seekers. Our argument is that underlying rationales for choice in Canada are increasingly infused with the language and ethos of concerted cultivation. Our data clearly show that more affluent and educated parents are most likely to exercise choice, but we bracket concerns about their ulterior motives to focus on their expressed intentions, thereby highlighting new directions in Canada's evolving choice debate.

Methods and Data

This study employs mixed methods (Jacobs, 2005). Since the conclusions of qualitative and quantitative studies in education are often discrepant (Lareau & Weininger, 2003), we attempt to triangulate our findings. The quantitative component comes from the Analyzing Change in Education survey conducted in 2005 (for discussion of all technical matters and for the questionnaire, see Guppy et al, 2005). We were part of a research team from five regions across Canada that devised a national survey of 2000 parents on a host of educational issues. Data were weighted to adjust for gender and for regions that were over-sampled, thus making the sample representative of Canadian parents according to census measures.

The survey asked respondents about the kinds of schools and programs attended by their children, and about their choice-related behaviours and attitudes. For the latter, we created three scales. First, a 'participation' scale was created to capture varying levels of involvement in school. Since qualitative research suggests that affluent parents are more likely to participate in school events (Lareau, 2000), we wanted to investigate whether choice-seeking parents are likewise more involved. We summed five dichotomous items: whether during the past semester the respondent had volunteered in the classroom/library/field trip or other; met individually with teachers; attended other school committee meetings; attended school events; or written a letter to anyone at the school. Second, we devised a scale of attitudes towards choice by summing five items: 'There should be an annual report card for schools'; 'Parents should be able to send their children'; 'There should be a greater variety of academic programs'; 'All parents should have the right to choose'; and 'Government funding/tax money should follow the student'. This scale captures perceptions of parental rights and the provision of educational variety or information. Third, we constructed a scale of attitudes towards accountability in schooling, focusing on the provision of measured outputs to demonstrate school performance, and procedures by which schools respond to stakeholders. Such sentiments are typically viewed to be compatible with pro-choice attitudes. A six-item scale was devised to capture attitudes toward accountability: 'Standardized tests should be used to assess changes over time in a school's performance'; 'The school principal should be accountable to parents for school performance'; 'Schools should do an annual survey of parent satisfaction'; 'Schools should have an annual improvement plan and report their progress'; 'Provinces should administer standardized tests (assessments) at key stages of schooling', and 'All students should pass a test of basic skills'.

Our statistical analysis consists of comparing the socio-economic status, demographics, and educational attitudes of choice-seekers versus other parents, and then running logistic regression models to examine the predictors of choice-seeking. We then deepen this analysis with a qualitative investigation.[4] Our survey was pre-tested in 20 focus groups in five cities. In the spring of 2005, we invited 32 teachers and parents to four focus groups in the Toronto area (other team members conducted 16 similar groups in Vancouver, Edmonton, Quebec City and Halifax). These groups were asked to identify the most important issues facing Canadian education, and discuss various issues surrounding student discipline, teacher training, parental involvement, and school choice. We draw mostly on our own focus groups, but also on the other team's written reports, and a policy forum that we conducted in Toronto in December 2005, which was attended by representatives from Ontario's Ministry of Education, local school boards, teacher associations, parent groups, and researchers. While these casual samples cannot offer representative views about choice, they are useful for illuminating some underlying meanings in choice debates.

	Attends Regular Public n = 1344	Public Religious n = 473	Private School n = 163	Private Religious n = 102	Non-religious Private n = 55
Family income	66,048	71,769[c]	80,675[c]	80,862[c]	82,944[c]
Years of school	15.22	15.14	15.94[c]	15.68[a]	16.48[c]
Rating of schools	73.06	74.13[a]	69.16[c]	68.37[c]	70.85[a]
Participate scale	3.14	3.20	3.57[c]	3.57[c]	3.58[c]
Choice scale	17.06	17.36[a]	16.96	17.07	16.65
Accountability	19.46	19.70	19.18	19.17	18.96
Check indicators	.497	.502	.594[b]	.621[c]	.532
Use to choose	.115	.116	.273[c]	.207[b]	.357[c]
Chose residence	.477	.485	.455	.439	.460
Close to home	.771	.786	.586[c]	.563[c]	.565[b]
For siblings	.489	.539[a]	.577[a]	.566	.566
For religion	.234	.631[c]	.443[c]	.533[c]	.208
Special theme	.517	.566[a]	.766[c]	.818[c]	.673[b]
Academic repute	.723	.730	.629[b]	.675	.554[b]

[a]denotes two-tail test significant at .05 level.
[b]denotes two-tail test significant at .01 level.
[c]denotes two-tail test significant at .001 level.

Table I. Difference of means (regular public schools as reference).

Findings

Quantitative Analyses

Table I shows the markedly differing socio-economic profiles of parents whose children are in different kinds of schools. Compared to parents whose youngest child is in a regular public school (column one), choice-seeking parents are significantly wealthier and more highly educated. Consistent with

American and British studies (Goldhaber, 1999; Gorard et al, 2001), Canadian choosers have a higher socio-economic status, particularly those in non-religious private schools. In terms of attitudes, parents with children in private schools rate public schools less favourably, participate more in school, are more likely to consult school performance indicators, and are almost twice as likely to use those indicators to choose schools. In contrast, these parents differ little on some of their expressed attitudes towards choice and accountability. The bottom six rows of the table compare rationales for choice, and reveal that public school (religious and non-religious) parents are most likely to choose a school close to home, and to choose their residence based on the quality of local public schools rather than a special theme. In sum, choice-seekers are distinguished by their backgrounds (income and education) and concrete acts (rating schools, participating, and using performance indicators) more than by abstract attitudes about choice and accountability.

	High participate	Child in private school	Check indicators	Chose on basis of indicators
Family income	.009[c]	.018[c]	.006[b]	.005
Years education	.037	.157[b]	.136[c]	.154[c]
Female	.361[b]	.021	.354[b]	.403[a]
Age	.019[a]	.026	.021[a]	.027
Community size	.002	.006	.005[a]	.013[c]
Quebec	.021	1.006[c]	.483[c]	.455[a]
Grade of youngest child	-.632[c]	.113	-.065	-.069
Scale of choice	.008	.021	.000	.149[c]
Scale of participation	-	.109	.180[c]	.127
Scale of accountability	.011	-.023	.028	.038
Rating of public schools	.003	-.058[c]	.004	.008
Child in private school	.006	-	.113	.907[c]
Nagelkerke R square	.062	.158	.102	.132
Chi square	62.91[c]	81.02[c]	105.22[c]	97.60[c]
n	1332	1332	1327	1329

[a]denotes two-tail test significant at .05 level.
[b] denotes two-tail test significant at .01 level.
[c] denotes two-tail test significant at .001 level.

Table II. Binary logistic regressions of forms of involvement and choice.

Table II explores predictors of choice using a series of logistic regression models. To establish a point of reference, the first column presents socio-economic, demographic, and attitudinal effects on parental participation, and the remaining columns display similar models for three dimensions of choice:

having a child in private school, checking performance indicators, and choosing with performance indicators. The first column shows that wealthier parents are more likely to participate in schools, as are female parents, older parents and parents with children in earlier grades. Parents who check and/or use school performance indicators and have children in private schools are wealthier and more educated, controlling for a range of attitudinal and demographic measures.[5] Thus, again, parents who engage in concrete dimensions of choosing (using performance indicators and enrolling in a private school) tend to be advantaged. Also, Table II shows that attitudinal measures are weak predictors of choice-seeking. Pro-choice attitudes are significant in only one model; attitudes to accountability are not significant in any model, and negatively rating public schools is a significant predictor of only enrolling a child in a private school.

	SD
Amount of choice in my district is sufficient	No
There should be a greater variety of programs	No
Government funding/tax money should follow the student	No
All parents should have the right to choose their child's school	Yes at .05 level
Choice matters little because most schools are pretty much the same	Yes at .001 level
Power of teacher unions to influence what happens in schools is too strong	No
How effective are teacher unions for contributing to school improvement?	No
Effectiveness of student improvement on standardized tests for evaluating teachers	No
Ranking performance on standardized tests is unfair to some schools	No
Importance of parent participation on school committees	No
Importance of parent participation on parent–teacher meetings	No
Importance of parent participation for hiring the school principal	Yes at .001
Importance of parent participation in school improvement planning	No
Parents' level of participation in schools is too low	No
Most often it is self-interested parents who participate	Yes at .005 level
Letter grade for public school	Yes at .001 level

Table III. Chi square analysis of attitudes of private school versus public school parents.

Since our scales may serve to conceal attitudes that differentiate choosers from non-choosers, Table III presents our search for 'wedge issues': the particular survey items that clearly distinguish private school from public school parents. The table lists 16 single-item indicators, including attitudes towards parental participation, public schools, teacher unions, and choice. Significant differences emerge for only five of the 16 items, but those five items reveal particular sources of contention. Namely, private school parents are significantly more likely to declare their 'right to choose', and to strongly disagree with the statement, 'Choice matters little because all schools are pretty much the same', These responses suggest that choosers believe more firmly in the right and necessity to choose. Turning to items about parental participation, only two statistically significant differences emerge. First, private school parents were far more likely to agree that 'parents should be involved in hiring a principal'. This highlights how questions of extending power over schooling to parents are highly contested. Second, private school parents are far more likely to disagree with the statement, 'It is self-interested parents who participate most in schools'. Finally, private school parents offer lower ratings of public schools compared to public school parents. Thus, while private school and public school parents agree on many issues, a select group of items reveals a substantial degree of discord. Most parents support forms of general forms of choice, parental involvement and accountability, but then disagree over issues of parental power and authority, rating schools, and assessing the motives of active parents. To further explore these 'wedge issues' we turn next to our qualitative data.

Qualitative Data: understanding the wedge issues

Discussions in our focus groups tended to centre on two issues: whether choice embodies consumerist or market thinking in education, and whether choice is a form of social elitism. These themes were strongly voiced by opponents of choice but were rejected by advocates, who offered counter-rationales for choice that drew on a language of concerted cultivation.

Market thinking or parental authority? As is common in choice debates, those participants who were sceptical of any further extension of choice warned of a consumerist 'market thinking' that is infiltrating schooling. Too many parents, they cautioned, are wrongly turning to the marketplace in search of superior accountability and school quality. These critics doubted the value of school-by-school comparisons or 'league tables' of standardized test scores, believing that such comparisons compel educators to 'teach to the test' and are often unfair to schools in disadvantaged neighbourhoods. A better way to improve schools, they reasoned, is to boost financial support for mainstream public education, rather than create a multi-tier system.

To our surprise, choice advocates responded with few allusions to market forces, competition, or consumerism. While some likened their fundamental right to choose schools to their right to choose a grocery store or car dealer, most choice advocates appealed to an overriding sense of parental entitlement. Their responses suggest that our survey did not capture nuances among choice-seekers, particularly their ambivalence toward accountability schemes. Indeed, choice-seekers in focus groups were not unquestioning supporters of school performance indicators. They echoed the fears of other parents (and especially teachers) that published rankings can be misleading if they fail to acknowledge the mitigating influence of neighbourhood affluence (and in our survey, private school parents were slightly *more* likely to agree with the statement, 'Ranking school performance on standardized tests is unfair to some schools'). All parents warned that some accountability schemes encourage educators to merely 'teach to the test' and pursue favourable test scores at the expense of more authentic forms of learning. As one chooser explained, the current emphasis on standardized testing proved that governments are 'only interested in a numbers game'. Market rationales did not emerge as a wedge issue that divided choosers from non-choosers, as choice advocates seldom expressed any undue admiration for any 'invisible hands' or any potential benefits from competition among schools.

Choosers in our focus groups did differ markedly in their beliefs about the proper role of parents, however. While all participants affirmed the necessity of parental involvement in school, they disagreed sharply over whether parent powers should be bolstered. Choice-seekers proclaimed their 'right' to posses more control over schooling, reasoning that parents, not teachers, best know the needs and wants of children. Public schools, they claimed, can offer only 'standardized solutions for standardized problems'. Choosers wholeheartedly embraced more directive forms of parental involvement, including hiring and firing principals, evaluating teachers, and influencing local school policy. They sharply condemned their 'token' roles in public schools, whether sitting on powerless advisory councils, volunteering for yard duty, or fund-raising for playground equipment. As one chooser explained, 'Too often parents are asked to be involved, only to find out they're needed to run a bake sale'. Another added, 'Everyone is for involvement, but it has to be meaningful'. Schools, they reasoned, must be more accommodating and responsive to parental values and the unique needs of their children.

Such views about parent power were hotly debated in our focus groups, and were sharply disputed by other parents. Non-choosers warned that a dominant few could impose their agenda upon the passive many. They called for a return to 'common-school' ideals in which the neighbourhood school was a meeting ground for all, and worried that further extensions of choice could divide neighbourhoods and corrode social cohesion. The following quotes illustrate such differences between non-choosers and choosers:

> We all have the right to education that meets our needs as parents, that reflects what we want for our children. (Chooser)
>
> Let parents prescribe for their children, not the state. (Chooser)
>
> Some of the school councils are given too much power. Some parents think that since they've been to school, they're [education]

> experts! ... I'm just saying that parents should not be driving school policy. (Non-chooser)

> I would not want to send my kid to a school where they taught mainly the views that I hold ... that only those views were right. That concerns me ... everyone needs to be in the same system to learn about what everyone thinks ... I'm talking about the whole world view, not just religion, but politics, economic, moral ... (Non-chooser)

In sum, while all focus group participants believed that parents should be active in schools, they disagreed over the proper amount of parental authority and power. Choosers repeatedly claimed that they, not bureaucrats, were best qualified to steer their children's educational trajectories, and articulated these beliefs less through a faith in the power of markets than in an assertion of the inviolable authority of parents.

Class elitism or parental responsibility? Choice-seeking parents also rejected another moral charge: that removing their children from regular public schools represents a type of elitism and retreat from public institutions (for discussions of this issue see Smith & Sikkink, 1999; Stevens, 2001). Sceptics in focus groups repeatedly worried that choice would further entrench socio-economic segregation and dilute the public sphere. But choice-seekers responded by pointing to their considerable participation in educational communities, noting their past roles as officials, researchers, members of school councils, or parent advocacy groups. Accordingly, they did not regard their own choice-seeking as a retreat from public institutions, nor as a form of class reproduction, but as a meaningful and grass-rooted form of involvement in schooling. Their ideal school was a vigorous polity and organic community where all stakeholders are intimately knowledgeable and empowered to craft sensitive policies, and where caring parents are placed at the core. In this view, schools ought to enjoy a modicum of autonomy from states, boards, and professional teacher bodies. Governments, they reasoned, lack sufficient information about local school communities to make effective pedagogical decisions.

Importantly, choosers reckoned that if parents' philosophies of education were at odds with their local school, then those parents were entitled to search for alternatives. Such challenging of experts like teachers and principals, they argued, was a reasonable extension of good, responsible parenting. As one private school parent explained, 'Parents are naturally more accountable when it comes to their children. They have to live with the consequences '. Further, they portrayed less-active parents who gladly hand over the responsibility of educating children to schools as negligent. As one chooser explained, educating children is the parent's responsibility:

> Parents are the primary educators. The analogy I like to use is that if you went to your doctor, the doctor isn't responsible for how healthy you are. They're a resource. Similarly, with education, it's the parent's responsibility. (Chooser)

Did these choice-seekers acknowledge that affluent parents are best positioned to take advantage of choice? Yes, but they portrayed themselves as merely privileged and fortunate enough to act in ways that *any* responsible parent should act if they could. In their minds, choosing itself is fully legitimate, since parents are responsible for finding an education that is tailored to the special needs of children. What is illegitimate in their eyes is the unequal distribution of opportunities to exercise such choice. Ergo, school choice should be made more available to all parents regardless of their wealth, they reasoned. By this counter-frame, choosers shifted the moral terms of the debate from those of 'elitism' to those of 'responsible parenting'. To address questions of parents' ultimate obligations, choosers pointed not to society per se, but to their children. To address questions of inequities, choosers pointed not to disparities between private and public schools, but to the lack of choice options for the poor. Thus, a key wedge issue emerged, as choosers reinterpreted notions of parent power in education as a call for responsible parenting and for responsive institutions.

The framework of concerted cultivation. These focus group debates encouraged us to look beyond market imperatives and socio-economic self-interest to comprehend choosers' own understandings. In public venues, they articulate school choice in terms of evolving notions of parental authority and responsibility. These understandings, we argue, are informed by emerging norms of intensive parenting. Virtually all parents in the focus groups and in the policy forum wholeheartedly embraced a version of Lareau's concerted cultivation. All admired those parents who assist children with homework, engage with teachers and principals, volunteer in schools, and are involved in school councils (and this was further confirmed by our survey data). Such activities were acknowledged to exemplify what good parents do. However, choice-seekers took the ethos of concerted cultivation further. Parents, they contended, should not merely comply with local schools, but also confront those institutions when necessary for the sake of their children's well-being. Being concerted cultivators, and viewing their children as projects in development, many choice-seekers believed *they* were the best assessors of schools, not external government bodies. Schools, they reasoned, should be accountable first and foremost to parents, and should align with parental goals, values and philosophies – not the other way around. Choosers extended the ethos of concerted cultivation to proclaim a need to actively manage their children's education careers, and a right to challenge professional educators. Our survey and focus groups detected many lines of consensus among parents, but also revealed particular divisions between choosers and non-choosers on questions of parental authority. While the vast majority of parents endorsed more limited forms of such authority, choosers embraced more intensive versions.

Conclusion: implications for theory

Canada represents a particular case of the globalization of school choice. Canadian advocates have largely imported a set of American policy options and cultural framings of choice, but have re-assembled them to suit their domestic context. Facing a difficult challenge of connecting choice to broad collective goals, legal principles, anti-state sentiment, or strategies for school improvement, their public discourse takes a more individualistic tenor, and embeds choice within emerging parenting sentiments. While racial and class inequalities may be underlying social forces that motivate the choice movement, Canadian advocacy for choice borrows idioms from evolving parenting norms. It is likely that these norms are spreading among the educated classes throughout the developed world, beyond any one national or ethnic heritage. Research in several countries on 'parentocracy' (Brown, 1990) and 'intensive parenting' (e.g. Zelizer, 1985; Hays, 1996; Stevens, 2001; Quirke, 2006) suggests that concerted cultivation is quite international and is perhaps intensifying.

This thesis has two implications for theorizing the cultural logics of class, parenting and schooling. First, our proposed link between concerted cultivation and school choice reveals the role of agency in class reproduction. It highlights cultural *production* – how advantages emerge through creative action. Beyond the upper class, school choice cannot be seen as a heritage that is being passed from generation to generation, since the vast majority of Canadian parents themselves went to regular public schools. Today's choice-seekers and concerted cultivators are relatively new species. Dance lessons, art camps, themed private schools and tutoring have been adopted en masse only quite recently. Few of today's parents lived a childhood that is as scheduled as their children's. Choice should be seen within a larger assembly of practices that is being invented by today's generation of parents.

Second, choice-seeking and concerted cultivation are nuanced activities that have strong non-rational qualities. While affluent families are more likely to engage in school choice, not all forms of choice are clearly oriented to reproducing status. Indeed, we are struck by the *lack* of calculative and instrumental reasoning that infuses much concerted cultivating and school choosing. Certainly, some forms are oriented to class reproduction, such as elite private schools that charge exorbitant fees in exchange for high-powered social connections (Cookson & Persell, 1985). But other forms are less attuned to class reproduction. The choice literature shows that academic outcomes for charter schools and voucher programs are typically weak or inconsistent (Goldhaber, 1999; Witte, 2000; Lubienski, in this volume). This equivocalness may partly reflect the fact that many schools of choice offer music or sports specialties rather than traditional academic subjects, and as such they pay rather ambiguous dividends. Quantitative research on the effects of parental involvement on school success has been similarly inconclusive, and suggests that payoffs vary by type of involvement (see McNeal, 1999; Muller, 1993; Kingston, 2001; Domina, 2005). The economic payoff from a practice like home schooling is highly indefinite, as are the benefits of various extra-curricular lessons or tutoring (Stevens, 2001; Aurini & Davies, 2005; Dumais, 2005). Thus, beyond sending one's children to elite private schools, it is difficult to regard these parenting practices as bequeathing a grand tradition or a set of tried and true strategies.

Accordingly, we emphasize the *expressive* dimensions of school choice. While middle-class parents certainly want their children to enjoy lifestyles comparable to their own, and seek school options that accord with their own socio-economic sensibilities, many pursue choice with great passion in the face of great uncertainty. Portraying choice-seeking as overly rational and instrumental, or focusing exclusively on its statistical links to class locations, may exaggerate its strategic intent and real efficacy. To understand the rising popularity of choice-seeking in Canada, we have attempted to balance a structural account with a description of its moral and expressive character. In future work we hope to further explore how idioms of concerted cultivation are affecting the provision of schooling by magnifying parents' sense of children's worth, individuality and self-actualization. We also invite scholars to explore whether this culture is increasingly transnational and perhaps even global.

Notes

[1] Home schooling is when a student receives instruction from a parent or guardian. Instruction may or may not be directed by schooling officials. While figures vary, home-school associations estimate there are 100,000 Canadian home-schooled students (http://www.life.ca/hs/).

[2] Charter schools are autonomous, non-profit public schools that operate under a performance contract approved by a school board or a ministry. Vouchers are monetary 'coupons' that parents can use toward an approved form of schooling of their choice. See 'Choice and Accountability in Canadian Education', at http://www.cup.ualberta.ca/resources_documents.html

[3] We use the terms 'choosers' and 'non-choosers' to differentiate parents who send their children to non-public schools and local public schools respectively. We recognize that public schooling parents have technically made a 'choice' to send their children to their local public school.

[4] We conducted the survey after several years of fieldwork on various forms of private education in the Toronto area. Along with our colleague Linda Quirke, between 2001 and 2004 we visited 50 private and public schools, 42 tutoring businesses and learning centres, interviewed many parents, activists and teachers and attended several events related to private education and school choice (for examples see Davies & Quirke, 2005; Aurini, 2006). Also,

the second author conducted a one-year participant observation study in which she tutored for a major learning centre franchise.

[5] Net of various demographics, Quebecois are more likely to enrol in private schools, to use performance indicators, and to choose on the basis of those indicators. Quebec is one of four provinces that partially fund private schools.

References

Adler, Patricia A. & Adler, Peter (1994) Reproduction of the Corporate Other: the institutionalization of after-school activities, *Sociological Quarterly*, 35, 309-328. http://dx.doi.org/10.1111/j.1533-8525.1994.tb00412.x

Arendell, Teresa (2001) The New Care Work of Middle Class Mothers: managing childrearing, employment and time, in Kerry J. Daly (Ed.) *Minding the Time in Family Experience: emerging perspectives and issues*. London: JAI Press.

Aurini, Janice (2006) Crafting Legitimation Projects: an institutional analysis of private education businesses, *Sociological Forum*, 21(1), 83-111. http://dx.doi.org/10.1007/s11206-006-9004-8

Aurini, Janice & Davies, Scott (2005) Choice without Markets: homeschooling in the context of private education, *British Journal of Sociology of Education*, 26(4), 461-474. http://dx.doi.org/10.1080/01425690500199834

Baker, David P. & LeTendre, Gerald T. (2005) *National Differences, Global Similarities: world culture and the future of schooling*. Stanford: Stanford University Press.

Brown, Phillip (1990) The Third Wave: education and the ideology of parentocracy, *British Journal of Sociology of Education*, 11(1), 65-81. http://dx.doi.org/10.1080/0142569900110105

Chin, Tiffani & Phillips, Meredith (2004) Social Reproduction and Child-Rearing Practices: social class, children's agency, and the summer activity gap, *Sociology of Education*, 77(3), 185-210.

Cookson, Peter W. & Persell, Caroline Hodges (1985) *Preparing for Power: America's elite boarding schools*. New York: Basic Books.

Davies, Scott & Hammack, Floyd (2005) Channelling Competition in Higher Education: comparing Canada and the US, *Journal of Higher Education*, 76(1), 89-106. http://dx.doi.org/10.1353/jhe.2005.0003

Davies, Scott & Quirke, Linda (2005) Providing for the Priceless Student: ideologies of choice in an emerging educational market, *American Journal of Education*, 111(4), 523-547. http://dx.doi.org/10.1086/431182

Davies, Scott, Quirke, Linda & Aurini, Janice (2006) Institutional Theory Goes to the Market: the challenge of new forms of private education, in Heinz-Dieter Meyer & Brian Rowan (Eds) *The New Institutionalism and Education*. Albany: SUNY Press.

Domina, Thurston (2005) Leveling the Home Advantage: assessing the effectiveness of parental involvement in elementary school, *Sociology of Education*, 78, 233-249.

Dumais, Susan A. (2005) Elementary School Students' Extracurricular Activities: the effects of participation on achievement and teachers' evaluations. Presented at the annual meetings of the American Sociological Association, Philadelphia.

Frones, Ivor (1994) *Dimensions of Childhood.* Brookfield, VT: Ashgate.

Goldhaber, Dan D. (1999) School Choice: an examination of the empirical evidence on achievement, parental decision making, and equity, *Educational Researcher*, 28(9), 16-25. http://dx.doi.org/10.3102/0013189X028009016

Gorard, Stephen, Fitz, John & Taylor, Chris (2001) School Choice Impacts: what we do know, *Educational Researcher*, 30(7), 18-23. http://dx.doi.org/10.3102/0013189X030007018

Guppy, Neil, Crocker, Robert, Davies, Scott, LaPointe, Claire & Sackney, Larry (2005) *Parent and Teacher Views on Education: a policymaker's guide*. Kelowna, BC: Society for the Advancement of Excellence in Education.

Hays, Sharon (1996) *Cultural Contradictions of Motherhood.* New Haven: Yale University Press.

Jacobs, Jerry A. (2005) Multiple Methods in ASR, *Footnotes*, 33(9):1, p. 4.

Kingston, Paul W. (2001) The Unfulfilled Promise of Cultural Capital Theory, *Sociology of Education* (Extra Issue), 74, 88-99. http://dx.doi.org/10.2307/2673255

Lareau, Annette ([1989] 2000) *Home Advantage: social class and parental intervention in elementary education*, 2nd edn. Lanham: Rowman & Littlefield.

Lareau, Annette (2002) Invisible Inequality: social class and childbearing in black families and white families, *American Sociological Review*, 67(5), 747-776. http://dx.doi.org/10.2307/3088916

Lareau, Annette (2003) *Unequal Childhoods*. Berkeley: University of California Press.

Lareau, Annette & Elliot Weininger (2003) Cultural Capital in Educational Research: a critical assessment, *Theory and Society*, 32(5/6), 567-606.

Lubienski, Christopher (2008) School Choice Research in the United States and Why it Doesn't Matter: the evolving economy of knowledge production in a contested policy domain. Chapter 2 of this book.

McNeal, Ralph B. (1999) Parental Involvement as Social Capital: differential effectiveness on science achievement, truancy, and dropping out, *Social Forces*, 78(1), 117-144. http://dx.doi.org/10.2307/3005792

Muller, Chandra (1993) Parent Involvement and Academic Achievement: an analysis of family resources available to the child, in Barbara Schneider & James S. Coleman (Eds) *Parents, their Children, and Schools*. Boulder: Westview Press.

Quirke, Linda (2006) 'Keeping Young Minds Sharp': children's cognitive stimulation and the rise of parenting magazines, 1959-2003, *Canadian Review of Sociology*, 43(4), 387-406.

Sayer, Liana C., Bianchi, Suzanne M. & Robinson, John P. (2004) Are Parents Investing Less in Children? Trends in Mothers' and Fathers' Time with Children, *American Journal of Sociology*, 110, 1-43. http://dx.doi.org/10.1086/386270

Smith, Christian & Sikkink, David (1999) Is Private School Privatizing? *First Things*, 92, 16-20.

Stevens, Mitchell (2001) *Kingdom of Children*. Princeton: Princeton University Press.

Witte, John F. (2000) *The Market Approach to Education: an analysis of America's first voucher program*. Princeton: Princeton University Press.

Zelizer, Viviana A. (1985) *Pricing the Priceless Child: the changing social value of children*. New York: Basic Books.

CHAPTER 4

No Choice but to Choose: selecting schools in Western Australia

MARTIN FORSEY

SUMMARY This chapter reports on research conducted among parents and their children regarding their educational choices in Perth, Western Australia. The people targeted for this research all chose to change systems, either from so-called 'private' schools to the government education system, or vice versa. While choice has always been part of Australia's schooling systems, governments of all political hues have been busily enhancing their commitment to opening up educational choices for parents and students through increasing funding to the non-government sector. Attempts to 'de-governmentalize the state' in education have led to parents, students, teachers, politicians and bureaucrats being drawn further into reproducing a social system that exacerbates social inequality. It is argued that Keynesian-style welfarism remains an influential element in the political machinations accompanying the reformation of Australian schooling. The free market is rarely ever free, and, as some of the parents interviewed found, the private sector does not necessarily generate greater levels of efficiency and accountability, nor are their standards automatically higher than those found in the public sector. Not only that, far from being the great source of openness, freedom and democracy that some would have us believe we will find in private enterprise, they are quite capable of squashing individual freedoms. As one would expect of any complex reform process, the results of recent neo-liberal reform to Australian schooling are at best unpredictable.

You know, when you are a little girl and you just want to wear one of those cool looking private school uniforms and you just want to, I don't know, go to a private school ... something about it which is

> just so ooooh, it's a private school. (Shannon, student, 15 years old)

> I knew that I wanted to go to places where I get a good education you know, and so private school, that's automatically what everyone thinks, you know, when it comes to good education. (Samuel, student, 17 years old)

> Liberalism depends upon a novel specification of the subjects of rule as active in their own government. (Rose, 1993, p. 291)

Asking Questions of the Here and Now

Jim is a teacher and parent.[1] He is one of 50 persons interviewed in 2005 as part of a research project conducted by me and a research associate investigating perceptions and realities of public and private education in Australia.[2] My interview with Jim took place on a student lunch table at Juniper High, where he works as an industrial arts teacher. Juniper High is a school with a reputation as one of the more academically successful government schools in the state of Western Australia. The research reported here involved a number of these in-depth, semi-structured interviews with teachers, parents, and students who reside in Perth, the state's capital. Jim was interviewed because he had recently taken the decision to remove his son from a low-fee Protestant high school that was run by the church of which he was a member, in order to enrol him at Juniper High.

Reflecting on this decision, Jim put it to me that a generation ago he would not have worried about where he sent his son to school – the local government school would have been good enough. Thinking further about the changes he has witnessed with regard to schooling and choice of schools, Jim made the following observation:

> What you're creating is little enclaves of like-minded, wealthy people and enclaves of people who are of all the same type and I think if we're not careful it's going to happen with our government schools, those who have no choice have just got to accept what's there and those who have got double incomes and highly motivated and ... I mean years ago most of those people would have been happy with a government school to be quite honest. I think schools like this [Juniper High] probably reflect what people were getting 20, 30 years ago to a certain extent ... What a lot of people are paying for ... is what they got for free 30 years ago. Does that make sense?

Jim's comment about what people were getting two or three decades ago suggests that while Juniper High is currently seen as exceptional in the government education system, it is what used to be more like the norm in the public system. What is now considered to be an outstanding educational institution was once more or less the standard offering among the government schools of Western Australia, or at least that is Jim's perception of what has happened to government schooling in the state.

Aware of how the choices he was making for his children were influenced by forces sweeping across Australian society, Jim was struck by how he was part of a significant historical development. As a product of a working-class family, who had attended his local Catholic school until Year 10 and which he left in order to take up an apprenticeship as a mechanical fitter, Jim was very conscious of how his own choices and decisions were influenced by what he saw as a competitive, materialistic ethos that has come to dominate contemporary Australian society:

> 30, 40 years ago parents didn't even take that active interest in what their kids did once they went out the door. They gave them their lunch and they went to school. I mean not even the mums were all that much involved really ... How has that shifted? I think because everything has become so much more competitive and the stakes ... I think we're a more materialistic minded society, you got to have a, you know, double professional income to get ahead and the whole thrust of everything has changed.

Neo-liberal Subjects

As Jim's comments help show, competition and choice have become significant catchcries in contemporary Australia. But they are more than public utterances; choice and competition policy have helped drive a raft of institutional reforms that are constituted by a neo-liberalist ideology that is extolled by politicians and activists across the very broad middle range of the political spectrum. The reforms are invariably aimed at making key public institutions perform in ways that are attuned to private enterprise with its emphasis on efficiency and a customer focus. Better outcomes are said to flow to citizens, who are now often construed as clients of the state, than were hitherto available when society was apparently under the spell of the stultifying orthodoxies of Keynesian welfarism.

As with its antecedent liberalism, neo-liberalism proposes that strong private property rights, open markets and free trade offer the basis for greater levels of social efficiency and wealth, and ultimately provide for human well-being and happiness (Harvey, 2005, p. 2). This is the orthodox economic position of our time and its effects on the organisation of schooling, among other public institutions, are profound. In the anglophone world it was Margaret Thatcher, the former Prime Minister of the United Kingdom, who led the charge by attempting to decentralise and privatise the British public education system. Or at least that was what her rhetoric suggested she would do. In reality, while she did have some success in disempowering various local education authorities and allowing individual schools to take charge of

N·C
9

their own destiny, she also helped produce a highly centralised national curriculum. The latter development reflected her conservative commitment to 'standards' far more than it did a liberal commitment to individualism and freedom of thought, a phenomenon that is more common than many commentators on neo-liberalism seem inclined to identify (Larner, 2005).

Anderson (1998, p. 577) argues that the global movements calling for increased decentralisation and privatisation were responding to 'a crisis of legitimation' that was felt at the level of the state and caused much greater scrutiny of the effectiveness and efficiency of public institutions (see also McLean & Laugo, 1985; Walford, 1996; Whitty et al, 1998; Pini & Ciglitutti, 1999). The increased public scepticism about the ability of government to look after the needs of its citizens led, among many other things, to an increased demand from parents for the state to loosen its control over education and to allow them to become more involved in decisions regarding their child's education (Gaynor, 1998). One of the most influential commentators on neo-liberalism, Nikolas Rose (1993, p. 296), argues that the main aim of this political formation is to 'de-governmentalize the state'. He describes a form of detachment of the centre from the various regulatory technologies that were assembled into a single functioning network over the course of the twentieth century which was steadily replaced by a form of administration that looked to govern by 'shaping the powers and will of autonomous entities'.

Jim's musings on the changes that he has seen in his lifetime with regard to attitudes and behaviours towards schools and choices of schooling encapsulate to some degree the transformations in the style of governmentality articulated by Rose. There is now no choice but to choose, or at least for the middle classes this is the case. I know that if I ask a parent for her or his choice story when it comes to the schooling of their child that they will have experienced some of the turmoil of school selection. In contrast with past practices, when only Catholics and/or the wealthy had either the cause or ability to choose schools, significant numbers of Australian parents now pursue involvement in the selection of a school for their children, especially when it comes to secondary schooling (Beavis, 2004, p. 5). In so far as they feel autonomous in their decision making they fit with Rose's depiction of neo-liberal subjects. But there is no straightforward translation of the shifts in practice to those effects that defenders of neo-liberalism describe in terms of increased efficiencies and commitments to academic excellence (Tooley, 1998), and which critics describe as the concentration of wealth and the restoration of class power (Harvey, 2005). As this chapter shows, the results of the education reforms described here are far more complex and nuanced than the polarities of either side tend to capture. In order to more fully comprehend the local issues affecting Western Australian people interviewed for this project about their choice of educational styles and systems, it is useful firstly to paint a broad brush stroke picture of some of the major changes in government policy leading up to the current policy regime affecting Australian educational practices.

Expanding School Choice in Australia

As has already been hinted, choice has always been part of Australia's schooling systems. Church groups were among the first to begin setting up schools in the six British colonies that were to become the states making up the Australian Federation that was formed in 1901. Catholic schools in particular came to have a significant presence across the length and breadth of the various states, so much so that towards the end of the nineteenth century they were drawing significant proportions of the population towards them, many of them non-Catholic. In Western Australia, for example, the state that is the main focus of this chapter, by the early 1890s some 34% of the population's school-going population were attending Catholic schools (Tannock, 1979). The drift towards non-government schooling that is currently causing a deal of consternation among those who support a strong public system is clearly not a new phenomenon in Australia. The main difference now is that, contrary to what happened in the 1890s, there is now very little political appetite for de-funding the schools in the so-called private sector (Forsey, 2007a).

Responsibility for administering the nation's public schools rests with the six state and two territory governments that make up the Australian Commonwealth. In the first half of the twentieth century government schooling in the various states developed into what a number of commentators have described as being amongst the most centralised systems on the planet (Chapman & Dunstan, 1990). As was the case in many other parts of the industrialised world, these highly centralised, state-wide bureaucratic systems offered a means of ensuring some level of equitable provision of educational opportunities and resources. In the Australian case this commitment to equity usually had to be pursued across vast geographic areas (Harman et al, 1991). However, the image of such a tightly controlled organisational structure is rarely portrayed in any sort of positive light. Indeed, critiques of various types of bureaucratic formations, which Rose (1993) suggests are viewed by many as inimical to liberty, are highly conventional and predictable (Herzfeld, 1992). Interestingly, the criticisms do not simply emanate solely from the conservative and the so-called 'right' side of the political field, they arise from most sections of the broad political spectrum.

In the recent past educational choice in Australia has been expanded via two main mechanisms. Firstly, since the early 1970s we have witnessed a steady increase in funding of non-government schools by the national (federal) government. These were initiated by the Whitlam Labor Government's policy of guaranteeing state aid to private schools, measures that were mainly aimed at redressing the inequalities extant in the severely under-resourced Catholic schools sector (Forsey, 2007a). Secondly, the various state governments progressively relaxed the rules that hitherto had compelled the majority of students wishing to access government education to attend their local school.

Since state aid to non-government schools was first guaranteed in the early 1970s, there has been a steady decline in market share for government education. In 1974 the proportion of Australian school students attending government schools was 78%; by 2004 the proportion had fallen to 68% (Burke & Spaull, 2001; Australian Government Department of Education, Science and Training, 2005). The vast bulk of non-government schools, regardless of their financial status, are now guaranteed some level of federal government support. Furthermore, over the last decade, especially under the leadership of the recently deposed Liberal government, the level of financial support to the private sector has increased quite dramatically (Megalogenis, 2006, p. 18). Given that secondary schools play such an important role in preparing students for university entrance, it is not surprising that it is in this sector that these shifts have been most profoundly felt. Currently 38% of Australia's high school students are enrolled in non-government schools (Australian Bureau of Statistics, 2006). However, as this research helps show, while undoubtedly the perception and realities of academic standards helped drive this significant shift, other factors drive parental and student choice.

These shifts in commitment to the various education systems among politicians and the Australian electorate reflect a growing loss of confidence in government schools. In 2004 the Prime Minister, John Howard, attributed this growing disillusionment with public education to the perception that government schools are simultaneously devoid of values and much too politically correct. Apart from the fact that the two descriptors seem to be at odds with each other, it is interesting to note that the issue of profound shifts in funding and resource bases to the different school sectors did not emerge in the Prime Minister's discourse as a significant contributor to the movement away from government education. Issues such as security in schools, facilities, perceptions about standards of teaching and care undoubtedly play a role in the directions parents lean in relation to public education.

The epigraphs opening this chapter help show that it is not just parents who are important decision makers when it comes to schools; student perceptions of the different types of schools are also potentially significant to the choices being made. The fact that both Samuel and Shannon ended up in public schools after trying their luck in the private sector offers some pause for thought. Their reflections will emerge in due course, but before moving to share more of the various insights regarding the selection of schools in Western Australia that emerged from this study it is important to outline how the research was conducted, who was involved and what it aimed to do.

The Study

Set against the backdrop of the fairly dramatic leakage of students out of public schools into the non-government sector, the interviews reported here focused on parental and student responses to the increased levels of choice available to them in contemporary Australia. Contrary to the impressions created by the current net flow towards the non-government sector, the stream is not unidirectional. Reflecting this fact, approximately half of the people interviewed for this project recently took the option to move from a private establishment to a government school. Clearly, the sample is neither random nor representative. We deliberately pursued approximately equal numbers of students, parents and teachers who have moved from the non-government sector towards government schooling and vice versa. We also partially relied upon the snowballing effects of recommendations from respondents we had already interviewed as to people we might contact for interviews.

Responding to his own extensive survey into parental reasons for choosing public or private schools, Beavis (2004, p. 5) acknowledges that we know quite a bit about the perceptions of the two main types of schooling, but little about how realistic such impressions are. Those who have changed their educational allegiances can take us beyond perceptions based upon singular experiences and stereotypes of the unknown 'other' system. By interviewing individuals who have switched systems, we have been able to capture some personal reflections on the realities of working, studying and overseeing the education of one's children in different types of school from the perspective of those who have actual experiences of government *and* non-government education. Table I summarises some of the various categories of contributors to this project. Given that the majority of respondents were self-nominated volunteers, it is not surprising that close to two-thirds of interviewees are female. As David et al (1997) note from their research with parents in England, mothers tend to do the *work* of school choice. This project reflects that trend.

	Parents (38%)	Teachers (34%)	Students (28%)	Total
Females	14	10	7	31 (62%)
Males	5	7	7	19 (38%)
Total	19	17	14	50

Table I. Interview sample by category and gender.

The interviews with the parents and students usually lasted at least 45 minutes, and were mostly conducted in the participants' homes. Each interview was audio-recorded and transcribed verbatim by a professional typist. While we occasionally spoke with couples, most of the interviews were one-to-one. Students were usually interviewed separately from their parents, but some times the parents stayed in the room when we interviewed their children. While the youngest student we interviewed was 10 years old and the oldest in her twenties, the majority of the students were of high school age.

In their extensive and important research into school choice in England Bowe et al (1994) highlight the significance of focusing on the social context of human thought and action, particularly when reporting the results of interview-based research. The conversations reported here aimed at locating the cultural context of the participant's decision-making processes through a deeper understanding of their biography – the beliefs, the values, the material conditions and structural forces underpinning their socially patterned choices. In moving to consider more fully the interview data generated for this project, I begin by telling the story of one of the teachers I met in 2005. I interviewed Kelly because she recently resigned her job as a teacher at a Catholic school and had taken up a posting at a government school, but it was her comments about the future schooling of her infant daughter that most intrigued me.

Kelly's Story

Kelly is in her mid-twenties. She is a mother and a music teacher. Her first teaching appointment to a Catholic school in the eastern suburbs of Perth lasted a little over a year. As is so often the case with first-year teachers it was a 'sink or swim' experience and it did not work out as she hoped. Her next job was a short-term contract at a government school near where she lives with her husband in the southern industrial zone of Perth. Her experience at the government school was quite different. Kelly found both the staff and parents to be more supportive there.

Kelly has a daughter who was two years old at the time of the interview. Interestingly, while Kelly would be happy to continue working at the government school in which she recently had a contract, she is not at all keen for her daughter to eventually attend there. 'I wouldn't want her in the classes of some of the teachers', she explains, 'they just haven't got a clue'. Kelly would prefer her daughter to start off in a private primary school, but she would not choose any of the non-government schools in the southern industrial zone. Her husband, who teaches in the public system, is deeply committed to government education and vehemently opposed to private schooling. He calls her a snob, 'because you know I've come from south of the river and now I'm down here and it's a totally different lifestyle, totally different outlook. The kids have different sort of ideas about things, a different home life to what I had'.[3]

What concerns Kelly most about the students she has taught in the southern industrial zone is their general lack of ambition. If her daughter were to be schooled in the area she would worry that she would not aspire to do anything that Kelly deems to be worthwhile: 'Down here you're lucky if you graduate school and don't get knocked up beforehand. 'Cause so many of the kids that you know get out of school the first thing that happens is they end up pregnant'.

Despite her husband's deeply held commitment to public schooling, he tends to concur with Kelly and they are seriously considering moving out of the industrial area in order to ensure that their daughter can attend a more acceptable school. They are contemplating enrolling her in a non-government primary school. As one who enjoyed her own government school education and who is happy enough to work in such schools, Kelly worries about her apparent hypocrisy; however, she is also aware of the changes that she has experienced: 'Twenty years ago you just went to the local school, but now, we just expect more. Private schools will have better resources and they'll have more competent teachers right throughout because they are able to weed out the undesirable teachers and the undesirable kids'. Her conclusion: 'if I want to give my daughter every opportunity I will be hypocritical'.

As with Jim, who was introduced at the opening of this chapter, Kelly speaks of a world that has changed in the course of her relatively short lifespan. Her comment about the ways in which 'we just expect more' amplifies what we often hear regarding consumer expectations in this neo-liberal age. This is what the shifts in policy are supposed to yield; in responding creatively to these changing expectations, schools will apparently wind their way down roads leading towards increasing levels of excellence.

The class prejudices, and their accompanying realities, that were expressed by Kelly were replicated on many occasions in the interviews conducted for this project. For example, a 12-year-old female student who had recently shifted from her local government primary school to a small Christian primary school and from there to an Anglican high school commented on the social differences she had noticed between parents in government and private schools. When I asked Louise to elaborate on this she suggested that there was a group of parents in the government school who stood out because they smoked and shouted out loud at their kids: 'They don't seem to take as much pride in themselves either like ... I mean because there's nothing wrong with coming not dressed up or not like ... but they just don't seem to have as much pride in what others think'. Louise was quite sure that there was no such group of parents in either of the non-government schools she had attended.

It is not simply class prejudice; there is something all too real about the sorts of chaos that the parents and students interviewed for this project seek to avoid in schools. As will become more apparent, it is particular government schools, those located in the poorer parts of town, that cause the greatest concern to this particular group of education consumers. Writing in defence of school choice policies in the USA, Almond (1994, pp. 70-71) identifies a commitment to altruistic ideals among the parents she has encountered, but this only goes so far; most 'are not prepared to sacrifice their own children's welfare for the public good'. The awkwardness felt regarding the implications of expressing support for the government system whilst rejecting particular types of government school for one's own child was also evident in the reflections of a number of the participants in this project, particularly those who had chosen to shift their children from government to non-government schools.

Going Private

Jonelle, who we interviewed because she had recently removed her two children from a government school in the same southern industrial zone in which Kelly lives, reflects Almond's observation very cogently. We pursued an interview with Jonelle because we had heard about how she drove around the suburbs with a bumper-sticker proclaiming her commitment to public education despite having sent her son and daughter to the local Catholic high school. When asked about this, it drew the following response:

> Yeah. I still run around with my government education sticker sitting on my car and people say, 'You're sending your kids private, why do you have this on your car?'
>
> And I say it's because the government system is still important and just because I don't want to send my kids in there to be the so-called sacrificial lambs to fix it doesn't mean I don't care about the kids that are in there you know! Like it's still got to be fixed and I think a lot of us have still got to lobby to get them fixed particularly for the funding and just the other things down here.

Jonelle comes from a family of teachers. Her mother was a principal in government schools and her sister and brother-in-law also teach in the public system. However, despite having a strong familial link to government education, when she was in her final year at a high school in rural New South Wales she transferred out of the government school she had attended for four years in order to enrol at a high-fee Anglican school in Sydney. She describes the move as like going from hell to heaven as she moved away from the prejudices and bullying she experienced as a consequence of being an academically inclined student with an interest in music.

Jonelle's own secondary school experiences undoubtedly guided her decision making as a parent of academically inclined children who were also interested in music. Like many Australian parents she was comfortable with them going to the local government primary school. It was when it became time for them to go to high school that she felt the need to change systems. Her eldest child won a scholarship to the Catholic school he now attends, which meant they only had to pay half of the required fees. Jonelle was particularly happy about this because not only did she judge St Margaret's to have the best music curriculum in the district, they also had the best pastoral care programme.

Four of the ten parents interviewed who had recently moved at least one of their children from a government to a non-government school were teachers in the public system. Along with Jonelle and two of the other parents in this cohort, they expressed strong support for the public system, and, as has been shown already, they explained the obvious tensions between their public mindedness and their parental interests in fascinating ways. To draw on one further example, Hayley is also a teacher in the government system. Like Jonelle, one of her parents, her father in this instance, had been a principal in the government school system. She had also been sent to public primary schools but made the switch to an Anglican grammar school as part of her transition to high school. Hayley and her husband were committed to following a similar pattern for their children, mainly because they felt that academic standards were higher in the private system, but they also felt that their children would get better options for playing sport in church-based schools. However, having grown disillusioned with the ways in which a new principal had reshaped their local primary school, they had decided to pursue the private option earlier than they originally intended. As was the case with Kelly, Hayley was a little concerned about the apparent hypocrisy of her choices, but she was also committed in a vague, slightly uncomfortable way, to a consumerist ethic:

> I have gone through this a lot, that is almost ... in some ways it's almost like hypocritical isn't it? You know, you're in one system but you've got your kids going somewhere else. And I do sort of think a lot about why you make those decisions but it's always the same, there's never anything really conclusive. [Pause]
>
> To me it's a bit like buying a car – you go and you shop around for the best deal or whatever. And it's the same, like I've never felt that I would send all my children to the same school; just because one was there, the others had to go there, you know! I really think that if somewhere offered a particular thing that was really good for one of your children, be it state or be it government, then that's what I'd go and look at it. And it may be that the other ones might be better off somewhere else.
>
> I think that that's how I think you should see it, they're offering you a service and you go and check them out. You line them up against everybody else.

What we hear from Jonelle and Hayley in these narratives, and they reflect the general pattern among the 10 persons we interviewed who have recently opted for non-government schooling, is a biography of choice. In a nation that has had a robust Catholic education sector, as well as a set of high-fee Protestant schools, for as long as there have been schools, there has always been some ability to select which school one wishes to attend. Clearly, both

Jonelle and Hayley were able to take advantage of this when they were students. There is now a greater ability to choose and this has intensified the desire among the likes of Jim, Kelly, Jonelle and Hayley to exercise their choices in the best interests of their children. For each of them, even for Jim who moved his child to a government school, their decisions produced some level of discomfort as they reflected upon the broader issues of the common good and social justice. But their decisions were not framed around narrow instrumental concerns associated with increasing their child's position on the academic ladder. In many instances the parents reported being influenced by the sense of community offered by the schools, by the extra-curricular programmes, the ways in which their child was welcomed into the school, and/or by the directions that their particular son or daughter wanted to pursue.

Laura and Colin, a married couple who are both teachers in the public system, capture this very well. They had moved to a particular suburb so that their son and daughter could be guaranteed a place at the government high school with the strongest academic reputation in the state. But their son had other ideas. Josh wanted to attend a particular Catholic school because of the sporting opportunities it offered. Both Laura and Colin agree that the Catholic school did not present the same academic opportunities as their local government school, but Laura now describes herself as a 'poster girl' for the school her son now attends. She loves the atmosphere of the place, the ways in which Josh is cared for by the teachers and the opportunities it provides him to get involved with a wide range of activities. Both of them suggested that this sort of care is rarely available in the public system.

Jim, whose thoughts on what has happened to government schools and how this is influenced by shifts in societal expectations helped open this chapter, moved in opposite directions to the ones taken by the other people introduced so far. Interestingly, he was concerned that his son's needs were not being met in the low-fee Protestant high school he attended mainly because it did not cater very well to those students who were not university bound. As the next section shows, this is not an uncommon story, but other concerns were also evident.

Going Public

Claire, Laurie and Sam's Story

Claire and Laurie were both in their forties at the time of the interview. They have four children. In 2005 their eldest child, Sam, was completing Year 12 at a government high school that was some distance from their home in the foothills on the east of the city. The government high schools in their immediate vicinity have a reputation for being quite rough and Claire and Laurie discouraged Sam from attending them. Laurie talks of the 'dirty big fence' that surrounds their local school, a security measure that caused both of them to feel decidedly insecure about sending their son there. Sam describes the school as a place in which drug users and 'pretty serious gangs' wielded a great deal of influence. To him it is 'dangerous'.

Interestingly, it was a fight with one of Sam's closest primary school friends that triggered his decision not to attend the fenced-off local high school. Up to that point he was intending to follow his friends there, but the divisions triggered by the conflict caused him to rethink his choices. This all happened when Sam was in Year 7 and Clair and Laurie recall a frantic last-minute search for a suitable school. Sensing that their lack of religious conviction would probably preclude the local Catholic school, and finding two other independent schools to be too expensive, they settled on a new low-fee Christian school that was just opening in a suburb about 15 kilometres from their house.

At first things went well. Sam enjoyed being at the school, describing it as a calm place, with no violence. Comparing the two and a half years he spent at the Christian school with the government school he moved to towards the end of Year 10, Sam speaks with residual surprise about how little homework he was expected to do when he first arrived at the government school: 'there was a lot of homework and stuff like that at the private school. But when I went to [the government school] it was just like you know sitting back doing nothing really in Year 10'.

Sam describes an elaborate set of rules and regulations at the Christian school that revolved around 'referrals', 'uniform defaults', 'letters home' and 'detentions' that were mainly associated with governing homework and school uniform rules. These rules tightened progressively over Sam's time at the school, reaching a point where a number of his friends started to react against the regulations. By about halfway through Year 10 they had all left the school. By the time Sam left, he calculates that there were only five boys left in his year group, and he was on friendly terms with only one of them.

In part Sam attributes his leaving the Christian school to having had his eyebrow pierced in Year 10. The teachers and the principal demanded that he remove it. Having spent $80 on the piercing, there was no way that Sam wanted to comply with this ruling. But, in Sam's words:

> Eyebrow thing or not I would have left there that year anyway cos I'd come home depressed and sad. You got to have your friends to talk to and you got to have friends there to stand by your side and stuff. But I just had no one there, it was just me. Cos it was school you know, but it wasn't school any more, it was just learning.

For most of the students interviewed as part of this project, a major factor governing their choice of school revolved around where their friends were going. In interview after interview, when students reflected upon their choice of school they reported being strongly influenced by what their friends were doing. If their parents selected a school to which few of their friends were going they often found this difficult to deal with. In turn they judged their reactions to the school according to how readily they formed new friendships.

As Sam's final comment so cogently puts it, for students at least, schools are about more than 'just learning'; they are deeply social places.

Parents are cognisant of this, and Claire and Laurie certainly responded to Sam's misery at the loss of his friends, but they were also concerned about the lack of resources available at the Christian school. The attrition rate, itself attributable to the lack of resources, only compounded their concerns. Without a critical mass of students going into Years 11 and 12, the school could not guarantee as wide a range of subjects as they would have liked and they were concerned that the university entrance subjects Sam wanted to take would not be available there. Shortly after we completed the interview, in fact, Claire emailed me to make sure I was clear about the various reasons they had for firstly seeking out a private school and then returning to the government system:

> Reasons for initial private school decision:
>
> – Perception of more accountability in the private system.
> – Belief that the private school would be working for us and our child, i.e. take more notice of input/concerns/needs.
> – An expectation of mutual respect and support of our family values.
> – Perception of better facilities.
> – Perception of better pastoral care for students, included in this, the view that private schools can readily expel troublemakers, thus creating a safer environment for other students.
>
> We came to see that all was not as we'd hoped and our perceptions were not the reality. The following outlines our negative findings:
>
> 1. The private school fell short of expectations, e.g. promises not kept on several issues.
> 2. There was overzealous policing of minor uniform infringements and unfair and inconsistent treatment of behavioural misdemeanours.
> 3. The school lacked adequate facilities.
> 4. No tertiary entrance examination subjects available to our child. A change to a sister college was offered, however, new uniform would be required and no subsidy or discounts were going to be forthcoming.

Another parent, Sarah, sent her son William to a Montessori school for many of the reasons listed by Claire and Laurie. Primarily she thought that an independent school would be more accountable to parents and that this would give her more control over her child's education. The three and a half years that her son was at the school caused her to rethink this perception quite drastically. She found the staff uncommunicative and unsupportive of her child's needs. The lack of testing, that sounded so positive when she first went to the school, bothered her in the end as it was never clear to her how her son was progressing as a student. A number of other parents shared this concern and gradually the numbers at the school dwindled.

Failing to reach a critical mass of students is significant in a number of the new independent colleges that have opened in the past few years as a consequence of increased federal funding. Half of the cohort under consideration here chose so-called alternative forms of schooling – Montessori and Steiner – for their primary school-aged children, with three of the four commenting that the main reason for leaving these schools revolved around their lack of resources. Sarah put this very clearly when she contrasted what she noticed in the public schools she started to visit when she was considering withdrawing William from the Montessori school he was attending. Noting the strong academic, sporting and cultural focus at the government primary school in which she eventually enrolled her son, Sarah observed that such programmes are not in the independent schools 'because they don't really have the resources to offer all of those things'.

Yvette is another mother who felt that the alternative school her daughter, Shannon, attended until Year 5 was severely limited by its lack of student numbers. The literature she was reading about schools suggested to her that single-sex schools were the most appropriate for girls and so, after agonising over the best school for Shannon, she decided on one of the high-fee United Church schools. She felt that they had better social policies than the other church schools, particularly in relation to Aboriginal people, women, lesbians and gays. Her choice was also influenced by the strong academic standards she believed the school set.

Shannon, whose romantic views of elite private schools helped open this chapter, loved her new school, but after a little while both she and her mother began to have some doubts. Yvette observed that Shannon had barely progressed in maths or English – 'Every student has a laptop in the school, but they cannot spell. They download their assignments from the Internet'. Shannon is quite a gifted musician, but even in that area she appeared to be underperforming. According to Shannon and her mother, the students at the exclusive private school were 'mollycoddled' and protected from failure. They both felt that the school valued presentation over substance and Shannon developed a growing distaste for what she saw as an elitist, 'snobby' attitude among many of her schoolmates. As a consequence of this variety of factors, Shannon wanted to leave and she chose to go to a government school with a specialist music programme.

Simone also moved her son Thomas out of the local Catholic school in the northern suburbs of Perth because she was not happy with its academic standards. Compounding this perception, she also felt that the classes, which sometimes had up to 35 students in them, were overcrowded. Simone works in the government education system and had some inside knowledge on which schools were best to go to, so when she transferred Thomas out of the Catholic school, he went to a hand-picked government school. Upon arriving at the new school she became immediately aware that Thomas's work was not up to the standard of his peers in the government school, and some of the teachers also told her this was the case.

Louise and Harry had an opposite problem. While their eldest daughter had sailed through the Catholic school close to their southern suburbs home, their son Bob really struggled. Bob told us how he was never really interested in school work or going to university. His parents felt that the school only cared about finances. The school offered little by way of vocational training. To all three of them it seemed that the main curriculum concern was to get as many students doing well in the tertiary entrance examinations subjects as possible, and forget about the rest. As was the case with Jim's son, this is the reason that Bob moved on.

As discussed earlier, school choice for parents and students has opened up on two fronts: by increasing funding to all non-government schools and by allowing students to attend the government school of their choice. Clearly, for the parents and students discussed in this section the private option did not work. The reasons are manifold, but revolve around curriculum and academic standards, as well as the lack of a critical mass of students, with its concomitant lack of resources and educational options. Most of the parents and students discussed here have therefore explored the second set of options open to them. They have shopped around in the government system and most of them have found this satisfying enough. But in all cases they did not choose to enrol their children in their local school. One parent put it to us that she chose a particular school for her daughter because out of all government schools in the state it is the one that is most like a private school.[4] As was the case with Jim, all but one of the parents choosing government education after their child had spent a period of time in a non-government school opted for places that were outside of their designated catchment zone. They were located in middle-class suburbs, had a reputation for being fairly strong academically, and for their friendly and safe atmosphere. As I have recently argued in relation to neo-liberal reorganisation of schooling (Forsey, 2007b) for all of the rhetoric of diversity and meeting individual needs that accompanies contemporary education reform, the homogenising effects of the market are strong (see also Blackmore, 1999).

As is always the case, contradictory and complicated forces are at play in the organisation of schooling. In drawing this chapter to a close I want to reflect briefly upon what the apparent anomalies discussed here indicate and what the parents and students interviewed for this project tell us about future directions for educational reform.

Choice and the Neo-liberal Consumer

> The deregulation and privatisation of schools shifts the responsibility for educational outcomes squarely on to students and parents ... If one's child does not perform and achieve to the expected level, then, as a parent one must look to oneself for the reason. Perhaps it is because insufficient attention was paid to the 'choice of school'. (Brown, 1994, p. 63)

In an era of expanding school choice, citizen-clients of a nation state can certainly develop the impression that they are acting as autonomous individuals. As this study helps show, many more Australian parents have become more active, conscious consumers of educational services than there were in the past. In so far as they have done this in the spirit of seeking 'self-reliance over community dependence' (Safire, 2004), we can argue that this is part of becoming a neo-liberal subject. It would be a mistake, of course, to assume that self-interest is re-emerging out of hibernation. We have not simply moved from a period of communal care and concern into an individualistic 'second modernity' (Beck et al, 2003). However, the argument offered by Beck and his colleagues, that those living in the so-called West are living through a period when individualism is pursued and constructed in some unique ways, offers useful ways of comprehending the present.

Bowe et al (1994) assert that choice draws parents (and I might add students, teachers, politicians and bureaucrats) further into a system of social reproduction. They ask, 'are we in fact witnessing not the devolution of power to the individual consumer but the exacerbation of social inequality through the unequal distribution of power in the mode of consumption?' (p. 66). While their answer is obviously an affirmative one, nevertheless, they also point out that parents and their children are not simply dominated by a new freedom of choice or by naïve consumerism (p. 76). Both of the realities reported by Bowe et al are clearly evident in the research reported here.

As Jim's comments indicate at the opening of this chapter, there is now no choice but to choose. The mere act of opening up public schools to the competitive forces of the market, of removing the boundary limitations compelling those living in set geographical spaces who wish to utilise public education to enrol children in their local school, causes most people to make a choice. Even remaining committed to one's local school becomes a choice one has to take, or at least in cities and larger towns it does. There is something compelling in Brown's (1994, p. 63) argument about the ways in which deregulation and privatisation of schools has shifted the responsibility for educational outcomes from governments to individual education consumers. This is a logical enough outcome of the predominant neo-liberal doctrine. However, there being no choice but to choose does not mean that people simply accede to the realities being constructed for them, nor do they necessarily behave in the manner hoped for by those enamoured of neo liberal ideals.

In warning against seeing the new political configurations of our time as 'monolithic projects imposed upon passive victims', Larner (2005, p. 12) urges social researchers to pay attention to the specificities of neo-liberal political economies, and to be sensitive to the complex, hybrid 'political imaginaries these new spaces, socialities and subjects are likely to embody'. One should focus on the historical continuities of social change at least as much as on the ruptures (Saussure, 1959). Even though so-called private schools are meant to be articulated through a market rather than a bureaucracy (Connell et al, 1982), as some of the parents we interviewed found in their encounters with non-government schools, they were not necessarily accountable to them as consumers of their product, or at least not as accountable as they may have wished them to be. At the same time, the non-government schools did not necessarily provide the level of commitment to excellence and service that the neo-liberal advocates of the private over the public suggest they would. As Beck and his colleagues (2003) predict in their outlining of the changes that have occurred in 'second modernity', this study does help reveal a group of parents and students who are primarily focused on their individual needs and aspirations in contemporary Australia. However, these needs and aspirations are rarely pursued to the exclusion of other families and students. We are not witnessing a straight reinforcement of class power. There is at least a consciousness among many of the common good and of the contradictory nature of the choices they are making. Commitment to egalitarianism has not been simply jettisoned in the rush to empower the individual to become a self-serving entrepreneur, and it is a mistake to think that parents and students choosing to attend non-government schools do so out of purely selfish motives. Many of the religious and alternative schools offer a strong commitment to social justice. Keynesian-style welfarism remains an influential enough element in the complex political struggle that accompanies the reformation of schooling in these neo-liberal times (Forsey, 2007b, pp. 160-161), something that was evident, however weakly, in the concerns raised by the parents interviewed in this project. Most, if not all of them, would favour a significant boost to the funding of government schools and a withdrawing of funds from schools that already receive more funds in student fees than the government pays in funding public schools on a per capita basis.

As this research project helps show, there are many parents who have moved their children from the public to the private system who are satisfied with the results of their decision. There are others, however, (a smaller minority) who have been far from content with what they have experienced on the other side of the fence. Contradicting what some of the more orthodox neo-liberalists might say, the private sector does not necessarily generate greater levels of efficiency and accountability; their standards are not automatically higher than those found in the public sector. Not only that, as Sam found out when he pierced his eyebrow, the private system can be intolerant of the sort of individualism he sought to express. Interestingly, it was in a school run by the apparently rigid, rule-bound bureaucracy that he found greater levels of tolerance for his slightly altered appearance.

Education cannot be run according to the rules of a pure market. Apart from the fact that schools offer services to the community, the sorts of products they deal with, such as knowledge, care and direction, are not easily commodified. Even those responsible for so-called private schools are rarely conducting a straightforward for-profit enterprise. More often than not they have a religious, or a quasi-religious, mission to fulfil that often reflects a complex mix of conservative and progressive values. Furthermore, it is not an open market. For many of the highly desirable traditional schools demand exceeds supply, so they can pick and choose who can enter and remain inside. A consequence of this is that far from being the great source of openness, freedom and democracy that some would have us believe we will find in private enterprise, they are capable of imposing rules that squash individual freedoms. The so-called free market is rarely ever free. They are eloquent fictions, as Apple (2001) has described them, and the effects of these fictions are at best unpredictable.

Notes

[1] All of the names of people and schools used in this chapter are pseudonyms.

[2] I thank Marnie Giles for her work on this project. Marnie conducted the majority of the interviews with parents and students, while I interviewed the teachers. Greg Martin also gave invaluable assistance in helping code and analyse a significant slice of the interview material.

[3] South of the river is a local expression that historically at least was suggestive of some of the more affluent suburbs of Perth.

[4] See Forsey (2006) for a discussion of Perth Modern School and its recent reinstatement as an academically selective school.

References

Almond, B. (1994) In Defence of Choice in Education, in J. Halstead (Ed.) *Parental Choice and Education: principles, policy and practice.* London: Kogan Page.

Anderson, Gary (1998) Toward Authentic Participation: deconstructing discourses of participatory reforms in education, *American Educational Research Journal*, 35(4), 571-603. http://dx.doi.org/10.2307/1163460

Apple, M., (2001) Comparing Neo-liberal Projects and Inequality in Education, *Comparative Education*, 37(4), 409-423. http://dx.doi.org/10.1080/03050060120091229

Australian Bureau of Statistics (2006) *Australian Social Trends.* Catalogue number 4102.0. Canberra: Australian Bureau of Statistics.

Australian Government Department of Education, Science and Training (2005) *Annual Report 2004-2005.* http://www.dest.gov.au/annualreport/2005/default.htm

Beavis, A. (2004). Why Parents Choose Public or Private Schools, *Research Developments*, 12. Australian Council for Educational Research.

Beck, U., Bonns, W. & Lau, C. (2003) The Theory of Reflexive Modernization: problematic, hypotheses and research programme, *Theory, Culture & Society*, 20(2), 1-33. http://dx.doi.org/10.1177/0263276403020002001

Blackmore, J. (1999) *Troubling Women: feminism, leadership and educational change.* Buckingham: Open University Press.

Bowe, R., Gewirtz, S. & Ball, S. (1994) Captured by the Discourse? Issues and Concerns in Researching Parental Choice, *British Journal of Sociology of Education*, 15(1), 63-78. http://dx.doi.org/10.1080/0142569940150104

Brown, P. (1994) Education and the Ideology of Parentocracy, in J. Mark Halstead (Ed.) *Parental Choice and Education: principles, policy and practice*, 51-67. London: Kegan Paul.

Burke, G. & Spaull, A. (2001) Australian Schools: participation and funding 1901 to 2000, *Australian Bureau of Statistics, 2001 Year Book Australia*, 433-446. Canberra: Australian Bureau of Statistics.

Chapman, J. & Dunstan, J. (1990) Introduction, in J. Chapman & J. Dunstan (Eds) *Democracy and Bureaucracy: tensions in public schooling*. London: Falmer Press.

Connell, R., Ashenden, D., Kessler, S. & Dowsett, G. (1982) *Making the Difference: schools, families and social division*. Sydney: George Allen & Unwin.

David, M., Davies, J., Edwards, R. & Standing, K. (1997) Choice within Constraints: mothers and schooling, *Gender and Education*, 9(4), 397-410. http://dx.doi.org/10.1080/09540259721150

Department of Education, Science and Training (DEST) (2003) *Parents' and Community Members' Attitudes to Schooling. Report of Scoping Study*. Canberra: DEST.

Forsey, M. (2006) Australian Public Schools and the Eloquent Fiction of the Free Market, in G. Willett (Ed.) *Thinking Down Under: Australian politics, society and culture in transition*. Trier: Wissenschaftlicher Verlag.

Forsey, M. (2007a) The Great Education Consensus: why do we no longer seem to be really interested in equity?' *New Critic*, 5 (May). http://www.ias.uwa.edu.au/the_new_critic/archives/issue_5

Forsey, M. (2007b) *Challenging the System? A Dramatic Tale of Neoliberal Reform in an Australian High School*. Charlotte: Information Age Publishing.

Gaynor, C. (1998). *Decentralization in Education: teacher management*. Washington, DC: The World Bank.

Harman, G., Beare, H. & Berkeley, G. (Eds) (1991) *Restructuring Management: administrative reorganisation of public governance in Australia*. Canberra: Australian College of Education.

Harvey, D. (2005) *A Brief History of Neoliberalism*. Oxford: Oxford University Press.

Herzfeld, M. (1992) *The Social Production of Indifference: exploring the symbolic roots of western bureaucracy*. Chicago: University of Chicago Press.

Larner, W. (2005) Neoliberalism in (Regional) Theory and Practice: the stronger communities action fund in New Zealand, *Geographical Research*, 43(1), 9-18. http://dx.doi.org/10.1111/j.1745-5871.2005.00294.x

McLean, M. & Laugo, J. (1985) Introduction: rationales for decentralization and a perspective from organization theory, in J. Laugo & M. McLean (Eds) *The Control of Education: international perspectives on the centralization–decentralization debate.* London: Heinemann.

Megalogenis, G. (2006) Government by Default, *The Weekend Australian*, February 4-5, p. 18.

Pini, M. & Ciglitutti, S. (1999) Participatory Forms and Democracy: the case of Argentina, *Theory into Practice*, 38(4), 196-202.

Rose, N. (1993) Government, Authority and Expertise in Advanced Liberalism, *Economy and Society*, 22(3), 283-299. http://dx.doi.org/10.1080/03085149300000019

Safire, W. (2004) Inside a Republican Brain, *New York Times*, July 21.

Saussure, F. (1959) *Course of General Linguistics.* New York: Philosophical Library.

Tannock, P.D. (1979) Catholic Education in Western Australia 1829-1979, in W.D Neal (Ed.) *Education in Western Australia.* Perth: University of Western Australia Press.

Tooley, J. (1998) The 'Neo-liberal' Critique of State Intervention in Education: a reply to Winch, *Journal of Philosophy of Education*, 32(2), 267-281. http://dx.doi.org/10.1111/1467-9752.00092

Walford, G. (1996) School Choice and the Quasi-Market in England and Wales, *Oxford Studies in Comparative Education*, 6(1), 49-62.

Whitty, G., Power, S. & Halpin, D. (1998). Devolution and Choice in Education: the school, the state and the market. Canberra: ACER Press.

CHAPTER 5

School Choice in England: globalisation, policy borrowing or policy corruption?

GEOFFREY WALFORD

SUMMARY This chapter reviews the history of school choice in England, focusing particularly on the motivations for changes in 1988 and in subsequent years. It argues that, rather than being a case of 'policy borrowing' from Australia, the changes that occurred in England were more a case of 'policy corruption'. England now has a well-established choice system in the state sector and there has been a considerable amount of research conducted on it. This chapter describes and evaluates several of these studies and discusses the relationship between greater choice of school and increased standards of attainment. It then examines the research work that has been conducted on the effects of choice on social segregation and finds mixed results.

Introduction

Over the last two decades England has experienced a variety of changes in education policy that has given greater self-management to individual schools and given families greater choice between schools. These changes were mainly made through the 1988 Education Reform Act that restructured the education system through grant-maintained schools, local management of schools and open enrolment. The Labour Government returned in 1997 made further changes through the 1998 Education Standards and Framework Act and further acts that have made the system even more diverse.

As in many other countries, school-based management and increased choice of schools was originally justified in terms of the effect that it is said to have on efficiency and effectiveness and, ultimately, on students' attainment. In England, as many of the changes to schools occurred at the same time, it is far from proven that any improvements are related to greater choice between self-managed schools as such. Indeed, it may be that regular school inspection by the Office for Standards in Education, the introduction of a National Curriculum and, more recently, a number of special initiatives such as the Literacy Hour and the Numeracy Strategy have had a more important effect on raising students' performance compared to that of increasing choice and competition between schools.

The educational policies of the New Labour Government since 1997 are mixed (Walford, 2004, 2006), but there has been an increasing emphasis on cooperation. While a basic belief in the benefits of school choice and diversity has been retained, there is also a recognition that no school exists in isolation. The Government has encouraged greater cooperation between schools, given more powers to the local education authorities (LEAs) to increase equity, and initiated several schemes to deal with groups of schools in poor areas.

The Historical Context

Diversity and division have long been central elements of English schooling. Prior to 1832 the Government was not involved in education at all (expect for some training in workhouses for the poor). Schools were provided by private initiative or charities, the majority being either Church of England or Catholic based. The first government schools did not appear until 1870 and were designed to fill the gaps in charitable provision especially in the new urban areas. The private and charitable sector remains and still provides places for about 7% of the population.

The 1944 Education Act established free secondary education within the state sector as a distinct stage for all children. In the years following the Second World War secondary schools were provided to 'accommodate all children according to age, ability, and aptitude', which, at that time, was generally interpreted in terms of meritocracy and beliefs from psychology about the necessity for separate provision for three types of pupil. In most LEAs separate grammar, secondary modern and technical schools were proposed to enable children to develop their talents and to fit them for their future place in the occupational structure.

The technical schools within the tripartite system did not last long, so that selection for secondary schools at 11+ became a contest where those who 'passed' went to grammar schools, but where the majority who 'failed' ended up in the secondary moderns. The rhetoric that these schools were 'different but of equal status' rapidly disappeared as it became evident that the two different types of school were offering highly unequal educational experiences. Moreover, during the 1950s and 1960s evidence showed that there was considerable class bias in the intakes to the two types of school. The selective system was reinforcing class differences rather than offering wider opportunities to all (Floud et al, 1957) and was largely gradually replaced by a comprehensive one over the 1970s and 1980s. It is an indication of the way in which power was delegated to the LEAs that this change took place authority by authority, and some LEAs still retain a selective secondary system to this day.

By 1979 when Margaret Thatcher's Conservative Government was elected to power, although the private sector still educated a small but significant number of children, within the state sector, selection of children for separate and unequally provided schools had decreased markedly and more children were taught in comprehensive schools than ever before. There remained some inequalities between schools, of course, and the use of catchment areas (or zones) as a basis for allocating children to schools meant that there were still considerable class and ethnic differences between the intakes of schools, but these differences were decreasing and the aim of most LEAs was to try to ensure greater equality in the educational experiences being offered.

Choice, Competition and Standards

During the early years of Conservative government there were several moves to increase competition between schools by giving greater choice to families over which school their children could attend. These included giving parents more information about schools and making it easier to appeal against school allocations. But it was not until 1988 that choice became linked with the idea of the 'self-managing school', competition between schools, and 'driving up standards'. What can be seen here is a distinct example of globalisation of policy or, at least, an extended case of international policy borrowing (Phillips & Ochs, 2003). It is also an example where the activities of a small group of people can be seen to have had a crucial influence in this process – at least in the initial stages. While it is impossible to understand all of the influences that led to the growth of the idea of choice in education, it is possible to see in England how the concept of the 'self-managed school' came to be associated with that of choice.

In their book of that name, Caldwell & Spinks (1988) define a 'self-managing school' as one where there has been a significant and consistent decentralisation to the school level of authority to make decisions relating to the allocation of resources. What is not widely remembered is that the original idea was developed through a study of Rosebery District High School in Tasmania, which, in fact, was highly isolated with no other competing public schools nearby. The original idea was concerned simply with giving more power to those within the schools to manage their own priorities. However, the New Right in England saw the potential of the concept during 1986 and 1987. Stuart Sexton, who was advisor to several secretaries of state for education in the early 1980s, had an important role in several New Right groups, including the London-based Institute for Economic Affairs. In 1987 the Institute published a booklet by Caldwell

(1987a) and also published Sexton's edited version of a conference on the funding and management of schools which included a paper by Brian Caldwell. Caldwell's paper was moderate in tone and explicitly denied the calls for privatisation of state-maintained schools (Caldwell, 1987b), but the same volume included a version of Sexton's own vision for a 'system truly based upon the supremacy of parental choice, the supremacy of purchasing power' (Sexton, 1987, p. 11). It was only during the policy-borrowing process that the idea of the self-managed school became intertwined with ideas of choice of school, competition between schools, and funding directly based on the number of students that the school could attract. Early English examples of delegation of funding to schools had, in fact, been more about cost-effectiveness than school improvement (Humphrey, 1988), which meant that it had been seen as a way of reducing spending on education but passing on the responsibility for continued success to the schools. These wider links to school choice and competition were originally made as part of a political process by New Right Conservative activists within the Institute for Economic Affairs and beyond.

Similar elements of globalisation and international policy borrowing can be seen in the idea of City Technology Colleges (CTCs) introduced in 1985 in advance of the 1988 Education Reform Act (Walford & Miller, 1991). This new type of school was to be supported by industry and commerce and be independent of LEAs. They were established in deprived areas and one international influence on the policy was that of magnet schools in the USA. A major difference, however, was that in the USA the idea was explicitly to reduce ethnic and social segregation by attracting white and middle-class children into poorer neighbourhoods. In England, the CTCs drew from a distinct catchment area of poorer people and attempted to provide a better schooling for those children (Walford, 1991a) without any magnetic effect. This particular policy was initially largely a failure, for there was little enthusiasm for supporting such schools by industry. Only 15 were eventually established. However, their longer-term effect was great for they served as models for the grant-maintained schools in the 1988 Education Reform Act and, much later, as models for the Labour Government's Academies.

The 1988 Education Reform Act for England and Wales introduced a wide range of different ideas at the same time – and there were contradictions between them. School-based management was introduced, which shifted power and control away from the LEAs towards the schools. Schools were given far greater control over the allocation of resources – including technology, power, materials, people, time and finance. They were still funded through the LEAs but the LEAs could only retain a small proportion of funding for their own uses. At the same time another new type of school with greater autonomy (grant-maintained schools) shifted power and control completely away from the LEAs to the schools and (in some ways) to central government, which funded each grant-maintained school individually.

The 1988 Education Reform Act was presented as a loss of confidence in the LEAs' abilities to raise standards and ensure quality. Instead, individual schools, whether they were given greater independence through grant-maintained status, or still remaining within the LEA sector, received their own delegated funds and became self-managed. The belief was that individual schools were better able to make decisions about their own priorities and activities than were bureaucratic local councils. Moreover, the increased power given to families over the choice of schools, by being able to express a preference for any school, was designed to ratchet-up quality through head-on competition between schools for students (Walford, 1994).

In fact, the Conservative Government itself quickly lost its faith in the market as the sole way of raising standards and ensuring quality. Whilst the ideology of the market was still evident in government rhetoric, the 1992 Education (Schools) Act established the Office for Standards in Education (Ofsted) and ushered in a new era of school inspection. Teams of registered inspectors conducting regular four-yearly inspections of all schools were now seen as the way to ensure quality. To report on the 'quality of the education' provided by the school is the first of the four general reporting duties of any registered inspector (Her Majesty's Stationery Office, 1992, p. 6). This is followed by the duty to report on standards, on finance, and on the spiritual, moral, social and cultural development of pupils. Here quality is to be maintained and improved by quality control through inspection.

The New Labour Government elected in 1997 had education as its major priority. Since that time there have been several major Education Acts and a great number of separate education initiatives from government. While many of these initiatives have been directly aimed at reducing inequality and providing better educational opportunities for the disadvantaged, other initiatives have unintentionally acted in the opposite direction. Many commentators have argued that there have been contradictions between many of the initiatives and a lack of overall coherence. However, there has been some encouragement of cooperation rather than competition between schools and a focus on improvement at the district level rather than at the school level alone.

There has been a focus on the disadvantaged and excluded in many of Labour's policies both in education and elsewhere. Very quickly after the 1997 election the Social Exclusion Unit was established within the Cabinet Office and this has been crucial in advocating many policies (not just in education) that have targeted the poor and excluded. In education, one of the main targets has been inner-city schools, which generally do not do well in the competitive league tables of results. It has also targeted particular areas of deprivation with its Education Action Zones and Excellence in Cities programmes (Adnett & Davies, 2003). There have been several initiatives designed to link schools more closely to their local communities.

At the level of rhetoric a similar change in policy can be seen in Labour's policy towards secondary specialist schools. Specialist schools were very much an invention of the Conservative Government, dating back to 1985 with the idea of City Technology Colleges (Walford, 1991b), and developing through Technology Colleges, then Technology Schools until finally becoming Specialist Schools. Nearly all of the secondary schools in England now have Specialist School status and are supposed to have an emphasis on specialisms such as technology, mathematics and computing, sport, the arts, modern languages, engineering or science. Under the Conservative vision, these schools were essentially competitive one with another and with other types of school, but under Labour their purpose has partly changed. They are still supposed to 'raise standards in the chosen specialism and across the school', but they also must now aim to 'work in partnership with their private sector sponsors, other schools and the local community' and 'act as a resource' for their 'family of schools' and the wider community (Bell & West, 2003). Adnett & Davies (2003) note that this change has not been completely successful and that there is a tension between the need to compete to attract students and the aim of cooperation, but clear examples where positive support and cooperation was occurring have been found (Bell & West, 2003, Penney, 2004).

The Academies programme, legislated in the 2002 Education Act, might be seen as a reversal in policy towards greater competition between schools. This new type of independent school, based heavily on the Conservative City Technology College model, has been controversial as it depends on sponsorship and extra funding from beyond the state (Hatcher & Jones, 2006). While the central government is providing current expenditure, some capital expenditure for the new-build or highly renovated schools is coming from private organisations. There are currently 83 Academies open and the Government wishes to see several hundred by 2010. Again this new type of school is designed to maintain and raise educational standards through extending choice to a new type of school, but there is little evidence so far that this is actually working.

The fact that Ofsted inspection was established so quickly after the introduction of market mechanisms into state-maintained schooling means that it is almost impossible to make judgements about the independent effects of these conflicting strategies for maintaining and improving quality. While several of these advocates have asserted that standards of achievement have indeed risen as a result of increased choice, but on a modest scale (Adnett & Davies, 2002), the situation is actually too complex to unravel (Walford, 2001; Gorard & Taylor, 2002). The period since 1988 has been one of constant change in education with a constant stream of new initiatives and little stability. There is no possibility of evaluating the effects of increased choice on academic performance in isolation. Adnett & Davies (2005) have questioned the very focus on competition between schools, arguing that, once adjustment is made for pupil characteristics, variation in pupil attainment levels between schools is small and unstable over time. They argue that choice within schools might be a more effective way of raising attainment than choice between schools.

However, it is certainly true that the overall academic performance of all schools, as measured by examination successes at age 16 and 18, has improved greatly since the introduction of greater choice, but this is not necessarily a causal relationship. The introduction of the National Curriculum with regular testing of all pupils, followed by two separate, yet linked, developments – the public publication of the examination results of all schools and the introduction of regular inspection of schools with, again, the results being made public – may well have had a greater effect on performance (Walford, 2001). More importantly, as Levačić & Woods (2002) have shown, individual schools have had differential rates of improvement. Those schools with low concentrations of social disadvantage relative to other local schools are likely to have higher rates of improvement. Those schools with high concentrations of social disadvantage are more likely to suffer the dual handicap of being low down the local hierarchy of schools and finding that this relative social disadvantage worsens over time. As other local schools are more able to select and shape their intakes, so it becomes more difficult for more disadvantaged schools to improve.

Segregation Effects of School Choice

In England, families have the right to 'express a preference' for a school for their child. They have no automatic right to have that child accepted. In a true quasi-market of schools it is inevitable that schools would attempt to choose the students as well as the families choosing a school. Given that schools with responsibility for their own admissions are more likely to act in their own interest and select advantaged students (West, 2006), the degree of control that schools have over their own admissions has thus been a focus of concern. The Labour Government has given power back to the LEAs to coordinate admissions, but there is still considerable diversity between schools in the procedures and criteria used for admission. Each school has to specify what criteria are used (which cannot include an interview with parents or children or any selection test), and these usually include distance from school or living within a defined catchment area, siblings already being at the school and medical or other special needs (West et al, 2004). Three LEAs in London continue to have a system of banding to ensure that all schools in their areas have a representative mix of children with differing academic abilities, but this cannot be extended as it is deemed to be inconsistent with the right to express a preference (West, 2006).

Opponents of greater school choice have been mainly concerned about the possibility that that it would lead to greater segregation between children from different social classes and ethnicities. As a result there were many studies of the effects of secondary school choice in the years following the 1988 Education Reform Act. These studies were both qualitative and quantitative, with the qualitative work focusing on the dynamics of choice through a series of case studies, and the quantitative research using published data sets at both the LEA and national levels. Both forms of research slowed dramatically in the early years of the century, as focus moved to choice of primary school and university rather than the secondary level.

The qualitative research by Stephen Ball and his colleagues has been particularly influential (Ball et al, 1995, 1996; Gewirtz et al, 1995; Ball & Vincent, 1998). In the main study, they interviewed a broad spectrum of parents who had recently decided which secondary school to send their child to, and examined in detail the ways in which various families responded to the market situation in which they found themselves. Ball argues that families are privileged or disadvantaged by the values that inform their conceptions of choice-making.

Gewirtz et al (1995) also indicate that, where curriculum specialisms were being introduced by schools, they were sometimes acting as selection mechanisms for high academic ability and middle-class children. In particular, the development of specialisms such as dance or music indirectly discriminated against working-class children, and allowed schools a greater chance to select what they deemed to be 'appropriate' children. However, they show that, despite the specialisms, rather than schools becoming more diverse, the pressures of competition between schools has led to schools becoming more similar in what they offer, but within a hierarchy of perceived ability to offer advantage. They conclude that local hierarchies of schools were developing where resources flowed from those children with greatest need to those with the least need. The finding that schools have become less rather than more diverse in their offerings is supported by considerable research, including that by Glatter et al (1997) and Halpin et al (1997).

While these case studies have been highly illuminating about the workings of the market at a micro level and have suggested an increase in social segregation as a result of greater choice, they have tended to be conducted in areas where competition between schools has been at its most fierce. The situation in London, for example, where there are many schools in relatively easy reach of most people's homes, is very different from that of rural Devon. Another limitation of these studies is that little attention has been paid to the level of segregation present *before* the introduction of greater choice. While some LEAs did use complicated catchment areas to encourage a diversity of social classes and ethnicities in all schools, most simply relied on geographical proximity to allocate children to schools (West, 2006). As much housing is socially selective through cost, this meant that many school systems were highly socially segregated prior to 1988. The introduction of greater choice seems to have done little to change this.

A series of quantitative papers from Gorard and his colleagues (Gorard & Fitz, 2000; Gorard, 2000a, b; Fitz et al, 2002; Taylor 2002; Gorard et al, 2001, 2002a, b, 2003) has partly challenged this general picture of choice leading to greater segregation. In their several papers they draw year-by-year comparisons using statistical data available from government sources of the social composition of schools. Using indicators such as the percentage of children in each school who have the right to free school meals (which is a commonly used indicator of poverty), they argue, amongst other things, that in most cases social segregation has actually decreased rather than increased as the qualitative studies have found. There has been considerable debate about the indicators that they use and their operationalised definition of segregation (Goldstein & Noden, 2003; Gorard, 2004), but their methodology is relatively simple. In most of their work they take the LEA as the unit of analysis and compute the 'expected' percentage of students eligible for free school meals in each school. They then compare the 'expected' percentage with the 'actual' percentage in each school in each year of the analysis and show that the differences have declined since families have been given greater choice of school. In their more recent studies they have also used alternative indicators of deprivation such as the percentage of children with a statement of special educational needs, or with English as a second language. In all of these cases their calculations lead them to conclude that, overall, increased marketisation has not resulted in increased segregation or, indeed, to some schools entering a 'spiral of decline'(Gorard et al, 2002a). While they do find some indications of a rise in segregation after 1997 (Gorard et al, 2002b), the balance of their evidence points in the opposite direction. One of their interesting arguments is that, while market forces may have a theoretical polarising effect, because they were introduced into a system that was already deeply polarised through 'selection by mortgage', the result has been that pre-existing polarisation has decreased. As they state in their book (Gorard et al, 2003, p. 186), 'What choice policies may do is change the rules by which segregation takes place, but without markedly increasing or eliminating levels of segregation that are largely shaped by structural factors'.

Another group of researchers (Bradley & Taylor, 2000; Bradley et al, 2000) have used data from the national Youth Cohort Survey to investigate changes in segregation in England during the 1990s. They use the same indicator of segregation as Gorard and his colleagues – the percentage of children eligible for free school meals – but find that, although small, differences in the social segregation of schools have widened during the1990s. Additionally, they found a significant positive relationship between school examination results and any decrease in the proportion of children eligible for free school meals in the schools. Expanding schools were found to be decreasing their proportion of children with disadvantage and thus increasing their examination results. Meanwhile, the less popular schools were increasing their proportion of such children. The differences between the various studies are well discussed in the work of Adnett & Davies (2002, pp. 196ff.), who argue that the differences between the various findings may not be as great as they believe. The main problem is that studies at the national and LEA levels may conceal results that would emerge from the study of identified local markets. They argue that the effects of choice on social segregation will be strongly affected by local conditions.

Recent work by Johnson et al (2006) has used government data collected on the ethnic origin of all pupils admitted over the period 1997-2003. They find some increase in ethnic segregation over this period in Greater London and some other cities, but only to the extent that is to be expected given the changing relative size of the ethnic minority populations there. They find that in these cases segregation is relatively high, but has only increased in line with the increase in the number of children of minority groups. It would seem that over this period, which is well after greater choice was introduced, there were no significant changes to the degree of ethnic segregation, and that residential segregation was the major cause of segregation in schools. However, school segregation is greater than residential segregation which could, they state, possibly be 'a result of parental choice using ethnic composition as a criterion in their selection process' (Johnson et al, 2006, p. 17).

However, there are two further comments worth making on this whole body of work on segregation. First, apart from the work of Johnson et al (2006) just discussed, the indicators used are all indicators of deprivation. Only about 20% of children are eligible for free school meals and the percentages of children with a statemente of special education needs or with English as a second language are smaller. These are measures of social disadvantage, not social advantage, and are used as bipolar either/or indicators. Further, taking 'English as a second language' as a single category, for example, conceals the known differences in academic performance of children from different backgrounds and ethnic groups. These single bipolar indicators do not give information on the whole distribution of social polarisation, but only on how particular extreme (but still sometimes heterogeneous) groups have coped with marketisation compared with the rest. It is certainly not unimportant that these groups may not have fared as badly as expected, but such data gives no information at all about how the most advantaged or even the average students have fared. We need research that uses the full range of social class, income and wealth variables to enable a true test of the polarisation hypothesis to be made. The qualitative and quantitative research is not necessarily in disagreement.

Second, while the usual social indicators of social class, income, wealth, ethnicity and gender are important, the detrimental effects of marketisation do not depend on disadvantage being linked to these variables. Several of the detailed small-scale studies already discussed have shown that families are differentially placed before the market. Choosing a school has now become a complicated process where local knowledge, interest in education, and degree of motivation of parents and children have become a vital indicator of successful acceptance of a child in a leading school. Children and families where there is a low level of interest in education simply do not give this process sufficient attention. Put crudely, if there is a hierarchy of schools, someone has to attend those at the bottom of the hierarchy if others are selected for those schools at the top. With a quasi-market, the children at the bottom are likely to be those with the greatest need for high-quality schooling – whether or not this need can be identified by standard social indicators of class, gender and ethnicity.

Conclusion

This chapter has reviewed some of the research literature on secondary school choice in England. The 1988 Education Reform Act made considerable changes to the educational system and encouraged competition between separately funded and managed schools. The aim was to improve efficiency and effectiveness and 'drive up standards' through the workings of a quasi-market.

In terms of examination successes at 16 and 18, there has been considerable improvement but, as so many changes were made at the same time, and as there have been continual changes since 1988, it is not possible to separate the effects of school choice and competition on this improvement. Similar improvements are noticeable in many other countries that have not introduced school choice. Although rather contradictory, the Labour Government of 1997 initially made some attempts to reduce the emphasis on competition between schools and encourage greater cooperation. More recent policy changes have given renewed emphasis to competition.

The chapter has also shown that the research findings on segregation are mixed. Local small-scale qualitative studies have shown that many parents 'play the market' and expend a great deal of energy ensuring that their child is accepted into what they perceive to be the 'best' school. Especially, in urban areas, there is an informal hierarchy of schools to which many parents subscribe. This research also indicates that there are class and other biases in the extent to which parents are informed about different schools and engage with the market. On the other hand, large-scale quantitative research indicates that there appeared to be relatively little change in the overall levels of segregation according to proxies for social class. This finding is probably related to the fact that segregation was far from unknown before the extension of school choice, and that the usual proxy used (eligibility for free school meals) is problematic – only identifying a small proportion of students. While we now do have information on ethnicity, there have been no quantitative studies that use an adequate social-class indicator simply because this information is not available in large-scale data sets. Moreover, inequality is still inequality whether it is related to social class or ethnicity or not. That parents who show the least knowledge or interest in the education of their children are most likely to 'choose' the nearest neighbourhood school, while others who already offer their children advantages are likely to be more knowledgeable and discriminating, leads to potential segregation and further disadvantage for those children already disadvantaged.

It is particularly interesting to consider the extent to which the changes in England are part of a globalisation process or, at least, related to a process of international policy borrowing. While the influences that led to an increase in the demands for greater school choice are myriad, it is possible to isolate the particular way in which the conjunction of the 'self-managed school' and school choice occurred. It has been shown that the original formulation of the concept of the 'self-managed school' was not at all linked to competition and choice, yet it became linked because a small group on the political New Right saw its potential in their campaign for a more privatised school system. Indeed, rather than being a case of policy borrowing, this was more a case of policy corruption, or policy incorporation.

Much the same might be said of the use of the American magnet school concept in the plans for City Technology Colleges. Again, those on the New Right made visits to magnet and Charter schools and encouraged the growth of something similar in England. Yet, while there were continuities with American practice, there were also great differences. In particular, there was no emphasis on desegregation of class or ethnicity in the English policy.

These two examples are suggestive of the need to carefully examine the influences of global phenomena in detail at the local level, and not to accept their power without question. Whilst England can be said to have been influenced by educational policies of other nations, there was no wholesale copying of policy, but more of an incorporation of elements of policies into particular political agendas.

Note

This chapter draws on and extends several of my previous articles (Walford, 1993, 2001, 2004, 2006).

References

Adnett, N. & Davies, P. (2002) *Markets for Schooling. An Economic Analysis*. London: Routledge.

Adnett, N. & Davies, P. (2003) Schooling Reforms in England: from quasi-market to co-operation? *Journal of Education Policy*, 18(40), 393-406. http://dx.doi.org/10.1080/0268093032000106848

Adnett, N. & Davies, P. (2005) Competition between or within Schools? Re-assessing School Choice, *Educational Economics*, 13(1), 109-121. http://dx.doi.org/10.1080/0964529042000325234

Ball, S. & Vincent, C. (1998) I Heard it on the Grapevine: 'hot knowledge' and school choice, *British Journal of Sociology of Education*, 19(3), 377-400. http://dx.doi.org/10.1080/0142569980190307

Ball, S., Bowe, R. & Gewirtz, S. (1995) Circuits of Schooling: a sociological exploration of parental choice of school in social class contexts, *Sociological Review*, 43(1), 52-78.

Ball, S., Bowe, R. & Gewirtz, S. (1996) School Choice, Social Class and Distinction: the realisation of social advantage in education, *Journal of Education Policy*, 11(1), 89-112. http://dx.doi.org/10.1080/0268093960110105

Bell, K. & West, A. (2003) Specialist Schools: an exploration of competition and co-operation, *Educational Studies*, 29(2/3), 273-289. http://dx.doi.org/10.1080/03055690303274

Bradley, S. & Taylor, J. (2000) The Effect of the Quasi-Market on the Efficiency–Equity Trade-Off in the Secondary School Sector. Lancashire University Management School Discussion Paper EC9/00.

Bradley, S., Crouchley, R., Millington, J. & Taylor, J. (2000) Testing for Quasi-Market Forces in Secondary Education, *Oxford Bulletin of Economics and Statistics*, 62(3), 357-390. http://dx.doi.org/10.1111/1468-0084.00176

Caldwell, B.J. (1987a) *The Promise of Self-Management for Schools. An International Perspective.* London: Institute for Economic Affairs.

Caldwell, B.J. (1987b) New Roles and Responsibilities for Resource Allocation: an international perspective, in S. Sexton (Ed.) *The Funding and Management of Education*. London: Institute for Economic Affairs.

Caldwell, B.J. & Spinks, J.M. (1988) *The Self-Managing School.* Lewis: Falmer Press.

Fitz, J., Gorard, S. & Taylor, C. (2002) School Admissions after the School Standards and Framework Act: bringing the LEAs back in? *Oxford Review of Education*, 28(2 & 3), 373-393. http://dx.doi.org/10.1080/03054980220143487

Floud, J.E., Halsey, A.H. & Martin, P.M. (1957) *Social Class and Educational Opportunity*. London: Heinemann.

Gewirtz, S., Ball, S.J. & Bowe, R. (1995) *Markets, Choice and Equity in Education.* Buckingham: Open University Press.

Glatter, R., Woods, P. & Bagley, C. (1997) Diversity, Differentiation and Hierarchy, in R. Glatter, P. Woods & C. Bagley (Eds) *Choice and Diversity in Schooling: perspectives and prospects*. London: Routledge.

Goldstein, H. & Noden, P. (2003) Modelling Social Segregation, *Oxford Review of Education*, 29(2), 225-237. http://dx.doi.org/10.1080/0305498032000080693

Gorard, S. (2000a) Here We Go Again: a reply to 'What's in a number?' by Gibson and Asthana, *Research Papers in Education*, 15(2), 155-162. http://dx.doi.org/10.1080/026715200402470

Gorard, S. (2000b) *Education and Social Justice*. Cardiff: University of Wales Press.

Gorard, S. (2004) Comments on 'Modelling Social Segregation' by Goldstein and Noden, *Oxford Review of Education*, 30(3), 435-440. http://dx.doi.org/10.1080/0305498042000260520

Gorard, S. & Fitz, J. (2000) Investigating the Determinants of Segregation between Schools, *Research Papers in Education*, 15(2), 115-132. http://dx.doi.org/10.1080/026715200402452

Gorard, S. & Taylor, C. (2002) Market Forces and Standards in Education: a preliminary consideration, *British Journal of Sociology of Education*, 23(1), 5-18. http://dx.doi.org/10.1080/01425690120102827

Gorard, S., Fitz, J. & Taylor, C. (2001) School Choice Impacts: what do we know? *Educational Researcher*, 30(7), 18-23. http://dx.doi.org/10.3102/0013189X030007018

Gorard, S., Taylor, C. & Fitz, J. (2002a) Does School Choice Lead to 'Spirals of Decline', *Journal of Education Policy*, 17(3), 367-384. http://dx.doi.org/10.1080/02680930210127612

Gorard, S., Taylor, C. & Fitz, J. (2002b) Markets in Public Policy: the case of the United Kingdom Education Reform Act 1988, *International Studies in the Sociology of Education*, 12, 23-41. http://dx.doi.org/10.1080/09620210200200081

Gorard, S., Taylor, C. & Fitz, J. (2003) *Schools, Markets and Choice Policies*. London: RoutledgeFalmer.

Halpin, D., Power, S. & Fitz, J. (1997) Opting into the Past? Grant-Maintained Schools and the Re-invention of Tradition, in R. Glatter, P. Woods & C. Bagley (Eds) *Choice and Diversity in Schooling: perspectives and prospects*. London: Routledge.

Hatcher, R. & Jones, K. (2006) Researching Resistance Campaigns against Academies in England, *British Journal of Educational Studies*, 54(3), 329-351. http://dx.doi.org/10.1111/j.1467-8527.2006.00350.x

Her Majesty's Stationery Office (HMSO) (1992) *Education (Schools) Act 1992*. London: HMSO.

Humphrey, C. (1988) *Financial Autonomy in Solihull*. London: Institute for Economic Affairs.

Johnson, R., Burgess, S., Harris, R. & Wilson, D. (2006) Sleep-walking towards Segregation? The Changing Ethnic Composition of English Schools, 1997-2003: an entry cohort analysis. Centre for Market and Public Organisation, University of Bristol, Working Paper No. 06/155.

Levačić, R. & Woods, P.A. (2002) Raising School Performance in the League Tables (Part 1): disentangling the effects of social disadvantage, *British Educational Research Journal*, 28(2), 207-226. http://dx.doi.org/10.1080/01411920120122158

Penney, D. (2004) Policy Tensions Being Played out in Practice: the Specialist Schools initiative in England, *Journal of Critical Education Policy Studies*, 2(1), 1-12.

Phillips, D. & Ochs, K. (2003) Processes of Policy Borrowing in Education: some explanatory and analytical devices, *Comparative Education*, 39(4), 451-461. http://dx.doi.org/10.1080/0305006032000162020

Sexton, S. (1987) *Our Schools: a radical policy*. London: Institute of Economic Affairs.

Taylor, C. (2002) *Geography of the 'New' Education Market. Secondary School Choice in England and Wales*. Aldershot: Ashgate.

Walford, G. (1991a) City Technology Colleges. A Private Magnetism? in G. Walford (Ed.) *Private Schooling: tradition, change and diversity*. London: Paul Chapman.

Walford, G. (1991b) Choice of School at the first City Technology College, *Educational Studies*, 17(1), 65-75. http://dx.doi.org/10.1080/0305569910170105

Walford, G. (1993) Self-managing Schools, Choice and Equity, in J. Smyth (Ed.) *A Socially Critical View of the Self-managing School*. London: Falmer Press.

Walford, G. (1994) *Choice and Equity in Education*. London: Cassell.

Walford, G. (2001) Does the Market Ensure Quality? *Westminster Studies in Education*, 24(1), 23-33. http://dx.doi.org/10.1080/0140672010240103

Walford, G. (2004) The Educational Policies of New Labour and the Old Problem of Inequality, in Karl Heinz Gruber (Ed.) *Bildung: Konsumgut oder Dürgerrecht* [Education: consumer commodity or citizen's entitlement]. Vienna: Oesterreichischer Bundesverlag. Reprinted in English in G. Walford (2006) *Markets and Equity in Education*. London: Continuum.

Walford, G. (Ed.) (2006) *Education and the Labour Government*. London: Routledge.

Walford, G. & Miller, H. (1991) *City Technology College*. Buckingham: Open University Press.

West, A. (2006) School Choice, Equity and Social Justice: the case for more control, *British Journal of Educational Studies*, 54(1), 15-33. http://dx.doi.org/10.1111/j.1467-8527.2006.00334.x

West, A., Hind, A. & Pennell, H. (2004) School Admissions and 'Selection' in Comprehensive Schools: policy and practice, *Oxford Review of Education*, 30(3), 347-369. http://dx.doi.org/10.1080/0305498042000260485

CHAPTER 6

The Introduction of Controlled School Choice in Tel Aviv, Israel: an attempt to attain a balance between integration and pluralism

IZHAR OPLATKA

SUMMARY Based on data gathered from school principals, parents of intakes, and written materials (school brochures), this chapter aims at examining the program of school choice in Tel Aviv, Israel, and at analyzing its underlying beliefs versus school reality. It is argued that whereas the advocates of the introduction of the school choice reform in Tel Aviv saw it as a result of a combination of integrative, egalitarian values with liberal, pluralistic ones, schools' responses to this major change in their external environment were inclined towards the intensification of market philosophy rather than towards comprehensive values. This kind of philosophy seems to guide the parents in choosing the junior high school for their child. Implications and meanings of this analysis for school choice policies worldwide are suggested.

Market forces, particularly apparent in school choice reform, have been introduced in many countries during the past two decades (Cookson, 1994; Walford, 1994; Bell & Rowley, 2002; Oplatka, 2006), including Israel where programs of school choice have been initiated in Jerusalem, Haifa and Tel Aviv (Haymann et al, 1997; Tel Aviv Municipality, 1999; Hoshen, 2004). The design of the educational market in Tel Aviv, the focus of this chapter, was influenced by new ideas imported, mainly, from North America and England (e.g. magnet schools, choice, decentralization), as well as, very reasonably, by some local cultural and structural features.

The purpose of this chapter is to examine the introduction in 1992 of school choice reform in Israel in general and in Tel Aviv in particular as an attempt to balance long-held views about the importance of social integration (the 'melting pot' policy) with new conceptions of pluralism, individualism and liberalism. It also discusses the major responses of schools and parents to arrangements brought about by this new reform.

While the pattern of school choice reform in Tel Aviv was a result of a combination of integrative, egalitarian values with liberal, pluralistic ones, I argue that the school responses to this major change in their external environment were inclined towards the intensification of market philosophy (e.g. liberalism, individualism, competition, excellence) rather than towards comprehensive values (e.g. collectivism, socialism, egalitarianism). Likewise, parents' considerations in choosing their child's junior high school were based, mostly, on individual factors (e.g. academic success, safety) rather than on social integration ones.

It is worth noting that the chapter was written against a background of the controversy arising between advocates and opponents of school choice reform. The latter group sees the introduction of market forces to education as a 'mechanism of class reproduction', legitimating and reinforcing the 'relative advantages of the middle and upper classes within state education' (Ball, 1993, p. 13). They believe that social class disparities are expressed in the way parents go about choosing a school (Taylor, 2001). This sort of assertion was taken into account when I read historical and empirical reports of school choice reform in Tel Aviv.

On a practical level, the chapter aims to contribute to our understanding of the ways policy makers and educators cope with dilemmas stemming from the need to incorporate contradictory values into the educational system. The context of the centralized structure of Israeli education on the one hand, and the conflicting demand for ethnic integration on the other hand provides unique insight into the complexity of school choice programs in multicultural societies.

In what follows, a historical and structural overview of the State of Israel and of its educational system is given to provide the international reader with the contextual background in which the school choice reform of Tel Aviv has emerged. Then, the process of introducing the school choice program in Tel Aviv is discussed, and its major underlying ideological ideas are highlighted. These ideas are compared with schools' and parents' responses to the new educational policy, and the chapter ends with some practical implications for policy makers and school managements.

The Israeli Educational System

Following large waves of immigration since its establishment almost 60 years ago, Israel is today a nation of immigrants, a bi-national, multi-ethnic and multi-religious state, with over seven million citizens. The state is divided into social, national and political enclaves (Eilam & Ben-Peretz, 2006).

Social scientists in Israel point to four major divisions in Israeli society: the national division between Jews (80%) and Arabs (20%); the religious division between Orthodox (14%) and secular Jews; the ethnic division between Jews of Middle Eastern and North African origin (Sephardi, about 50%) and Jews of European and American origin (Ashkenazi); and the most recent division, between new immigrants, mostly from the former Soviet Union (17%), and old, established immigrants. These divisions are also reflected in the Israeli educational system.

Education in Israel is segregated by nationality and degree of adherence to religious practices, with separate school systems for religious and secular Jewish children and separate State and Church religious schools for Arab children. Consequently, there are four distinct sub-educational systems: the state educational system, the religious state educational system, the Ultra-Orthodox educational system, and the Arab educational system. Parents have the legal right to enroll their child in any of these systems, provided that he or she accepts the basic requirements of the chosen system (e.g. modest garb in the religious systems). This is the basic choice of every parent in Israel.

The introduction of school choice policy in Tel Aviv occurred within the state educational system to which most schools in this city belong. The school structure in this system is mostly arranged in three units: six years of elementary school (age 6-12), three years of junior high school (12-15), and three years of high school (15-18). For many years, this system has been highly centralized both in structure and procedure. The Government was the major provider of education, which was (and is) ideologically geared towards matriculation examinations at the age of 18 (parallel to General Certificate of Education [GCE] A level in England) that usually take place at the end of secondary school and are necessary to gain entrance into higher education institutions (Iram & Schmida, 1998). All high schools are required to follow a basic national curriculum devised by senior officials in the Ministry of Education. Likewise, a policy of fixed catchment areas designed to prevent free movement of students from one school to another has dominated the educational system for many years in Israel – admittedly another expression of a centralized educational system.

Consistent with past assumptions underlying the educational system in Australia (Forsey, 2004), a centralized educational system and uniformity in the state schools has long been considered the suitable means by which to achieve the social and educational aims of Israel, such as the integration of immigrant groups into one society and the pursuit of equal educational opportunities for disadvantaged children coming, chiefly, from immigrant families originating from North Africa or Asia (Goldscheider, 1996). The ethos of equality has been a driving force in Israel's educational system since the establishment of the State. This ethos is legitimated by the view that education is the main vehicle for consolidation of Israel's highly diverse immigrant population into one nation.

In this respect, the reform of 1968 aimed at increasing student achievements as well as at decreasing social and ethnic gaps in educational outcomes and life chances, i.e. it aimed to introduce integration into the educational system. Greater equality in education, minimizing ethnic gaps and the promotion of social integration were its major purposes. To this end, students from disadvantaged families were granted the right to study in schools located in the more advantaged areas. The local education authority (LEA) was responsible for free bussing services.

This educational policy was for many years in conjunction with major Israeli ideological values that have tended to emphasize the importance of collectivism and social cohesiveness (Gardinger, 1993), rather than self-development and pluralism. However, there is considerable evidence that middle-class families that resisted this policy either moved to small, 'upper-middle-class' towns, or established magnet schools so as to avoid any integration with other social groups. The public in general tends to view school integration as an unsuccessful enterprise (Chen, 1997).

The spirits of globalization and privatization accompanied by values of individualism and diversity have brought about some changes in the state educational system since the early 1990s. The Ministry of Education has begun to encourage schools to specialize and offer unique subjects out of a predetermined list of subjects taught for matriculation examinations. Furthermore, many secondary schools are increasingly becoming autonomous and self-managed, providing enough freedom for school staff to build a vision and mission for their schools, based on their values, communal needs, and ethnic characteristics of their students.

The new value system coupled with policy shifts enabled, by and large, the introduction of school choice reform in Tel Aviv, as long as it adheres to collective, egalitarian values. I elaborate on this point in the next section.

The Introduction of School Choice in Tel Aviv

School choice is historically a common practice in Israel. Parents, first of all, choose one of the sectors of elementary education at the first grade (and even in the pre-school system). Some of them make an additional choice of a magnet school, or a special program of study within their sector (Chen, 1997). Those parents who live in Tel Aviv have been allowed to choose between a neighborhood junior high school and other junior high schools in different parts of the city since the early 1990s.

The debate over choice policies in Israel has turned to a heated ideological debate between choice protagonists and supporters of a 'school integration' policy (Yogev, 1997). The advocates of school choice reform in Tel Aviv highlight the long years of disappointment from the reform of integration mandated in 1968. Similar to what happened in other Western countries (Walford, 1996), the discomfort of many 'players' in the educational arena about public schooling (e.g. due to high levels of student drop-out and low levels of ethnic integration in Tel Aviv) pushed local policy makers to initiate the reform of school choice (Iram & Schmida, 1998).

The opponents, in contrast, claimed that the school choice policy is virtually a retreat from the official policy of equity, as expressed in ethnic integration, which was expected to be accomplished by means of diverse classrooms, enforced zoning of school catchment areas and bussing (e.g. Yonah, 2000). Note that the call for parental choice is gaining popularity at a time when we witness the decline of social democratic elites in Israel, together with an increasing challenge to the idea of the welfare state. As a result of this debate, the final structure of the school choice reform in Tel Aviv was a compromise between egalitarian, integrative values and liberal, individual ones.

Understanding the educational arena of school principles in Tel Aviv, however, needs further discussion on the particular social, cultural and demographic fabric of Tel Aviv. Like metropolitan cities worldwide, Tel Aviv consists of neighborhoods that are largely homogeneous in socio-economic terms. The city is divided into three social-geographical areas, marked by large socio-economic gaps: the north (the high socio-economic area), the center (moderate socio-economic area), and the south of the city (the low socio-economic area populated by a high percentage of Jews originating from North Africa and Arab countries). Substantial gaps exist among the areas in terms of schooling, occupational status, wages and computer use and, to a lesser extent, in dwelling density, family car use and percentage of women in the labor market (Tel Aviv Municipality, 1999).

The socio-economic gaps find expression in the educational system. There are higher percentages of disadvantaged pupils in schools in south Tel Aviv than in the center and north of the city. The schools in the south, therefore, have a low public image. Subsequent to the reform of 1968 (integration in education) high achieving students from the south were bussed to junior high schools (and high schools) located in the north of the city. Each school was forced legally to have 30% of its student population from the south.

Due to the unique social mosaic of Tel Aviv and in light of the new spirit of education indicated above, its education authority devised, in September 1992, a plan to reform the city's educational system. The launch of this plan was followed by a decision of the Israeli Government to allow LEAs to open enrollment zones and establish school choice programs in the country. Prior to this policy change, the Tel Aviv education authority had no legal right to introduce a school choice program of any kind. In this respect, the year 1992 was a changing point, at least in part, due to the establishment of a new government that supported liberal reforms in the educational system.

The title of the Tel Aviv plan was: 'There are other ways – Tel Aviv believes in education'. The purpose of this plan was to raise the standards of education and student achievement, and its planners assumed that this could be accomplished through 'the creation of a broad range of educational options, suited to the educational, cultural and social pluralism of the population, while taking into consideration the students' needs and areas of interest' (Haymann et al, 1997, p. 91).

However, the declared aims were not to encourage competition for improvement alone. Committed to egalitarian values on which the Israeli educational system is based (e.g. integration, equal educational opportunities), and to relatively new values of 'excellence in education', the Tel Aviv LEA introduced (in September 1992) the program of 'controlled school choice'. As this kind of program was theoretically intended to give all pupils in a community equal access to every public school (Boyd, 1998), the program planners believed that a better balance of ethnic and social integration would be achieved and the quality of instruction would increase (Tel Aviv Municipality, 1992).

The emphasis was on integration that, it was assumed, would be strengthened by the market, not only the market for its own sake. Some of the planners argued ardently that controlled choice of schools in Israel could increase integration by bringing together pupils of different social groups on the basis of a common curriculum (Shapira, et al, 1995). In order to accomplish this aim, the planners emphasized the need to differentiate one high school from the other in terms of their curriculum, extracurricular activities and teaching methods, as well as the need to establish clear criteria for student selection.

Note that the program of controlled choice did not propose giving schools freedom to select their pupils. Rather, the choice is controlled by the LEA, so that the demographic make-up of each school is a fair representation of the population of the city as a whole. In meeting the need to ensure equal educational opportunities for children from all groups, the controlled choice reform tended to negate free and open enrollment. The model suggests that within heterogeneous districts, school choice is controlled so as to allow different social groups the opportunity to study together while sharing their school's orientation (Shapira et al, 1995). This orientation would hopefully contribute to the creation of a common denominator that cuts through different strata, thus increasing integration within the school.

The program of controlled school choice in the high school sector was gradually implemented from 1994 to 1999. It started in the south, where every child was granted the choice of a junior high from a list of five potential alternatives, and went on to include the north and the center of the city. At the end of the process, the city was divided into six areas of enrollment, in which every student was given the same alternatives of school choice. In general, every student was allowed to choose a school from a formal list of five schools published by the LEA – some in his/her neighborhood and others outside, some in the north and some in the south. The LEA decides the actual allocation according to various criteria (e.g. a reflection of the community's composition in school, with priority given to lower status families' choices, proximity to home, and having relatives who already attend the school). Before actually choosing, parents are supposed to receive proper information and guidance about the schools and the choice process from an information center for parents set up within the framework of the program, and transportation was provided for the students.

In sum, the controlled choice reform was an attempt to emphasize the values of equity and equality in education, to ensure a certain level of social integration in school, and at the same time to grant parents and children some freedom in choosing the school. According to the choice advocates in Israel, school choice would be implemented under conditions designed to prevent any possibility of utilizing the system to advance class interests: First, admittance to schools would not be conditional on achievement tests or on material advantage. Second, all schools, especially the prestigious ones, would be obliged to admit a sizable quota from underprivileged neighborhoods in order to guarantee an integrated environment in school. Third, catchment areas would not be abolished altogether, but would become more flexible. Parents would be able to choose a school from a defined cluster of schools which exist within certain geographical boundaries. Each school would be allowed to develop its own unique identity, climate and set of goals. Have school managements and parents adopted the integrative, egalitarian value system? Have they shared an ideology of equity and equality? Answers to these questions are the topic of the following sections.

Schools' Responses

To this point we have seen how profoundly the values of social integration, equity and equality were embedded in the planning phase of the school choice reform in Tel Aviv. Social integration, in the views of the reform's planners, refers largely to the combination of students from disadvantaged areas with students from the advantaged areas, on the grounds that the high achievers (mainly from the latter group) will help the students from the former group to raise their academic achievements considerably. Likewise, integration was connected to equal educational opportunities and social justice.

Interestingly, from the launch of the implementation phase of the school choice program in Tel Aviv, when a pilot program included only several neighborhoods in the south, opponents of this market-led policy emphasized that no student from the north chose to study in the south, which, in their view, means one-way integration. They also indicated that a hierarchy of schools emerged based on reputation and location instead of particular curriculum and subject matter. Yonah (2000) reported that parents from the north forced the LEA to limit the rate of students from the south in a certain northern school, or else, they explicitly threatened, they would not enroll their children in this school. Unfortunately, their case is not exceptional and implies, in some sense, the limited adoption of integrative, egalitarian values among parents in Tel Aviv.

When viewing the criticism of school choice policy in Israel and worldwide, I develop a slightly different approach here to explore issues of integration in the controlled school choice program. Instead of counting how many students from the south study in the north and vice versa, a common measure of social integration in education, understanding the dominant value system not merely of the policy planners, but of the key players in any local education arena, i.e. schools and parents, might shed light on the integration-choice controversy. I assume, though, that an integrative, egalitarian value system shared by educators and constituencies is likely to promote a successful implementation of a controlled school choice program in any particular city. One lesson from the 1968 reform was that institutional arrangements are insufficient for ensuring social integration and equal educational opportunities.

In my view, then, any incorporation of an integration policy should partially be expressed by schools' responses that are inconsistent with the spirit of egalitarian, collective values. Thus, if schools adhere to the dual value system embedded in the controlled school choice reform introduced in Tel Aviv, one would expect to find verbal, symbolic and ritual expressions of both systems of values. For example, schools' marketing messages should address equally both the development of individual competencies and the generation of a collective society. However, in the educational market of Tel Aviv, this kind of dual incorporation is less likely to appear; rather, the opposite is more likely. The marketing-like orientations of many schools in Tel Aviv put much emphasis on the glorification of individual achievements, individual well-being, personal development, competition, and the like. I develop this argument in the next section.

It is worth noting, however, that marketing messages represent the rhetoric, ideal aspect of education policies, not necessarily the practical ones. I am fully aware of the potential gaps between schools' rhetorical messages and practical aspects of integration. The reader should bear this gap in mind when reading the analysis that follows.

Marketing Messages: the individual in the center

An interesting way to trace any incorporation of integrative, egalitarian values into junior high schools in Tel Aviv, the target of the controlled school choice reform, is to look at their descriptive brochure, a marketing tool through which the school presents its educational ideology and activities. A qualitative content analysis that I conducted on 13 secondary school brochures out of the 15 secondary school in Tel Aviv (Oplatka, 2002a) provides insight into the minor place given to social egalitarian, integrative values. Let us start by looking at the schools' aims and ideologies as they appear in the brochures.

Schools' Aims and Educational Ideologies

Several issues of school aims and ideologies were inductively exposed in the brochures of the junior high schools. The four elements relating to the individual, liberal value system were common to most schools – the pupil in the center (11 schools), creating schools' domestic environment (10), promoting academic achievements (11), and maximization of self-development and growth (10). Note that one element (which is partially in relation to an integrative value system) – reinforcement of pupils' social respect and consideration for others – was less prevalent (7).

The ideology of 'the pupil in the center' is well expressed in many statements in the brochures. 'Every pupil is unique and special in our school' or 'the school is dedicated to the uniqueness of the individual' both illustrate the almost sacred standing of individualism and a student-oriented image that the school would like to convey to its prospective parents. It is not surprising then that school efforts are described as completely oriented towards the individual pupil: 'the pupil's needs determine the school policy', 'school staff believes in your uniqueness and aspires to create an atmosphere which enables you to express yourself and your competencies'. This supportive atmosphere is commonly illustrated in phrases such as 'warm family', 'open door', 'positive climate' and 'supportive environment', which highlight the schools' domestic and happy environment contributing to the student's self-fulfillment.

Arising from this individual-oriented attitude are the aims concerned with promoting achievements and desirable qualities in the pupil. The schools express the significance they attach to personal academic achievements in one word that is common to all of them: 'excellence'. Slogans such as, 'excellence is our school', 'in our school every pupil finds his or her own way to personal excellence', and 'personal excellence and social values' stress the valuable role the schools attribute to academic achievements in the image-building and marketing of the schools. In addition, high achievement is depicted as the central aim of the schools, where 'everybody does their best to get the best results' and 'our school assists our pupils in fulfilling themselves in their pursuit of high academic achievements'.

As regards maximization of personal development enabling the young to enter the adult community, 10 schools conveyed messages of self-development and growth, transmitted through sentences such as 'we pursue humanistic and personal excellence', 'our aim is to raise a sensitive and holistic adult', and 'promoting curiosity, activism, and flexibility in youth'. Furthermore, as part of schooling's contribution to the pupils' self-development, the brochures provide statements that highlight the need to advance the young towards being adults in a changing technological society. Many slogans illustrate this notion: 'the year 2020 is in school X', 'the third millennium is already in our school', 'training for the future is our goal'.

Whereas the individual, liberal value system repeatedly appears in the brochures, the following value-labeled element – reinforcement of pupils' social respect and consideration for others – appears in seven schools only, most of them in the south and center of Tel Aviv (only one, which has a female principal with a strong egalitarian ideology, was in the north). This element refers to the schools' pursuit of democracy, multiculturalism, tolerance and patriotism. The schools that choose to highlight these values in their brochures demonstrate their concern for the education of 'society-oriented adults' in many forms. For example, 'we want to see our graduates more tolerant and open to the other', 'we aim at developing an adult who espouses social and universal values', 'we educate our pupils to be good citizens', 'we develop adults who contribute to their community'.

While there are some traces of views expressing egalitarian, integrative values in the brochures, they are overshadowed by the great emphasis being given to individual purposes. A similar pattern is found when reading about the schools' competitive advantage.

Schools' Competitive Advantages

Three major themes in regard to schools' presentations of their advantages were revealed in the brochures: high results and achievements (11), unique structure and organization (9), and winning in competition (5). For the purpose of this chapter, two of them are briefly discussed.

Eleven schools report the high academic achievements of their pupils, and the professional success of their graduates: 'since the establishment of our school 94 years ago, many of our graduates have attained positions in politics, universities and business', 'for many years our school has obtained the highest results of Tel Aviv's matriculation exams', 'excellent pupils study at our school'. This, in turn, enhances their image and constitutes evidence of their good schooling.

Another advantage adopted by schools in their brochures was 'winning a competition'. Nonetheless, only five brochures provided information about their pupils' victories in various competitions. They included sentences such as, 'school's team won first place in a nation-wide math Olympics', 'from its establishment the school is known as the leader in sports competitions in Tel Aviv', 'our pupils win the best places in many prestigious competitions'. Here again, no school chose to display its competitive edge in terms of ethnic integration or equal educational opportunities, but rather in terms of individual success and career aspirations.

The Image of School Staff

Another way to trace the values of the school management is to examine the preferred image of the teacher. Six brochures describe the schools' staff as competent and skillful, and nine brochures depict their staff's commitment to the advancement of the pupils. The qualifications and skills of the staff are presented without specifically mentioning any role incumbent or teacher by name, but the adult community is described in general terms. For example, 'excellent teachers', 'our teachers have PhD degrees', 'in our school you study with the best teachers in the city', 'young staff', 'up-dated teachers', and 'expert teachers', are some of the phrases indicating the importance attached to the staff's high instructional qualifications in the schools' image-building.

The high qualifications are displayed as a human resource oriented towards the promotion of the pupils in the schools. These themes seem to be connected to the ideology of putting 'the pupil in the center' to whom schools direct their efforts and activities. The schools emphasize the various ways the staff may contribute to the education of pupils. In particular, they use the word 'caring', which symbolizes their perceptions of the 'correct' relationships between the staff and the pupils. Furthermore, the staff's aim is exhibited in sentences such as 'the staff is here in order to teach, assist and support the pupils', 'the staff accompanies the pupils through their various stages of growth by means of support, caring, personal attention', 'the staff is totally involved in your progress', and 'we are totally committed to your advancement'. There is no doubt that when so much is devoted to the individual pupil, then the adult staff is presented as one of many other means to fulfill the pupils' individuality. Note, however, that an ideal teacher is less likely to be constructed in terms of creating a multicultural classroom, or helping the disadvantaged students to 'fit into' the class. In marketing terms, it is improper to give any indication of the percentage of enrollment of underprivileged students in the school.

Extracurricular Activities

The majority of schools provided information about the extracurricular activities regulated by the Ministry of Education. These are part of the social education in Israel aimed at strengthening moral and civic values through a variety of activities. Schools are required to incorporate these activities into their structure on a class and school level. It is implicit that every school should adopt the same activities; however, every school chooses to highlight rhetorically different aspects of the national program in its brochure. Thus, most of the brochures include statements about 'theater', 'hikes', 'lectures', 'Aids prevention programs', 'preparation for the army', and 'sex education'.

Non-regulated extracurricular activities of the Ministry of Education are less prevalent in the school brochures, leaving enough room for diversity among the schools. Only here we find direct reference to issues of social integration, yet, to a limited extent. Six schools depict a project called 'getting to know others', which includes dialogues with pupils from different ethnic and social groups in Israel, like Arabs, Bedouins, religious Jews, and pupils from development towns.

Verbal Messages

The preceding section illustrated the major place given in school brochures to liberal, individual values, while integrative, collective values are left relatively untouched in this kind of written marketing tool. In this section, I underscore the lack of integrative spirit in schools, in spite of the central place given to this spirit in the controlled school choice program. Using voices of junior high school principals from Tel Aviv (Oplatka, 2002b), the language of those who are responsible for the implementation of the controlled school choice program in reality is analyzed.

The Principals' Subjective Interpretations of the New Environment

In general, similar to findings from England (Oplatka & Hemsley-Brown, 2004), most of the principals describe the relationships among high schools in Tel Aviv in terms of competition, war, struggle, and lack of cross-cultural collaboration. One principal commented:

> Competition is intense. A huge struggle means not a personal struggle ... but rather, alienation among the school principals, no relations, no information sharing. Everybody is closed in his place.

By the same token, the description of war is manifested even more acutely in the words of principals from schools less in demand. Thus, one of them stated that '235 pupils graduate from the elementary school [in his area], and they are the target of the war'. Another principal emphasized that 'the competition with the north is very acute and therefore I don't have much chance to win this competition'.

For the purpose of this chapter, the emphasis the principals put on competition in their accounts manifests the internalization of market-led values, which, in turn, might overshadow values of integration and egalitarianism. Some questions may sharpen the assumed association. For instance, will principals give priority to integration and equal educational opportunities to all in their school's image-building, when they have to compete in the educational marketplace? Will they insist on recruiting less advantaged students when this might diminish their school's image and, in turn, weaken their competitive advantage? Competition usually forces companies to respond to clients' needs and desires, not to be protagonists of old social ideologies.

The Incorporation of Marketing Ideology

If one believes that one's organization is in competition with other organizations, marketing reasonably surfaces. Consistent with findings from England (Gewirtz et al, 1995), there are two seemingly contradictory points of view concerning the concept of marketing among Israeli school principals

– a negative term but rather indispensable for the school. The following quotes demonstrate this duality:

> I strive not to think of myself as a salesman. There is no reason to perceive myself as a salesman because I do not employ marketing tactics. I know I should convince parents to choose my school, but not as a salesman ... for example, I don't say that my school is the best, I think that most of the schools are good.

However, marketing is also conceived of as a vital element in the recruitment of prospective students, as well as a revealing means through which the community is informed about the school's aims and activities. This is evident in the following:

> I find it very important to let the parents be informed about the school, what my school's values and visions are. For example, I want them to know that we deal with disciplinary problems with a tough hand, no compromises.

> At the first stage of the open enrollment reform, I was strongly convinced that I have the best school, that pupils will join us because they know that we can offer the best for them ... unfortunately, I was wrong. I didn't go to meet advantaged parents and no one registered for the school. The next year I understood the significant role of marketing.

The principals undoubtedly hold negative attitudes towards the concept of marketing, but, at the same time, they cannot deny its impact upon their school life and success. However, when marketing is considered to be a vital tool without which the school will not survive, this implies, in some sense, that the recruitment of the students from the advantaged areas is the preferred option, at least in the schools located in the center and the north of Tel Aviv. If principals believe in the key role of marketing to communicate their school's advantages and activities to the target market (i.e. the more advantaged families), will they let integration and equality divert their attention from the real purpose? If marketing is glorified, which means that the school principal strives to appeal to the best students (why should he market the school to those who will apply to it in any case?), we would not expect him/her to pay much attention to egalitarian values.

When asked about their goals following the policy of open enrollment, the principals stated that they were: to permeate a new market, to increase the number of students, to recruit the needed minimum number of students, and so forth. The principals of the schools in more demand also emphasized their desire to attract more of the high-achieving students, although some of them tended also to stress the importance of integration of students from the south and the north of the city. One must consider whether their last remarks were merely rhetoric, because the value of integration is deeply rooted in

Israel, or rather, were they an authentic belief? The brochures depicted above cast doubt on the latter possibility.

In sum, while some of the planners (e.g. Haymann et al, 1997) claimed that a process of reorganization took place at the school level in several domains, such as diversification of learning frameworks, curricula and teaching methods, support for underachievers, and promotion of positive attitudes towards social integration among students, the brochures produced by schools in Tel Aviv, and the principals' views of the reality in terms of competition, marketing and individualism undermine this claim.

Parents' Responses

Similar to the responses of school management, parents in Tel Aviv also tend to highlight individual-oriented choice factors such as the child's well-being, academic results, and the academic reputation of the school (Oplatka, 2003; Hoshen, 2004), factors similar to those indicated by parents in other Western countries (Foskett & Hemsley-Brown, 2001). In so doing, they seem to internalize market-led values rather than collective, integrative ones which the planners of the controlled school choice program in Tel Aviv addressed in particular.

Of the various factors affecting the school choice process of parents from north Tel Aviv (Oplatka, 2003), and congruent with parents choosing magnet schools in the USA (Maddaus, 1990), school curriculum was a key motive. This is evident from one mother:

> *Q*: What did you think of the third option?
> *A*: The three schools differed in the subjects they offered; in the third school there is an academic track that is not present in the other schools. They don't have that option. Perhaps that is the reason my daughter wanted to be there.

Indeed, the children interviewed indicated certain subjects that had exerted influence upon their decision to choose a certain school, among them communications, art, physical education, languages, music and economics.

Particularly striking was the impact of the child's classmates in making a school choice, although it played a contradictory role in the choice process. Similar to findings from England (Gorard, 1999), the sixth grader's classmates, and especially close friends, are conceived of as a sizable source of impact upon school choice among parents and children who chose their catchment (neighborhood) high school. One father, for example, indicated that 'the most important thing in my eyes was that she would be with her friends', and two children emphasized their need to apply to a school that their friends from the sixth grade would attend:

> *Q*: Why didn't you choose, finally, the other school?
> *A*: Because all my friends decided to go to that school.

A prominent rejection factor was the type of population that makes up the student body in the high school, a key factor identified also elsewhere (Maddaus, 1990; Gorard, 1999). Thus, despite planners' attempts to encourage social integration, a school could be rejected because its pupils are of low socio-economic status or vice versa, as is reflected from the following extracts:

> There is also a low-rated school that I think is also pretty open-minded, the school where we went, we know that the population which goes there has gone right downhill.
>
> When he [the child] heard about the many snobs studying there, he decided to forget it ... I know a women whose child said they measure you by the size of your apartment, and it is funny that teachers in that school ask the kids not to leave school for ski vacations during the academic year.

Parents' adoption of the individual value system is also reflected in a few studies undertaken subsequent to the implementation of the controlled school choice policy in Tel Aviv. It was found that parents usually preferred schools that would promote their children academically and emotionally, and that issues of equal opportunities, integration and promotion of disadvantaged classes were of less importance for the parents in Tel Aviv (Marko-Shoham, 1996). Furthermore, a major factor found to have a considerable influence upon the choice process was the local community of parents. Thus, parents from the northern part of Tel Aviv tended to choose a school in the north or the center, whereas only 50% of the parents from the south preferred their children to study near home (Haymann et al, 1997). Less educated parents (coming mostly from the southern communities) preferred the academic factor and the integrative one in choosing a school. They saw the school as a means for social mobility, whereas more educated parents did not take this factor into account at all in their choice process (Marko-Shoham, 1996).

To sum up, when academic factors (achievements, curriculum), composition of student population, and a desire to be with their friends (i.e. remaining with the child's original social group) are of high priority in the school choice process, it reflects, in my view, the glorification of individual needs and development rather than any other values, including integration. Furthermore, when composition of student population plays a key role in the school choice process, this indicates explicitly a resistance to integrative, collective values. Thus, the parents do not appear to take the spirit of integration, equity and equality into much consideration. Instead, they are likely to prefer, to a great extent, a liberal, individual and market-led value system.

Concluding Comments and Implications

At the outset of this chapter, I premised that local policy makers' attempts to preserve the main essentials of the integration reform of 1968 in the new school choice reform in Tel Aviv have not been inculcated into the local educational environment in an adequate manner. In reality, educators, stakeholders and constituents in this city adopted, by and large, the market-led value system, while paying minimal attention to an integrative, egalitarian value system, at least in their marketing efforts or school choice decision.

Underpinning my conjecture are local planners' notes and working papers reviewed by some of the participants in the new reform's planning phase (e.g. Shapira et al, 1995; Haymann et al, 1997), and marketing messages and interview data conducted among school principals, parents and students. What has come to light is the emphasis being given to social justice and integration in the controlled school choice program in Tel Aviv, on one hand, and a focus on individual, market-led values among those who had to implement the reform in reality, on the other hand.

It is apparent that institutional arrangements are a necessary, but insufficient, condition for preserving what seems to be an old-fashioned value system. Culture plays a significant role in this respect. Since the early 1990s the Israeli Ministry of Education has aimed at restructuring the educational system, using concepts such as 'school-based management', 'empowerment', 'choice', 'autonomous schools' and 'accountability' (Iram & Schmida, 1998), concepts that are in sharp contrast with values of the comprehensive school and integration. The new dominant terminology, coupled with constraints stemming from the characteristics of the marketplace (competition, survival, efficiency), appears to promote individual, liberal ideologies. Schools' strong need to survive the inter-school competition and to exhibit a good image in the community might lead principals to emphasize those values they believe attract prospective students or are in conjunction with current social myths, definitions and constructions of the 'efficient' school.

In times when education is socially constructed to promote growth and development, schools cannot adhere principally to integrative values, or they might be seen as inefficient and have to cope with a decline in enrollment rates. In light of institutional theory (Oplatka, 2004), parents whose system of values corroborates the new market ideology tend to reinforce the school's new 'ideal' image and vice versa. A similar cycle was observed a decade ago in England, where Gewirtz et al (1995) illuminated a transition from comprehensive values to market values in the English educational system. They showed that schools moved from an agenda of social and educational concerns to one of image and budgetary concerns, from an orientation to serve community needs to attracting 'motivated parents/able children'. In their terminology, schools in the marketplace highlight an exclusive, academic ethos rather than an integrationist, caring ethos.

The data and analyses in this chapter tend to align with some major conjectures in the criticism of school choice policy (e.g. Ball, 1993; Yonah,

2000; Taylor, 2001), especially in that school choice is held responsible for increasing ethnic, racial and religious segregation and not minimizing it, as some advocates of this reform maintained. Indeed, some opponents of school choice in Israel have long maintained that school choice is incongruent with values of equality, equity and social integration, questioning its ability to promote these values. In their view, school choice discourages equal opportunities in education, and contributes to the interests of the upper classes, which in turn increases social segregation and educational gaps, mainly due to the content of the school curriculum and the selection procedures used by the sought-after schools (Yonah, 2000; Hoshen, 2004).

Nevertheless, I cannot accept the black-or-white notion coming from this criticism. In my view, segregation and choice are not necessarily incompatible. They can go hand in hand if some conditions are met. One could learn, though, some lessons from the attempt conducted in Tel Aviv to combine the two ostensibly contradictory philosophies into one reform.

First, it is not easy to combine two contradictory standpoints into one reform by means of institutional arrangements solely. While market ideology usually promotes values of individual success and excellence in education, values of social integration encourage equity and equality, two basic concepts that are in stark contrast with market ideology due to their emphasis on the unifying and common base rather than competition and the glorification of individual achievements.

A review of the deliberations of the Israeli Supreme Court over a period of 25 years shows that it has become commonly accepted that school integration, as an operational definition of educational equity, and school choice, as an operational definition of freedom to choose, are two contradictory concepts (Chen, 1997). Therefore, I believe, policy makers need to pay much attention to a controlled school choice program, which is an attempt to remain attentive and committed to social justice and integration in the era of accountability and marketization. The development of strong awareness among policy makers and educators to these difficulties seems warranted.

Compared to open school choice programs, and despite the difficulties of inculcating egalitarian, integrative value systems in a market-led education environment, it is likely that 'controlled choice' minimizes the establishment of a stratified education arena within which elite schools operate, leading to extreme social equality. Besides, 'controlled choice' might convey pro-integrative notions to schools and parents, either by the establishment of centralized procedures to select intake, or by explicit declarations of the significant role of egalitarian values in the local educational system. In this sense, schools and stakeholders are socially 'expected' not to hold individual values when playing in the new education market, and to bear social values in mind.

Second, as institutional arrangements aimed at bringing about some sort of integration within a school choice program are not enough; it is necessary to complement these arrangements with cultural ones. One lesson from the Tel Aviv case is the great influence of cultural scripts upon school management, stakeholders and even intake. Thus, prior to the introduction of controlled school choice, it is recommended to establish in-service training to explain the importance attached in the new reform to making collective values prominent and the need of every school management to accentuate integrative, collective values in their marketing messages and activities (e.g. 'Every student is invited to our school', 'Our students are exposed to other cultures and lifestyles'). In so doing, schools will certify their commitment to integration regardless of fashions or parents' beliefs about the 'right school'. LEAs, then, have to supervise the marketing messages of schools and confirm compliance with the local education policy.

Third, in open evenings usually organized at schools during the school choice process to provide prospective parents and children with information about the school's curriculum, ideology, structure and so forth, the meaning of so-called 'elitist' choice to the student and to society should be illuminated. School staff and LEA officials should emphasize the great significance of integration in the educational system to the local community and the development of citizens sensitive to social issues and multiculturalism. It is hoped that some parents' consideration of the school's ethnic or religious composition will be insignificant subsequent to this activity/information.

Finally, Yonah (2000) indicated that diversification in education, a precondition in the introduction of school choice reform, has not occurred in Tel Aviv. This led, among other things, to isomorphism of the schooling processes and curriculum among junior high schools in Tel Aviv. In this case, students from various social and ethnic backgrounds were less likely to meet each other in a certain school to which they applied due to an attractive, common curriculum. Policy makers have to pay increased attention to this aspect of school choice if social integration is to be their guiding principle.

My basic belief in presenting these implications is that social integration is really the aim of policy makers in many multicultural societies, i.e. it is not merely rhetoric. However, this issue is left for further inquiry.

References

Ball, S.J. (1993) Education Markets, Choice and Social Class: the market as a class strategy in the UK and the USA, *British Journal of Sociology of Education*, 14, 3-19. http://dx.doi.org/10.1080/0142569930140101

Bell, L. & Rowley, A. (2002) The Impact of Educational Policy on Headship in Primary Schools in England, 1994-2001, *Journal of Educational Administration*, 40(3), 195-210. http://dx.doi.org/10.1108/09578230210427145

Boyd, W. (1998) Markets, Choices and Educational Change, in A. Hargreaves, A. Loeberman, M. Fullan & D. Hopkins (Eds) *International Handbook of Educational Change*. Dordrecht: Kluwer.

Chen, M. (1997) School Choice as a Bargain in a Sectarian Educational System, in R. Shapira & P.W. Cookson, Jr (Eds) *Autonomy and Change in Context: an international perspective.* Oxford: Pergamon.

Cookson, P.W. (1994) *School Choice: the struggle for the soul of American education.* New Haven: Yale University Press.

Eilam, B. & Ben-Peretz, M. (2006) The Israeli Educational System's Response to Current Societal, Economic and Political Changes, in J. Earnest & D.E. Treagust (Eds) *Education Reform in Societies in Transition: international perspectives.* Rotterdam: Sense.

Forsey, M. (2004) Equity versus Excellence: responses to neo-liberal ideals in a government high school, *Anthropological Forum*, 14(3), 283-296. http://dx.doi.org/10.1080/0066467042000269530

Foskett, N. & Hemsley-Brown, J. (2001) *Choosing Futures: young people's decision-making in education, training and careers markets.* London: RoutledgeFalmer.

Gardinger, M. (1993) Thoughts toward the Formation of an Israeli Management Model, in A. Shenhar & A. Yarkoni (Eds) *Israeli Management Culture.* Tel Aviv: Cherikover.

Gewirtz, S., Ball, S.J. & Bowe, R. (1995) *Markets, Choice and Equity in Education.* Buckingham: Open University Press.

Goldscheider, C. (1996) *Israel's Changing Society: population, ethnicity, and development.* Colorado: Westview Press.

Gorard, S. (1999) Well. That about Wraps it up for School Choice Research: a state of the art review, *School Leadership & Management*, 19(1), 25-47. http://dx.doi.org/10.1080/13632439969320

Haymann F., Golan, H. & Shapira, R. (1997) School Autonomy and Parental Choice: steps in local educational planning, in R. Shapira & P.W. Cookson, Jr (Eds) *Autonomy and Change in Context: an international perspective.* Oxford: Pergamon.

Hoshen, M. (2004) *Parental Choice: a literature review.* Jerusalem: Szold Institute (in Hebrew).

Iram Y. & Schmida, M. (1998) *The Educational System of Israel.* Westport: Greenwood Press.

Maddaus, J. (1990) Parental Choice of Schools: what parents think and do, in C.B. Cazden (Ed.) *Review of Research in Education.* Washington, DC: American Educational Research Association.

Marko-Shoham, H. (1996) Personal, Communal and Institutional Characteristics and Patterns of Parents' Choice in High Schools, MA dissertation, Tel Aviv University.

Oplatka, I. (2002a) Secondary School Brochures: what they tell us about diversity in a local educational arena, *Education and Society*, 20(3), 45-60.

Oplatka, I. (2002b) The Emergence of Educational Marketing: lessons from the experiences of Israeli principals, *Comparative Education Review*, 46(2), 211-233. http://dx.doi.org/10.1086/340477

Oplatka, I. (2003) Choosing the High-School in Open Enrolment Areas: voices of Israeli parents and children, *International Journal of Educational Reform*, 12, 289-306.

Oplatka, I. (2004) The Characteristics of the School Organisation and the Constraints on Market Ideology in Education: an institutional view, *Journal of Education Policy*, 19(2), 143-161. http://dx.doi.org/10.1080/0144341042000186318

Oplakta, I. (2006) Teachers' Perceptions of their Role in Educational Marketing: insights from the case of Edmonton, Alberta, *Canadian Journal of Educational Administration and Policy*, 51. http://www.umanitoba.ca/publications/cjeap/articles/izhar.html (accessed 7 February, 2007).

Oplatka, I. & Hemsley-Brown, J. (2004) The Research on School Marketing: current issues and future directions, *Journal of Educational Administration*, 42(3), 375-400. http://dx.doi.org/10.1108/09578230410534685

Shapira, R., Haymann, F. & Shavit, R. (1995) Autonomy as Ethos, Content as Commodity: an Israeli model for controlled choice of autonomous schools, in R. Kahane (Ed.) *Educational Advancement and Distributive Justice: between equality and equity*. Jerusalem: The Magnes Press.

Taylor, C. (2001) Hierarchies and 'Local' Markets: the geography of the 'lived' market place in secondary education provision, *Journal of Education Policy*, 16(3), 197-214. http://dx.doi.org/10.1080/02680930110041024

Tel Aviv Municipality, Education Authority (1992) *There are Other Ways – Tel Aviv believes in education*. Tel Aviv: TAMEA (in Hebrew).

Tel Aviv Municipality (1999) *Tel Aviv-Jaffa: major trends and characteristics*. Tel Aviv: Center for Social-Economic Studies (in Hebrew).

Walford, G. (1994) *Choice and Equity in Education*. London: Cassell.

Walford, G. (1996) School Choice and the Quasi-market, *Oxford Studies in Comparative Education*, 6(1), 7-15.

Yogev, A. (1997) Autonomy and Choice as School Strategies for Peripheral Communities in Israel, in R. Shapira & P.W. Cookson, Jr (Eds) *Autonomy and Change in Context: an international perspective*. Oxford: Pergamon.

Yonah, Y. (2000) Parental Choice in Israel's Educational System: theory vs. praxis, *Studies in Philosophy and Education*, 19(5-6), 445-464. http://dx.doi.org/10.1023/A:1005223312650

CHAPTER 7

School Choice and Quasi-State Monopoly in Education Systems in Latin America: the case of Argentina

MARIANO NARODOWSKI

SUMMARY Latin American educational systems experienced a large increase in the number of private schools and students throughout the second half of the twentieth century. This process of privatization of schooling is not a product of the recently labelled 'neo-liberal wave' of the 1990s – its roots go further back in time. The increase in the choice of private schools in Argentina can be observed even though there are no economic incentives, specific programmes or even 'experiments' stimulating this practice. This chapter analyzes two models of educational supply – public (or state) monopoly and educational markets and quasi-markets – and develops a third theoretical option, the quasi-monopoly, useful to understand these processes. National educational systems in Latin America continue to be based on a model of provision that is centrally guaranteed by the state in what pertains to its financing, regulation and provision. However, it seems hard to maintain that it is monopolistic if one considers the educational system as a whole and not just the sector of the school that is operated directly by the state.

Educational Systems in Latin America

Latin American educational systems have experienced an increase in their private supply of schooling over the last few decades. Even countries like Argentina and Uruguay that were dominated by a public supply of schooling during the first half of the twentieth century have seen a large increase in their numbers of private schools and students throughout the second half of the century. Since the roots of this schooling privatization go further back in time, these changes do not appear to be a direct product of the recently labelled 'neo-liberal wave' of the 1990s (Narodowski & Nores, 2003).

Private education in Latin America is not a minor phenomenon, and consideration of this sector is essential to understand the character of each educational system. According to World Bank and UNESCO data, the 2004 enrolment rate for private education was 12.4% at the primary level and 16.3% at the secondary level. These figures are significantly higher than those found in other world regions: 1.1% in Europe, 1.4% in Central Asia, 6.9% in the Middle East, and 6.0% in North Africa (World Bank, 2006). Even more significantly, private enrolment accounts for half or more of the total number of students in some of the larger Latin American cities.

With their large and rising private sectors, Latin American educational systems can be considered to be 'hybrids'. To understand their full complexity and the evolving and dynamic relations between both sectors, this chapter offers a theoretical model that draws on recent academic debates about the introduction of market reforms in various educational systems, and combines two images of educational supply that are usually contrasted in the literature: a public (or state) monopoly on the one hand, and markets and quasi-markets on the other.

State Monopoly

The model of the *state monopoly* was defined by Milton Friedman (1982), and was more recently updated by Chubb & Moe (1990). Also labelled as 'public school monopoly' (Everhart, 1982), the state in this model funds schools and provides service through its bureaucracy. In theory, monopolies create great homogeneity in school knowledge, cultural norms, and discipline. Public monopolies are seen to have evolved out of local traditions, and to have later consolidated into powerful systems with an enormous capacity to homogenize the education for the entire population (Archer, 1979; West, 1994). In Argentina as in other Latin American countries, this monopoly should be seen in the context of the historic civilizing mission granted to public education in a nation that was constituted through a massive migration and a cultural and linguistic diversity that was seen to threaten its territorial integrity. Even today, many of the poorest families have only recently gained access to the educational system, and they hold relatively humble expectations for their offspring's schooling.

Schools in public monopolies or the 'one best system', according to critics like Chubb & Moe (1990, quoting Tyack [1974] with irony), are deprived of managerial autonomy. Decisions are made at macro-political or intermediate bureaucratic levels, far from the interests of families or the professional opinions of teachers. From a political standpoint, this public monopoly is supposed to guarantee that the educational system provides the positive externalities associated with democratic life and with the needs of the national economy, as stipulated by state bureaucracies.

In this model, as in any monopoly, demand for a service is met by a sole supplier: the public school that the state bureaucracy assigns to each family, usually based on geographical regulations and their place of residence. However, theorists of state monopolies acknowledge the limited existence of private education. While most families can access only a predetermined school as regulated by the state, a minority of the population can buy its way out of this monopoly. The existence of private education options becomes a problem when those options move beyond the confines of a small minority. At some point there is no longer a state monopoly *strictu sensu.* This is now the case in most Latin American countries, and even in other nations, such as the United States, when compared to fully monopolistic systems such as the old Soviet one, or even those that maintain stricter control over discipline and schooled knowledge. For this reason I will later introduce the concept of quasi-monopoly. This concept will help us better understand the problem of the emergence of educational systems in which two subsectors of school provision coexist.

Quasi-Market

A 'quasi-market' is a hybrid made up of institutions that behave according to market rules but are also somewhat coordinated by state bureaucracies. In this model, schools are financed by the state on the demand side, but compete for students, at least when the relationship between demand and supply allows (Whitty et al, 1998; Minvielle, 2004). In this model, schools require ample autonomy to offer a type of education to appeal to its potential clients while using its resources efficiently. According to proponents of quasi-markets, incentives to compete serve to improve the quality of education and its efficient use of funds (Chubb & Moe, 1990). From an ethical point of view, choice of schools gets democratized, since all families are supposedly equally able to choose the school that is best suited to their interests, rather than just those families that can afford such schools (Everhart, 1982; Brighouse, 2000).

In reality, few Latin American countries actually conform to a pure state monopoly or a quasi-market. On the state monopoly side, only Cuba lacks a private sector (Gasperini, 2000). At the same time, most countries have also failed to adopt market reforms on a large scale. Only Chile (Narodowski & Nores, 2002) is part of the small group of countries in the world where schooling is completely regulated by educational quasi-markets (along with England and Wales, Sweden, New Zealand and Holland; see Whitty et al, 1998). In Argentina, some schools face little regulation, while others face a lot. As I discuss below, Argentina's and other Latin American systems have responded to the 'quasi' state monopoly by reaching a sort of equilibrium, where having wealthier parents opt out of the public system has allowed the public system to spend more dollars per pupil than it could otherwise.

In Latin America, the clearest examples of market-oriented educational reforms have been introduced at a sub-national or local level, such as the case of Bogotá. These reforms have often been labelled as 'experiments' given their restricted nature. Smaller scale market reforms have also been recently attempted, such as alternative schools in Nicaragua, El Salvador and Guatemala, but these reforms have not reached national scales, despite the aspirations of their proponents (Caballero, 1998; De Olivera, 1998). These restricted experiences show that it is very difficult to create educational markets. Very often, traditional political practices and the social conditions of public schooling clash with pro-market rhetoric. As correctly pointed out by several authors (Vandenberghe, 2002; Minvielle 2004), the creation of a quasi-market has so many institutional requirements that it is hard for any of those countries to implement it according to the image of the orthodox model.

But as the upper and middle classes opt out of the public system and send their children to private school, new providers of educational services are emerging. In Latin America, many examples can be cited, such as the schools of the 'Sin Tierras' movement in Brazil, the Piqueteros movement in Argentina, the Fe y Alegría movement in many countries and a few home-schoolers. In many ways, these new educational strategies share something in common: they are defined by what they *don't want to be.*

National educational systems in Latin America, then, continue to function on a model of central state provision of financing, supply and regulation (Narodowski & Andrada, 2004). However, the rise of private sector participation is not a trivial fact, not only because of its quantitative significance but also because its size and characteristics tell us something about the whole.

In this chapter I first analyse the processes of privatization and school choice in the Argentine case to cast light on the relation between the growing private sector and traditional state provision of public education, as well as the regulation and funding of the private sector. Second, I review recent research on the behaviour of families vis-à-vis school choice. Finally, I introduce the concept of state quasi-monopoly in order to understand how education is being currently distributed. In Argentina, two school subsectors coexist, both significant in size, but differing in terms of their financing, regulation and the amount of organizational leeway allowed for each school.

Privatization of the Argentine Educational System

A look at privatization within the Argentine educational system reveals two important phenomena. First, private education has been growing steadily over the past 50 years, not only in absolute terms but also in its share of total enrolment. Various studies (Morduchowicsz et al, 2000; Narodowski & Andrada, 2001) show that while in the 1950s the share of private education enrolment – for pre-school, primary and secondary levels – was around 8%, that share had tripled by the beginning of the twentieth century, bordering on 25% for the whole country. According to UNESCO and World Bank data, it had reached 20% for primary school and 26% for secondary school by 2004 (World Bank, 2006). This steady increase has survived the political and economic crises that the country has undergone in the last 30 years: neither the political violence of the 1960s nor the deep economic crises of 1989 and 2001 [1] have directly affected the behaviour of the groups that tend to choose private schools. The private sector is of considerable magnitude in certain geographical areas. Research suggests that the largest private enrolment rates are in the largest urban centres (Buenos Aires, Rosario, Córdoba, Mendoza and Tucumán), in which the enrolment share rises to over 50%, reaching as high as 70% (Narodowski, 2002).

At the same time, private enrolment is clearly a function of a family's socio-economic level. Studies show that private enrolments concentrate in wealthier areas (Narodowski & Andrada, 2001). For instance, 92% of households in the highest income quintile sent their children to private schools in 2003, compared to 75% of households for the second income quintile. Around 80% of the wealthier households (40% of all households) have practically exited the public education system. At the other end of the spectrum, only 8% of the 20% poorest households send their children to private schools (Instituto Nacional de Estadística y Censos [INDEC], 2005).

Similarly, parental education is related to private enrolments. Two studies of the education demand of families in the city of Buenos Aires and the district of Quilmes in greater Buenos Aires (López, 2002; Scialabba, 2006) show that 78% of the parents who had obtained higher education in López's study and 91% in Scialabba's sent their children to private schools. The latter study found that as the number of years of education attained by the parents increased, so did the chances that they would choose a private school for their children. These findings underscore the high level of socio-economic segregation in the Argentine educational system. It is fair to say that as the mid and high socio-economic level groups increasingly left public education, public schools have basically become an option attended solely by the poorest. On the other hand, private education increases in urban areas, and in areas where wealthier and better educated families live. [2]

In Argentina there are no voucher programmes or 'school choice' programmes for public or private schools that are funded by either government or private institutions. The demand for private schools is no longer directly influenced by tax incentives. In 1991 school payments were made tax deductible, but this benefit was abolished in 1993. Thus, given that public schools are funded entirely by tax monies, paying for a private education means that families are declining a state benefit in favour of funding education out of their own pockets. The system thus offers 'school choice without vouchers' (Narodowski, 2002) or 'school choice by default' (Davies, 2004). The main state incentive for private education comes from a 1966 law that allows the state to fund teachers' wages totally or partially in some private schools. This funding offers an incentive to create private schools by reducing school operation costs. As a result, the main obstacle to opening a new private school is real estate investment. This funding offers an indirect and partial incentive for choosing private schooling by theoretically reducing its price and in many cases making the service either free or one for a very low price.

In the city of Buenos Aires, for instance, where total private enrolment reaches 50%, 828 private schools (64%) out of a total 1292 receive some kind of state funding to cover teachers' wages. However, only 26.8% of all private schools receive 100% funding for teachers' wages; 23.8% receive a subsidy corresponding to 70-80% of the wages; and 13.3% receive a subsidy corresponding to 40-60% of the wages (Gobierno de la Ciudad Autónoma de Buenos Aires [GCABA], 2006). Evidently, as state funding decreases, the contribution of the family increases – although some studies (Morduchowicz et al, 2000) show that the relationship between family contribution and subsidy received (in those cases where it is present) is not always directly proportional.

The state support of religious education does not fully explain the large state funding of private education. For instance, according to 2004 data, 27% of all subsidized schools in the city of Buenos Aires were non-religious. On the other hand, among those private schools that do not receive any kind of state support, a little less than half are religious (GCABA, 2006). Even those private schools that receive 100% state funding for teachers' wages also need private funding to cover their operation costs. State support does not cover other financial costs, real estate investment, support personnel costs, and all the daily recurring costs that schools face. State funding of private education is not a priority in the public budget, even in the city of Buenos Aires, where private enrolments equal the public enrolment. In Buenos Aires, private schools receive only 18% of all public funds allocated to education (GCABA, 2006).

To what extent, then, does private education in Argentina represent a market? Although there are no definitive studies, it is evident that those schools that do not receive any public subsidies are forced to seek funds in the marketplace by charging fees to students. Such schools compete not only against each other but also against schools that receive state funds and can charge a lower fee. They can have profits that they do not necessarily reinvest and can go bankrupt. In fact, during the 2001 economic crisis many private schools were forced to close down. Since the number of students in the sector did not change, we can conclude that those displaced were transferred not to public schools but to other private schools.

Among the private schools that receive funding to cover 80-100% of their teachers' wages, competition is less intense. These schools can complement their funds with very low fees (with no real market value) and do not go bankrupt because state funding is not strictly contingent on their numbers of students. These conditions suggest that strict competitive market mechanisms are present only in a small portion of the private sector.

The differences between public and private schools' internal organization and decision-making capacities in administrative and pedagogical issues have been studied by several authors (Morduchowicz, 2000; Narodowski & Andrada, 2001; Narodowski, 2002). All conclude that private schools enjoy more decision making, and that public schools face more bureaucratic restrictions and limits to teachers' autonomy. In some provinces, private non-subsidized schools have even more leeway than private subsidized ones. However, private schools are mostly equal, whether they receive state funding or not. In many Argentine provinces, private education even has its own system of state inspectors, separate from that for public schools. However, there is no evidence that these higher organizational capacities over private schools are actually exercised.

On the issue of students' performance in standardized tests, available research is scarce. Such evaluations have been implemented only since the 1990s in Argentina, and there are questions about the reliability of data in these evaluations (Narodowski et al, 2002). This situation has worsened since 2001 due to the constant interruptions and discontinuities in the national campaigns to evaluate educational quality. Nevertheless, available studies conclude that student outcomes in private schools are higher than those in public schools, even when socio-economic background is held constant (McEwan, 2001).

Yet, neither school organization nor student outcomes in standardized tests can explain families' decisions to send their children to private schools. These characteristics of schools are known to academics and some government administrators, but are not normally made available to the media, so they can hardly be known to families. Similarly, Argentine officials have not published school performance rankings, and publish test outcomes only by province and region, not by school (Narodowski et al, 2002). Thus, to understand the reasons behind school choice it is necessary to turn to research that goes deeper into the reasoning of families.

Keys Factors in the Behaviour of Families

In the last few years, studies in several Argentine cities have examined how families decide to send their children to either private or public schools. Some studies investigate the reasons why middle and upper class families choose mainly private schools, while others examine how poorer families view public versus private schools.

The first question has two important presuppositions. First, as mentioned above, families have few economic incentives to choose private schools, and face sunken (hidden?) tax costs by declining a free place in a public school. Second, public opinion studies suggest that public schools enjoy a positive image compared to other public and non-public institutions

(Narodowski, 2002). 'Defending the public school' is an important slogan of every campaigning political party in Argentina (the apparent contradiction between this pervasive ideological discourse and the actual decision of many middle-class families to send their children to private schools is discussed by Scialabba [2006]). Yet, these studies show that lower-income families view public education as 'worse' than private education in terms of teaching quality, teachers' abilities, and especially school climate and discipline. Parents from the middle and upper classes observe that private schools teach English more intensively, and have more usage of personal computers. Those who choose private schools view public education as fraught with difficulties, believing that public schools have fewer class days as a consequence of frequent teacher strikes, and shorter school days. These studies show that adherence to a given religion does not adequately explain families' preference for private schools.

A recurring theme in these studies is that many parents who chose a private school for their children themselves attended a public school in their childhood, and in some cases strongly identified with the idea of public education. Nonetheless, these parents typically state that public schools have 'lowered their quality' and are 'not the schools they used to be' (Scialabba, 2006). This evidence of an intergenerational change in preference and a waning of a strong identification with public education is consistent with the transformation of the Argentine education system where a large private sector coexists with the public sector.

Some qualitative studies (Svampa, 2001; Del Cueto, 2007) link the rise of private school choice among the middle and upper class families to urban changes over the last 15 years. Since the 1980s, a sizable portion of middle-class families in the biggest cities have been opting to live in so-called 'country-clubs' or 'gated communities', which are large real estate developments located in the city outskirts that allow open access only to residents and their guests. These families increasingly demand private schools, many of which are located inside these gated communities.

These qualitative studies suggest that the choice of private schools is part of a social process of self-segregation wherein higher income groups attempt to differentiate themselves culturally and socially from lower socio-economic groups. They build peer group identities by believing in the necessity of protecting children in a suitable environment that is far from the social conflict and multiple forms of street violence they have associated with public spaces since the 2001 economic crisis (Veleda, 2007). Veleda also finds that while middle-class families claim to seek the 'best schools', be they public or private, the seekers of prestigious public schools are decreasing in number.

Peer identities and perceptions of school prestige seem to be, therefore, one mode in which groups seek a form of *distinction*, in Bourdieu's sense (1979). This powerful symbolic incentive to choose a private school overcomes the direct economic incentive that would otherwise persuade families to choose a free public school. In any case, these families expect their return on investment in private schools (which charge considerably high fees) to be high enough to justify its costs. The idea of 'economic sacrifice in favor of the offspring' comes up clearly in these studies (López, 2002; Veleda, 2007).

How do lower-income families who send their children to public schools view public and private education? Surveys show that a significant percentage (38% in López's study and 42% in Scialabba's) report being dissatisfied with their children's public schools, and that many say they would choose a private school if they could afford it. Although the majority of those who send their children to public schools are satisfied with their school, this percentage is always lower than that among private school users, where only a very small percentage of parents (4 and 7% respectively in López and Scialabba's studies) would transfer their children to a public school. These studies suggest a high percentage (though not a majority) of the families that send their children to public schools do so even though they are dissatisfied, and that they perceive their children as receiving an education that is inferior to those who attend a private school.

Further evidence for this comes from a recent qualitative study (Narodowski & Gómez Schettini, 2007) of very low-income families living in so-called 'villas miseria' or slums in Buenos Aires. These are precarious settlements where thousands of people live in a state of overcrowding, without access to running water, electrical power or sanitation systems. Mothers who were interviewed said they were very dissatisfied with their children's neighbourhood school, and that they would prefer a school that offered a better education. These mothers were often not capable of exactly identifying those 'other' schools, or even whether they were referring to private or public schools. Despite only recently gaining regular access to the public system, these mothers did intuit that there was a 'different' school out there to which their own children lacked access.

School Choice in a State Quasi-Monopoly

The evidence discussed in the previous sections highlights the complexity of the Argentine educational system in terms of its supply and the behaviour of families. Clearly, the Argentine case is not a 'state monopoly', given the proliferation of private schools, including free or low-cost alternatives, which dominate in certain geographical areas. Argentine education has two further important characteristics. First, not everyone has the capacity to exit public schooling. Consequently, the choice of alternatives to the monopoly is an unequally distributed social good. Second, the public school sector continues to behave monopolistically towards those who cannot choose a private school, in that public schools are strongly organized and regulated by public bureaucracies. Yet, the Argentine case is also not best seen as a 'quasi-market'. State funds are allocated to public and private schools, though the funding mechanism is always on the supply side, thus inhibiting free choice in the public sector, leaving free flow of demand and supply only to some realms of the private sector, as discussed above. The principle of state subsidy for schools (Scheerens, 1997) only pertains to those private schools whose wages are funded completely by the state. Most private schools also need private funds for their initial investment and for their operational costs – including human resources – which the state cannot cover.

Therefore, the concept of a 'quasi-monopoly' allows us to adequately fill this theoretical void. Jean D'Aspremont & Jaskold Gabszewicz (1985) describe how an increased demand for a segment within a monopolistic structure can generate a new closed structure, one that does not directly compete with the old monopoly, and, on the contrary, can actually contribute to its endurance. They label the whole set – the old monopolistic sector plus the new structure – a 'quasi-monopoly'. Any attempt by the old monopoly to accommodate the new demand with its existing regulations could result in a crisis due to an excess of demand for that good. On the contrary, the quasi-monopoly produces a balance by restricting the old monopoly to the demand segment that it actually can satisfy.

Figure 1. The 'quasi-monoploy'. As shown in the figure, the 'quasi-monopoly' is constituted by the old monopolistic sector plus the new structure, in such way that the whole is a functional and balanced structure.

Quasi-monopolies in education are not what in macro-economics are called 'duopolies' – two monopolies competing against each other (Gannon, 1972). Argentina's private sector does not behave like a monopoly, unlike the public sector, which has a captive demand from parents who lack the resources needed to exit public schools and enter the private sector. Although the private sector is somewhat regulated and funded by the state, its own provision mechanisms are increasingly autonomous from state bureaucracies. Private schools have more leeway to offer a differentiated education to accommodate the needs of potential clients, and form markets through competition.

D'Aspremont & Gabszewicz's (1985) model of a quasi-monopoly describes a dynamic balance between the old monopoly and the growing private sector. This balance allows the traditional sector to continue its traditional monopolistic practices, since any unmet demand is absorbed by the rising private sector. By being restricted to wealthier families, the private sector does not push the monopoly to the point of crisis. Studies of educational funding in Argentina show a structural efficiency in the use of public funding for private education, and even posit a virtual collapse of the public sector if the private sector were to disappear. In other words, the quasi-monopoly allows the middle and higher classes to fund their own education, leaving public funds mostly for public schools, given the relatively insignificant state funds allocated to private schools as a proportion of total public spending.

For example, per-student public spending for the public sector in the city of Buenos Aires is AR$1586 per year. This figure goes down to AR$869 for students in the subsidized private sector. However, private sector funding in relation to the totality of the private sector enrolment is even more efficient, reaching only AR$498 per student (GCABA, 2006). Thus, the state allocates to the private sector just one-third of what it allocates to public schools per student. Evidence suggests that the cultural processes among the middle and upper classes help structure the quasi-monopoly. The symbolic incentives discussed above allow any unmet demand to flow to the private sector while allowing the old monopoly to continue addressing the needs of the poorer population.

A state quasi-monopoly in education, therefore, solves two problems for the Argentine educational system. First, it solves the problem of political governability. The unmet demand is able to find its own outlet, one that is less regulated and more autonomous. This private sector can count on its own funding and its own administrative and inspection system, and has more leeway to make pedagogical decisions. Second, the quasi-monopoly provides an efficient solution to the problem posed by deficits in state funds for education. By funding itself, the private sector reserves resources for needier groups in public schools.

In sum, applying the model of a state quasi-monopoly to the Argentine case allows us to explain the co-existence of two education sectors, one monopolized by state funding and regulation, having little leeway to make educational decisions, and targeted towards the poorest population, the other mixing self-funding and state funds, having more autonomy, targeting wealthier social groups, and enjoying higher prestige, despite a lack of clear indicators of their actual performance. However, in spite of the later tendencies, we cannot conclude that only families who have exited the public system benefit from this model. The poorer sectors of society also stand to benefit. These families have only recently gained access to the educational system, and hold lower expectations for their offspring's schooling.

Notes

[1] In both cases, national governments were virtually deposed after a strong economic crisis. In 1989, President Raúl Alfonsín left the government to his already elected successor, Carlos Menem. Twelve years later, President Fernando De La Rua resigned and left the Pink House while a massive popular protest (called by the 'cacerolazo') took place in the streets.

[2] This increase in Argentina's private school sector has occurred even though there are no economic incentives, specific programmes or even 'experiments' to stimulate this practice. However, monopolistic control of demand is increasingly weaker. Some provinces maintain a policy of restricting enrolment to one's neighbourhood for only pre-school and primary levels. This restriction is applied flexibly, not throughout the country.

References

Archer, M. (1979) *Social Origins of Educational Systems*. London: Sage.

Bourdieu, P. (1979) *La distinction. Critique sociale du jugement*. Paris: De Minuit.

Brighouse, H. (2000) *School Choice and Social Justice*. New York: Oxford University Press.

Caballero, P. (1998) *La autonomía escolar en el marco de la descentralización*. Santa Fé de Bogotá: Instituto SER de Investigación.

Chubb, J. & Moe, T. (1990) *Politics, Markets, and America's Schools*. Washington, DC: Brookings Institution.

D'Aspremont, C. & Gabszewicz, J. (2006) Quasi Monopolies? *Economica*, 52(206), 141-151. http://dx.doi.org/10.2307/2554416

Davies, Scott (2004) School Choice by Default? Understanding the Demand for Private Tutoring in Canada, *American Journal of Education*, 110(3), 233-255. http://dx.doi.org/10.1086/383073

Del Cueto C. (2007) Fragmentación social y estrategias educativas en urbanizaciones cerradas, in M. Narodowski & M. Gómez Schettini (Eds) *Escuelas y familias: problemas de diversidad y justicia social*. Buenos Aires: Prometeo.

De Olivera, F. (1998) Vanguardia del atraso o atraso de la vanguardia: globalización y neoliberalismo en América Latina, in E. Sader (Ed.) *Democracia sin exclusiones ni excluidos*. Caracas: ALAS, CLACSO, UNESCO, Nueva Sociedad.

Everhart, R. (1982) *The Public School Monopoly: a critical analysis of education and the state in American society*. San Francisco: Pacific Institute for Public Policy Research, and Cambridge, MA: Ballinger.

Friedman, M. (1982) *Capitalism and Freedom*. Chicago: University of Chicago Press.

Gannon, C. (1972) *Consumer Demand, Conjectural Interdependence, and Location Equilibria in Simple Spatial Duopoly*. Regional Science Association. Papers and Proceedings, 28, 81-107.

Gasperini, Lavinia (2000) *The Cuban Education System: lessons and dilemmas*. Country Studies: Education Reform and Management Publication Series, 5(1), 2-41. Washington, DC, The World Bank.

Gobierno de la Ciudad Autónoma de Buenos Aires [GCABA]: Informe ertadéstico en base a datos Relevamiento Annual (2006) *Dirección Nacional de Información y Evaluación*, Ministerio de Educación, Ciencia y Tecnologia de la Nación.

Instituto Nacional de Estadística y Censos [INDEC] (2005) *Encuesta Permanente de Hogares*. http://www.indec.gov.ar

López, C. (2002) Comportamiento de las familias ante elección de escuelas y micro-mercados educativos. Estudio del nivel de la Educación General Básica (EGB) en el Partido de Quilmes (Buenos Aires-Argentina). MA Dissertation, Buenos Aires.

McEwan, P. (2001) *Private and Public Schooling in the Southern Cone: a comparative analysis of Argentina and Chile.* Occasional Paper 11. New York: National Center for the Study of Privatization in Education, Teachers College, Columbia University.

Minvielle, Lucila (2004) El Cuasi Mercado Educativo: acerca de sus condiciones de posibilidad. MA Dissertation, Buenos Aires.

Morduchowicz, A. et al (2000) *La educación privada en la Argentina*, Buenos Aires: Fundación Gobierno y Sociedad.

Narodowski, M. (2002) Socioeconomic Segregation in the Argentine Education System. School Choice without Vouchers, *Compare*, 32(2), 181-191. http://dx.doi.org/10.1080/03057920220143165

Narodowski, M. & Andrada, M. (2001) The Privatization of Education in Argentina, *Journal of Education Policy*, 16(6), 585-595. http://dx.doi.org/10.1080/02680930110087834

Narodowski, M. & Andrada, M. (2004) Cuasi monopolio estatal y descentralización educativa. Una exploración sobre América Latina *Revista de Educación*, 333, 97-219.

Narodowski, M. & Gómez Schettini, M. (2007) *Escuelas y familias: problemas de diversidad y justicia social.* Buenos Aires: Prometeo.

Narodowski, M. & Nores, M. (2002) Socioeconomic segregation with (without) competitive education policies. A comparative analysis of Argentina and Chile, *Comparative Education*, 38(4), 429-451. http://dx.doi.org/10.1080/0305006022000030720

Narodowski, M. & Nores, M. (2003) Searching for 'Neoliberal' Education Policies: a comparative analysis of Argentina and Chile, in S. Ball, C. Fischmann & S. Gewirtz (Eds) *Crisis and Hope: the educational hopscotch of Latin America.* New York: Routledge.

Narodowski, M., Nores, M. & Andrada, M. (2002) *La evaluacion educativa en la Argentina. Desde los operativos nacionales hasta los boletines escolares.* Buenos Aires: Prometeo.

Scheerens, J. (1997) *The Foundations of Educational Effectiveness.* Oxford: Pergamon.

Scialabba, A. (2006) La elección de escuelas de las familias de la Ciudad de Buenos Aires. MA Dissertation, Buenos Aires.

Svampa, Maristella (2001) *Los que ganaron. La vida en los countries y barrios privados.* Buenos Aires: Biblos.

Tyack, D. (1974) *The One Best System: a history of American urban education* Cambridge, MA: Harvard University Press.

Vandenberghe, V. (2002) Combinación de los controles urocrático y de mercado en educación: Una respuesta a as deficiencias burocráticas y de mercado? in M. Narodowski, M. Nores & M. Andrada (Eds) *Nuevas tendencias en políticas educativas. Estado, mercado y escuela.* Buenos Aires: Granica.

Veleda, C. (2007) Entre querer y poder. Las clases medias y la elección de la escuela en el conurbano bonaerense, in M. Narodowski & M. Gómez Schettini (Eds) *Escuelas y familias: problemas de diversidad y justicia social*. Buenos Aires: Prometeo.

West, E. (1994) *Education and the State: a study in political economy*. Indianapolis: Liberty Fund.

Whitty, G., Power, S. & Halpin, D. (1998) *Devolution and Choice in Education: the school, the state, and the market*. Philadelphia: Open University Press.

World Bank (2006) Global Country Data. http://devdata.worldbank.org/edstats/cd.asp

CHAPTER 8

Cultivating Choice: the invisible hands of educational opportunity in Tanzania

KRISTIN D. PHILLIPS & AMY STAMBACH

SUMMARY This chapter examines the relevance of the concept of choice to the educational context of the United Republic of Tanzania, where secondary school enrollment opportunity remains low and fees for study are prohibitive. In Tanzania, the concept of choice remains peripheral, not only to debates at the national policy level, but also to the way that parents and communities frame their claims to educational opportunities. Drawing on ethnographic research in two contrasting regions – Singida and Kilimanjaro – the chapter describes not how people 'choose' between their given options or rate the 'choices' open to them, but rather how they produce educational opportunities through social interaction. People cultivate and strengthen a variety of relationships, including those that involve putting oneself at the debt and the mercy of benefactors, and those that involve creating horizontal relationships of reciprocity, where people call on those with similar means and help them in turn. It is argued that it is through these relationships – rather than through a disinterested educational 'market' – that people in Tanzania access educational opportunity.

Once, when asked what the benefits were of having many children, a Nyaturu woman replied, 'If I have many, maybe one or two will succeed and come back to help me. If I only have three, and none succeeds, what's the point?' Her explanation continued with a metaphor: 'Here in Singida Region, people plant many seeds ... maize, sorghum, millet ... If one dries up in the sun, perhaps God will help and another will flourish'.

Success for this woman, whom we call Nyamichaeli [1], and for many parents in Tanzania, means that at least one child completes primary school – and if fortunate, secondary school – and then goes on to find employment.

Ideally, the educated child will earn enough money to live independently and to help her or his parents in the village. In Singida – as in many places across rural eastern Africa – poverty refers not only to a state of destitution brought on by having too many children to feed and educate, but more often to having too few children to support parents in old age. Parents will plant many seeds, knowing that, to continue Nyamichaeli's metaphor, the ground is not fertile enough for all to germinate. This 'wealth in people' model (cf. Guyer, 1995) conceptualizes educational opportunity in terms of being chosen, not in terms of consumerist principles that treat schooling as a commodity.[2].

Success, in this model, is neither a small nor an individual feat. In Nyamichaeli's village in 2006, for instance, 20 of 60 students sitting for the national Standard 7 examination passed, and only 10 students obtained a place in the nation's secondary schools. Such access rates mirror the national scene where 62% of those who passed the examination in 14 of mainland Tanzania's 21 regions failed to find places in secondary schools, and less than 10% of children complete a secondary education at all (Rajani, 2006).[3] A lack of wide-open educational opportunity means that obtaining a space in a school, paying fees, and finding safe lodging at or near a school (most likely far from one's home village or region) requires lifelong work by families and students. Cultivating educational opportunities requires building social relationships, amassing favors from extended kin, and securing gifts from various sources, near and far.

Typically, the post-exam scramble for placement occurs within a complex hierarchy of government and private schools that is similar to other educational contexts described in this volume. While some Tanzanian families are relieved when their children get any place at all, other families settle for nothing less than an English-language 'Academy' or overseas education. No matter how rich one is, however, one can never afford the education one values. Educational opportunity, as the major key to social mobility and claims to a precarious middle and upper class in Tanzania, is always relative to one's social position. While rural and poor families face the greatest challenges in cultivating success due to a lack of funds, appropriate social connections, and proximity to schools, all families, rich and poor, are confronted with this task of building relationships, by stacking up favors, calling on extended social networks, and seeking patronage in a variety of ways. Indeed, the 'planting of many seeds' in central Tanzania's adverse farming conditions is an apt metaphor for the lifetime of work required to cultivate educational opportunity and pursue upward mobility in Tanzania, which has been designated one of the poorest countries in the world, ranking 164 of 177 countries on the United Nations Development Program's 2005 Human Development Index (2005) and 175 of 177 for gross domestic product per capita.

As Jansen (2005) notes regarding the international policy of 'Education for All', our research shows that the concept of 'choice' as a means of organizing and implementing access to education has not played a central role in the national policy context of Tanzania. This does not mean that Tanzania is exceptional in every way to global discourses regarding education. Indeed, the Tanzanian context is in some ways representative of trends in international education: discourses of decentralization, devolution, and parent and community participation all emerge as central concepts to education reform in Tanzania today. Yet the concept of choice remains peripheral, not only to debates at the national policy level, but also to the way that parents and communities frame their claims to educational opportunities.

Hence, we focus here not on how people 'choose' between their given options or rate the 'choices' open to them, but rather on how they cultivate relationships in order to reap potential opportunities. This chapter points to the fact that neither the centrality of the concept of choice in educational policy, nor that people frame their claims to education as 'choices', may be taken for granted. Drawing specifically on intensive field research conducted in two socio-economically contrasting areas of Tanzania – Kilimanjaro and Singida – and reflecting on the history and contexts of formal schooling and sponsorship in these places, this work explores the various 'hands' at work in Tanzania's educational marketplace. In appropriating Adam Smith's famous phrase (Smith, 1904) into an ethnographic essay, we are not asserting that self-interest makes the world go round. Rather, we find that the notion of 'invisible hands' underscores the human interaction, agency, and relationships that occur behind the depersonalized, almost mystical market terms such as 'capacity', 'demand' and 'cost-sharing' in which educational opportunity is generally discussed (see also Sanders, 2003).

Historical Background and Current Landscape

British, French, and German missionaries introduced the first formal schools in Tanganyika Territory. When control of Tanganyika passed from Germany to Great Britain in 1920, the British Colonial Office began constructing government primary schools, many of them administered by mission associations and British-designated Native Authorities. The aim of schooling under British rule was to quell the rumblings of the Maji Maji rebellion that had erupted then simmered under the Germans and to teach Tanganyikans to work as manual laborers in a cash economy. For this latter reason, the British concentrated most schools in the fertile farming belts along the northern and southern mountain ranges, where the export of coffee, sisal, and bananas soon proved profitable.

In 1961, the first president of independent Tanganyika, Julius Nyerere, was elected. Three years later, Tanganyika and Zanzibar united to form present-day Tanzania. Nyerere socialized the Tanzanian economy and nationalized all schools except for seminaries. He called for the abolishment of primary school fees and for universal access to primary education.

Between 1962 and 1976, Nyerere concentrated nearly all government spending for education at the primary level, and his work was championed worldwide as a successful socialist experiment. By the early 1980s, however, Nyerere's programs began to crumble. Responding to International Monetary Fund Structural Adjustment Programs, Tanzania cut its spending on education in the mid 1980s and implemented 'cost-sharing' reforms (i.e. school fees) by the early 1990s. Although school fees were heaviest at the tertiary level, cost-sharing requirements trickled down to primary education (Buchert, 1994, p. 4). By the 1990s, the United Nations' call for 'Education for All' again turned policy makers' attention to questions of educational access (United Republic of Tanzania, 1995). Both the Tanzanian Primary Education Development Plan (United Republic of Tanzania, 2001) and the Tanzanian Secondary Education Development Plan (United Republic of Tanzania, 2005) have used basket funding from external donors to construct schools, increase access to basic education, and deal with the problem of what Robert Serpell (1993) has called 'squeeze-outs' – those who pass their primary examinations but fail to obtain placement in secondary school.

Today, students who wish to attend secondary school in Tanzania, whether government or private, must pay fees. Private schooling is, generally speaking, significantly more expensive. Religious organizations that sponsor such schools, however, sometimes offer scholarships to students directly. Government schools are less expensive, but finding funds for boarding or residence near the school can be difficult for families. Various factors make certain institutions (or kinds of institutions) more desirable than others (Lockheed & Jimenez, 1994). But instead of an 'all else equal' model of choice envisioned by some researchers (see Good & Braden, 2000), in which one might prefer a church-sponsored school over a public school, a number of factors (such as resources, science laboratories, English proficiency of teachers and students, socio-economic status, the degree of 'protection' offered to girls, hours spent teaching) create a difference in schools' desirability, and also in their fees. Educational opportunity in Tanzania is therefore rooted in a hierarchy of schools, differentiated by their cost, their currency in the Tanzanian economy, the moral status of the kinds of students they produce, and by the kind of teaching and learning they promote.

Further, and as may be expected, Tanzanian schools are clustered in urban areas where people and employment are concentrated, in areas historically settled by missionaries, and in areas highly attractive to international tourists, some of whom establish connections with communities and return to found schools and other development projects. This intensely regionalized educational development should be understood as the articulation of geo-political relationships, not as a function of geography per se. Individual families and students are mapped into the educational system by their relationships much more than by their physical location. Proximity to schools or urban centers allows one to build the necessary relationships to secure a place, find sponsorship, or afford housing and travel costs. However, neither geographical location nor land ownership entitle one to certain educational services or rights (as they do in the United States, for example). Tanzanians are mapped into this highly regionalized and highly differentiated system of secondary education through their relationships and resources, not through their property or through a guarantee of educational 'rights'.

Cultivating Choice in Dry and Fertile Lands

To illustrate how educational opportunity is conceptualized in much of Tanzania, consider two contrasting regions, Singida and Kilimanjaro. Singida, a semi-arid, boulder-strewn region abutting the Great Rift Valley, is known as one of the poorest and least educationally developed of mainland Tanzania's 21 regions. Singida region primary students were placed last in 2002 on the Standard 7 national examinations (*The African*, 2003). Kilimanjaro, on the other hand, is recognized throughout Tanzania as one of the country's wealthiest and most educationally advanced regions. Consistently, Kilimanjaro ranks among the highest nationally in school enrollment and students' performance (Ministry of Education and Culture, 1996, 1999). To paint ethnographic pictures of life in Singida and Kilimanjaro we present narratives by Phillips on Singida, and by Stambach on Kilimanjaro.

Singida

Singida's poverty is relatively stable, which is to say, entrenched. Both the colonial fortune-seekers of the past and today's international investors have steered clear of Singida's dry climate and sandy soil, and its residents eek a living from the land by farming millet, maize, and beans. Rural dwellers have made slow gains since independence – building schools and clinics and digging deep water wells – while other problems have intensified – the increasing frequency of drought and subsequent famines, the impact of cattle disease, and the number of malaria-driven deaths. Villagers live far from water sources and grinding mills, with electricity in neither their homes nor their schools. Most possess no more than two acres of land to feed their large families, and in a good year, cultivate only enough to eat for half the year. At school, however, kindergarten and primary students receive two meals a day through the United Nations World Food Program, which feeds schoolchildren in drought-prone and pastoralist regions of Tanzania.

Urban residents of the metropolitan cities of Dar es Salaam and Arusha consider Singida's towns and villages alike as 'the bush', the unworthy reward of a grueling (14-hour and 7-hour respectively) bus ride *ndani* – 'to the interior'. Yet Singida also possesses the power to charm visitors with sweeping landscapes of dramatic rock outcrops, the bustling frontier-like atmosphere of Singida town, and the self-deprecating humor and lack of pretension among its residents. Langilanga village perches on one of the great valleys of Singida. It lies not far from the regional capital of Singida Municipality, a large town of approximately 115,000 residents. Relative to the villages near Singida town, Langilanga is considered rural but not *ndani kabisa* ('totally interior'). Its 2000 residents live in large family homesteads that are scattered over an area of some 40 square kilometers. It borders on an inter-city transportation route which, though simply a two-lane dirt road, provides villagers with access to local mini-buses traveling to town, or the option to hitch a ride with a passing truck.

For the majority of Singida Rural District's 400,000 residents, subsistence farming, small agro-business, and local trading do not yield enough cash to educate one's children. Success in finding support for secondary education relies on additional work by students and their parents to develop the strength of personal relationships with potential sponsors; to increase the legitimacy of claims on particular relationships by stacking up favors and strategically accumulating debt; and to manipulate the timing of requests to coincide with moments when resources are available.

A visitor cannot be long in Singida before finding herself implicated in a number of schemes to secure educational sponsorship among its residents. Whether purchasing produce at the local Saturday cattle auction or wandering the labyrinth of sorghum-lined paths connecting Nyaturu homesteads, one is likely to make new acquaintances among friendly Singidans. Nyaturu are known to be very curious at the arrival of guests, who are said to be 'sent by the sun' (Jellicoe, 1978) and therefore beneficent and generous. This somewhat mythic aura surrounding strangers leads to startlingly speedy attempts to extract promises of future sponsorship for education. Moreover, the more recent history of missionization and volunteerism for educational development in Tanzania has led to a widespread belief that foreign visitors must be wealthy and seeking beneficiaries.

The more subtle and successful approach of initiating sponsorship, however, is also replicated between and among Tanzanian friends and acquaintances. It involves developing long-term relationships of exchange, support, and patronage, often between socially and economically unequal persons. People initiate such relationships by offering little favors, and in return, asking for bigger favors. In this way, lending a small amount of money to someone for the treatment of a sick child inevitably leads to requests for greater and greater amounts for school supplies or fees. Instead of the borrower feeling bad for already having outstanding debts, the benefactor finds himself enmeshed in a relationship in which his 'protection' is now understood. Third and fourth requests might be introduced after initial greetings with: 'I have a problem with you', or more pointedly, 'I have your problem'. Relationships merge with responsibilities and allegiances and demands grow greater and greater over time, as do the presentation of gifts, the offering of favors (taking over child care or assistance with household chores) and professions of loyalty and affection.

Nyabaraka was the second wife of a businessman in Langilanga, who purchased finger millet from local farmers and then transported and resold it in Dar es Salaam to urbanites who buy it to cook *uji*, a breakfast porridge. The profits from this business (which required capital beyond the means of most Singidans) were enough to construct a 'modern' house with a corrugated tin roof and cement floor, to furnish it with locally crafted 'modern' furniture, and to imagine that in the future they might be able to educate some of the businessman's 10 children that his two wives had borne. In the meantime, Nyabaraka enjoyed the status of Tanzania's rural middle class, who through the power of patronage, find themselves endowed with household assistance in return for their financial support.

Nyabaraka's best friend was the widow Nyalissu, brewer of millet beer and proprietor of one of the several *kilabu* (or beer 'clubs') in the village. While Nyabaraka enjoyed financial security, Nyalissu had but little. So each afternoon Nyalissu sent her oldest daughter Gili to fetch water for Nyabaraka, which Gili often accomplished with Nyabaraka's youngest child tied to her back with a brightly colored *kanga*. Some evenings Gili came to Nyabaraka bearing *mchicha*, the meaty wild spinach leaves her mother picked to eat with their maize-meal *ugali*. On other days, Nyalissu herself would come to visit Nyabaraka, taking over the household chores as they gossiped. Nyalissu then tapped into Nyabaraka's resulting sense of responsibility for the family when Gili passed her seventh grade examination but did not procure a place in an affordable government school but rather in an expensive and unprestigious private school. Nyalissu – marginalized as a beer-brewer and single mother from religious sources of educational support – commenced a frenzy of activity as she scrambled to collect on debts, drew on patrons (like Nyabaraka) and debtors that she had developed, wove a web of lies to make immediate claims on briefly available resources, and plagued the district office with requests for reconsideration of Gili for a government school.

Similar relationships developed between a neighboring Christian mission school, Grace Girls' Secondary, and people from Langilanga. While we do not mean to argue that people's religious preferences are shaped by potential educational opportunity, educational opportunities are certainly enhanced through a family's perception as devoted members of a congregation. Nyamattias was a devout widow whose daughter, Florencia, was not selected for pre-secondary studies at Grace, which is known nationally for its strong academic preparation and its fierce protection of its all-female student population. Nyamattias went to see a school official to beg for reconsideration. The administrator exclaimed, 'Oh, if I had known she was *your* daughter ... we don't like to accept girls if we don't know who their parents are'. It was acceptable that Nyamattias was poor, but necessary that she be pious. Florencia was then accepted.

Grace Girls' Secondary, like many private schools, relies on revenue-generating admissions from families who can afford to pay (so generally from

Arusha, Kilimanjaro, and Dar es Salaam). This part of the student population is generally diverse, both in terms of ethnicity and religion (as required by Tanzanian law). However the school maintains a mission to assist local girls from Singida, whom they accept with financial assistance. One teacher emphasized that with these admissions they try to help particular families: the children of local church members, guards, cooks, and others who work at the school or otherwise serve the church. These preferences are widely known, and villagers court the mission's attention in a variety of ways. The previously mentioned Nyalissu sent Gili and her younger sister Katherina to church every Sunday. Nyalissu did not attend, however, since she relied on her Sunday morning beer business. Her children were therefore considered 'children of the congregation' by the church leaders, but also marked as having an immoral mother, affecting their chances of being accepted at the school.

Timing was essential to strategies to procure financial assistance by students and their parents. Singidans, when pressed for the rule of thumb by which they offer and refuse assistance to needy neighbors and kin, consistently say, 'If you can help them, help them. If you can't, you don't. One day maybe you find you have the ability. Another day you don't. You just do what you can'. The general logic of requests further illuminated this vague advice: 'You can make claims on money that you know is there; you cannot make claims on money you know is not there or money that you do not know is there'. For this reason, people shrouded their own financial transactions in secret, while they aggressively sought to 'catch' others with cash. Phillips was surprised to learn after several months of work that one research assistant had told everyone that she was working for her voluntarily, as a representative of the village government. The assistant did this in an attempt to save her income for her own precarious situation as the widowed mother of seven children, trying to gain independence from her parents, and attempting to send two children to secondary school. One wealthier man in the village related that when he paid a male farm laborer for his services, he would often call the man's wife in to be present as well (without the man's prior knowledge or consent). In this way both would be present and the wife could make her claims on the money for household needs or school fees before the husband spent it on less noble purposes. If the wife did not know if or when he was paid, she would be unable to claim some of the money. In the same way, taxes for development projects would always be demanded during the harvest months, when people had more cash or assets on hand. Whatever debts remained past the months of September and October were understood to be lost until at least the harvest of the following May and June.

Assistance was not only sought through vertical patronage (sponsorship in the context of unequal social relationships), but also pursued from one's friends and allies. Friendship in the village was marked by reciprocal exchange: 'One day I give some of my valuable resources to you because you really need it. Another day, I can expect the same of you'. In some ways this storing up of favors and assistance functions as a savings – one knows one has allies that cannot refuse you. The Nyaturu say that '*Hiri ngwari*' – 'a debt is wealth ... the creditor has a bank in other people's pockets' (Olson, 1964, p. 74). However, this relies on one's ability to successfully make claims on past favors. Nyalissu endeavored unsuccessfully to collect on debts so she could put the 'down payment' on Gili's place at the private secondary school. Upon seeing her coming, people would leave their house to avoid having to make good on what they owed. '*Igutambaa igufahiwaa*', she said – 'the bird which soars overhead will be made of arrow feathers' (Olson, 1964, p. 75). Local wisdom taught her that the man with a debt cannot stay away forever, he must come home at some time.

Not all assistance was sought honestly or to great effect. Nyabasili – whose husband had long since run off – had a son who worked in the tanzanite mines of Arusha and contributed to his younger sister's secondary education. Young Magda met a young man who lived near her school, however, and soon became pregnant. Her mother allowed her and her lover to move home during her pregnancy, with the promise that Magda would return to school after nursing the baby. Basili returned from Arusha one weekend to his mother's home, and found his sister and a man they claimed to be a cousin living there. Nyabasili aimed to conceal the truth about Magda's condition so that he would continue to send support for her school fees. When Basili's grandmother revealed to him the truth, he 'went crazy'. After a wholehearted but fortunately failed attempt to kill his mother, his sister, and her lover and a more successful destruction of their house, he escaped the village authorities and ran off. Neither he nor his money were seen again. The village government eventually arranged for Magda and her mother to move near the village office for protection, but many villagers sympathized with Basili's rage, arguing that he had been deceived by his mother and that the money he had unproductively spent to educate his sister would have sufficed to purchase the roofing material for his own modern house. The aborted education of his sister released him of his familial obligations.

In Langilanga, education, and the rare hope of success it offers for many families, is often held up as *kazi ya Mungu* – 'the work of God'. It is therefore not surprising – with education the work of God and itself a scarcely available commodity in Tanzania – that those who successfully gain access to education or help to provide it are endowed in the social imaginary with a moral superiority. The acceptance of financial assistance is often accompanied with a sigh of relief and a '*Mungu akubariki*' – or 'may God bless you' – while one's own or one's children's educational success would be humbly explained by '*Mungu ametusaidia sana*' (God has helped us a lot'), or '*Tumebarikiwa sana na Mungu*' ('we have been greatly blessed by God'). Mzee Leonardi, a former village leader and the oldest and arguably most well-off man in Langilanga, described his family's success in the following way: 'I've educated my children until all have finished studying, even though it was with hardship that I educated them. Now I am thankful to God [*namshukuru Mungu*] that I have begun to receive the good fruits of that education ... a modern house, as you see'. Mzee Leonardi explained his success, often targeted by jealous neighbors and kin as the product of corruption or sorcery, as the work of God.

On the other side of this, people often attributed their own failure to succeed in secondary school to witchcraft or other foul play, in which unexplained sickness or blindness brought on through a jealous curse by a clansman prevented one from advancing. Blinding headaches forced Mama Mary to drop out of secondary school. Upon explaining her sickness to her parents, they exclaimed, 'This cannot be the work of God. It must be a human that refuses that you study! When you went to Form One, there was one person who said, "We've never seen a female child of our clan study ... why should this one?"' And so they concluded it was he who had cursed her. Such stories of witchcraft preventing educational advancement circulated widely in Langilanga. If education was the work of God, its cruel sabotage was the work of God's antithesis.

Kilimanjaro

As we noted earlier, the seeking of patronage is not limited to the poor. No matter how well-off or rich one is, educational opportunity often appears to be an unattainable good. In this regard, the experiences of many people living in Kilimanjaro Region provide illuminative contrast to those of Singida residents. As previously mentioned, Kilimanjaro is known throughout Tanzania as one of the country's wealthiest regions, and is often seen to be at the opposite end of the spectrum from poorer areas such as Singida. Early nineteenth-century caravan trade, linking the Swahili coast with interior places, passed through *mangis*' (chiefs') lands on Mount Kilimanjaro. *Mangis* presided over a system of lineage-divided land that was highly fertile and irrigated year-round. Kilimanjaro communities' political centralization and the temperate climate of the mountain attracted the attention of early European explorers. Many of these explorers regarded the *mangis'* system of governance as evidence of a kind of bureaucratic rationalization commensurate with – if not, they believed, an earlier historical representation of – European civilization and its reproductive mechanism: schooling. Depending on one's source of information, whether colonial archives or local memory, the first school established in Kilimanjaro was initiated either at the invitation of a particular *mangi or* at the insistence of Leipzig Lutheran missionaries. In any event, formal schooling flourished by the turn of the twentieth century, and the rest, in a sense, is history. For much of the past one hundred years, Kilimanjaro, and Chagga people living there, have been associated in the collective national imaginary with educational opportunity, advancement, and exceptional resources.

Today, Kilimanjaro Region is regarded as at the forefront of a movement toward new variations of private schools. Whereas in the 1980s, many privately funded community schools were registered in Kilimanjaro to accommodate children who did not qualify for government schooling (for reasons of regional quotas meant to curtail ethnic imbalance), today, highly selective and for-profit private schools are opening in areas surrounding the regional capital, Moshi. Called 'Academies', in keeping with a particular international parlance that re-imagines basic education as a prep-school opportunity, these schools are typically English medium. That is, instruction occurs not in the national, official language of Kiswahili, but in English – the language of business and world markets.

Increasingly, people in Kilimanjaro associate these two types of schools – community-based private schools and private English-medium academies – with an emerging two-tiered aspect of society.[4] Twenty years ago, community leaders pooled their resources and used their political clout to establish community-based private schools. They typically registered these schools through a religious organization – more for practical reasons than as a statement of faith – and saw these schools as solutions to years of socialism during which their children had been excluded from government secondary schools. Some of these leaders belonged to a group known locally as 'the Front Line' – wealthy business men and women who had houses in the village *and* second houses in the national capital (Stambach, 1998). In the capital, these leaders held occasional fundraisers for their 'poorer brothers and sisters' in Kilimanjaro. Fund-raising support stemmed from a sense of obligation to one's home and family. 'A child must come home to die', people say, meaning that no matter how far from home an educated person travels or lives, he or she will be buried at home, near the graves of ancestors, and thus will, and must (at the risk of being ostracized, possibly cursed), continue to support his or her home community.

But the power of cursing or of social exclusion depends on the extent to which inclusion matters. A younger cohort of educated professionals, whether living near or far from home, are pooling their resources not to build community schools but to invest in English-medium academies. Whereas leaders 20 years ago explicitly envisioned, in the written proposals they submitted to the Ministry of Education, that their model of schooling would foster community development and advance local ideas of communalism, founders of academies today stress the value of education for individual mobility and participation in a global economic market. This is not to say there is a simple shift from communalism to individualism. The picture is more complicated. But where 20 years ago local leaders were holding fundraisers for private community schools in rural areas, their progeny, in a certain sense, are now prioritizing English academies. To illustrate this picture, we detail some of the strategies parents use to enroll children in these two kinds of schools, showing that despite a shift toward investment and savings, and toward a greater number of educational models in the region, the cultivation of good will and positive social connections remains important in *all* conceptions of school opportunity.

Enrolling a child in community school is often a matter of being at the mercy of teachers, headmasters, village leaders, and, on the grander scheme of things, at the mercy of and in the grace of God – called variously *Mungu*, *Allah*, *Iruwa*, and God, depending on one's language and orientation (Tanzanian national Kiswahili, Islamic international Arabic, regional-traditional Chagga language, international market-oriented English). In contrast, enrolling a child in an Academy is often a matter of being at the mercy of markets, which are themselves often conceived of as controlled by a higher agency and moral order ('Or why else would they be so volatile?') Beginning as early as three months before the school year, parents – typically mothers, because they more than fathers want both sons and daughters to be educated and employed so as to support them in old age – might fix an appointment to see the headmaster of a community school. 'I have an envelope [*bahasha*] to give to you', a woman might say, passing the headmaster on a footpath one afternoon. To which the headmaster might respond in passing that he is 'too busy' and doesn't have a moment to spare. The woman might pass him again another day, perhaps now standing in his way, insisting that she see him, or perhaps arriving at school *ghafla*, unannounced, looking both nonchalant and intentional, looking out for the headmaster's whereabouts until he can be cornered in his office. On such occasions, one might also see the headmaster carefully avoiding the parent, perhaps knowing the 'envelope' she carries does not have contents he desires.

'Having an envelope' means 'having some money' and may refer simply to school fees that are owed. Or, it may refer somewhat ambiguously to an extra gift. Such a gift is not simply a bribe. It is not like the money one might pass to a police officer in order that he overlook a broken headlight; or the money one would give to a civil servant at the time of applying for a business licence or plot of land. It is an expression of thanks, of recognition for the headmaster's work, not only because he is himself known to be underpaid, but because the parents wish to demonstrate their appreciation for education and their understanding that education has a value that in itself goes beyond what is taught and learned. The envelope is necessarily an airmail one, with blue and white striped trim. Few parents would think of giving an ordinary brown domestic envelope to a teacher or headmaster unless, to begin with, that parent did not know that schooling carried promises of mobility. A domestic envelope, after all, 'might contain nothing more than millet seeds!' In any event, whether given an appointment or forced to corner the headmaster – or for that matter a teacher or member of the school board – parents are often at the mercy of someone within the school. This is so because most community-based private secondary schools are highly over-enrolled. Student–teacher ratios are as high as seventy to one in Form 1. Not every applicant can get in.

Bahasha, however, are just one strategy for entry. Others are less directly monetary. In advance of school enrollment, many students and parents might ensure – as do many in Singida as well – that their lives are in good social order (this is also sometimes the case in advance of students taking national examinations). For some children living in Kilimanjaro, this might involve taking a small dracaena branch to grandparents (dracaena is a conventional sign of good will and respect) or helping an old grandmother or grandfather clean, farm, or take care of livestock. For children living in town, it might mean sending a card or a message to a grandparent in the village, asking for blessings and prayers with regard to school. To be in a person's debt and good grace is to confer social power on that person and to augment that person's social standing. That person, in turn, will look favorably on the student, perhaps offering a blessing or prayer, or sending some money.

Some families might also slaughter a goat or chicken, although most will do so without overt symbolic gesture, for to 'slaughter a goat to the ancestors' in the eyes of most school-oriented people is past- and not future-oriented. Yet there are many ways to skin a goat, as it were, and one way is to assemble one's neighbors and kin, thank them for their blessings and camaraderie – and for their generosity in the past – and to announce that a particular child in the host's household is in urgent need of school fees. It would not be inappropriate – in fact, it has been done many times – to ask for small contributions in the course of or after the proffered meal. Gift-giving here is an indication of relations of reciprocity, not in the sense of fair trade for a meal, nor of commitment to equal return for guests' children later, but of partnership and commitment to (in this case) schooling, again as a means for raising up the community.

English-medium academies are a slightly different matter. Fund-raising is more typically a private affair, and enrolling a child in an Academy depends upon having made successful personal financial investments, less on the goodwill of teachers and headmasters. Mama Shiitrande's last born child, Jeremy, attended an English-medium private academy. Although Mama Shiitrande eventually withdrew her son (perhaps out of a not uncommon social concern that the school was 'taking him away from his family – he couldn't speak with his grandparents in the village!'), she enrolled him initially so that his schooling might advance him in business and internationally. She herself had been one of the first business persons in Tanzania to trade on the national stock market, which opened about five years ago. Around that time, the national bank of Tanzania was opened to international competition: a South Africa-based Standard Charter Bank opened branches in the country and soon after established a 'school fee loan' program that encouraged parents to start saving for private education. 'Secure his future', a Standard Charter Bank billboard read, 'make his dreams come true today'.

School fees at the Academy were about 1000 US dollars per year in 2003, plus room and board for most students. Mama Shiitrande did not need to take out a school loan; her business was well established – although South African investment in a rival local tourist hotel had created heavy competition for her own. Indeed, it was her to whom village mothers came to ask for money – both outright and in exchange for work. In one case, Mama Shiitrande bought a quarter-acre plot of land from a widow who wanted to use the fees to send her daughter to the local community school.

Figure 1. Billboard in Dar es Salaam, 2002. Photograph by Amy Stambach.

On many days, and for many years, women would congregate on her porch in the mornings, waiting to be handed a crumpled five-hundred shilling note as a gift. Mama Shiitrande frequently hired neighbors to help cook for communal meals that she then hosted for these women's families and others in the village. At various times, a migrant child would pass through her compound, looking for some work, and she hired them – not because she needed help but because they needed work. But Mama Shiitrande occasionally needed money herself, and for this she prayed and strategized. With few to whom she could put herself in debt, she extended and offered up her work to God. 'My God will Supply all Your Needs', read a sign in her hotel lobby. And 'My Redeemer Lives'. Not unlike Nyamichaeli, who sowed many seeds and thanked God for their germination, Mama Shiitrande sowed many investments and saw their growth as the work of a higher moral agent. Economic opportunity, like education, to her was a reflection of her being chosen, not a reflection of her own skills and interests as consumer or investor. Perhaps this is why Mama Shiitrande said she saw educational opportunities as *nafasi* – a chance, a gift, even a gift from God/Mungu/Iruwa – and as more an obligation than a right which she herself had to cultivate and see grow.

Relations of support and inclusion for families like Mama Shiitrande's are much more horizontal than vertical, as are relations between parents and the village leaders and community school teachers that we described earlier. In church, parents of Academy children tend to congregate together, and for that matter – according to one of their teachers – Academy students, who are chaperoned in church by their Academy teachers, actively seek to distance themselves from their Swahili-speaking peers. And yet it is not unexpected that in socially anonymous settings, wealthy parents should seek assistance from wealthy strangers – including from visiting American researchers or missionaries or volunteers. One European donor and advisor to the Tanzanian Government related an extreme example of this (to Phillips) during an interview. He had a very strained relationship with a notoriously difficult government Minister, no doubt one of the most powerful people in Tanzania. One day, this donor was called to the Minister's office, and he came prepared for a continuation of their usual sparring. However, upon his arrival he was startled to find that the Minister was requesting personal financial assistance for his child's overseas education. The Minister drew on the leverage of his professional relationship and his notoriety for making things difficult to extract a personal financial favor that his colleague could assume would result in some reciprocal good turn in their working relationship.

Another civil servant family (that Phillips encountered) in Dar es Salaam was known for its beneficence to foreign researchers, to the point that they almost seemed to 'collect' them. Though they repeatedly confused the names of their *wazungu* ('white') visitors and one had the sense they could not keep them all straight, Mama and Baba Deo were well loved and respected, and their house was often abuzz with guests at varying stages of research and a wide variety of topics. Subsequent to leaving Tanzania, most of their guests contributed to the parents' continuing education: Baba Deo is now pursuing a Master's in Norway, and Mama Deo an MBA in the United Kingdom. The friendships Mama and Baba Deo forged were neither disinterested, nor purely utilitarian; rather, they combined affective inclination with interested exchange. Friendship was articulated through favors, while favors deepened the friendship. It may be that this kind of interested exchange was not so foreign to the foreign researchers who so enjoyed their company.

The ethnography of these two regions highlights contrasting ends of the educational spectrum in Tanzania. In Singida, the lack of educational infrastructure, economic opportunity, and food and water security present huge obstacles to rural villagers and people must contend for finite community resources through developing certain kinds of relationships – some more likely to generate assistance than others. Our discussion of the cultivation of educational opportunity in Kilimanjaro showcases a very active yet also changing private sector of education in Tanzania, in which a former model of schooling that proposed to foster community development and advance local ideas of communalism has given way to academies that today stress the value of education for individual mobility and participation in a global economic market. There have been shifts toward investment and savings and toward a greater number of educational models in the region. Yet despite these contrasts, our ethnography demonstrates how the cultivation of good will and positive social connections remain important in all conceptions of school opportunity. Additionally, in both Kilimanjaro and Singida, we see a moral narrative about educational opportunity emerge in which opportunities are understood to be *nafasi*, bestowed by God, Mungu, Iruwa, Allah, or the ancestors, and in which 'obligations', 'debts', and accumulated commitment are more significant than 'rights' or 'entitlements'.

Concluding Remarks

Under the umbrella of 'choice', important conversations have come to light in the field of education. These include questions of rights, access, and equity in the distribution of educational services, and debates about the role of the state and the private sector in education (Lawrence, 2005; Stambach & David, 2005; Bagley, 2006; Stambach & Becker, 2006; West, 2006). While 'choice' increasingly may be a concept around which educational policy and funding are organized around the globe, we find the notion of choice itself to be peripheral from the educational, policy, and everyday contexts of Tanzania.

Choice, if we try to imagine it in the logic of internationally circulating ideas that currently shape educational policies (see Hoxby, 1998; Tooley & Dixon, 2002; E.G. West Centre, 2007), suggests a free-standing subject exercising her or his right to education through selecting from a free-floating range of educational options. As we have shown, that is hardly the case in Singida and Kilimanjaro (and – we could argue elsewhere – not even the case in other contexts, despite the rhetoric). There is little that is 'free' about educational opportunities in Tanzania, in any sense of the word. We refer not only to prohibitive school fees and merit-based selection, but also to the sense that opportunities for secondary schooling are rarely 'open' chances for enrollment. Indeed, educational opportunity in Tanzania sometimes reminds one of riding a public mini-bus or *daladala*. Just when one thinks there is no more room for even another chicken – let alone another person – the conductor defies the laws of physics and, with one hard shove, two more people squeeze in.

Second, options are not 'free' in Singida and Kilimanjaro in the sense that opportunities, as they materialize, are not untethered to personal and social connections needed to obtain enrollment or financing. Opportunities surface only *in the context* of social relations, not separate from them. Our ethnography describes how people cultivate and strengthen a variety of relationships, including those that involve putting oneself at the debt and the mercy of benefactors, and those that involve creating horizontal relationships of reciprocity, where people call on those with similar means and help them in turn. In building both types of relationship, people draw on a moral narrative of obligation and debt, in which one either looks to God for assistance *through* patrons, or in which one *is* a patron and therefore in the debt of God. This moral language also seeks (if unconvincingly) to reframe the seeming anti-sociality of educational success by attributing power and wealth to a socially acceptable and benevolent source and therefore obliging the wealthy to repay their debt through assisting others. In any case, one's own educational opportunity – always conceived in terms of social mobility and therefore relative to one's social position – unavoidably depends on others. As we have shown, the important question in Tanzania is not how people 'choose' between their given options or rate the 'choices' open to them, but rather what they must do to cultivate relationships in order to reap potential opportunities

Finally, 'choice' implies that at some given moment, one is faced with a number of paths, all possible. One has a moment – or several – to weigh one's options, and pick the path most fitting to one's goals. Yet the opportunities sought and seized in Singida and Kilimanjaro are not fixed; they have no guarantee of concurrence. Rather, as we have shown, opportunity opens as fleeting chances, windows that open and shut, each in their own time, in the context of social intercourse and calculated action. Indeed, educational opportunity in Tanzania is embedded in a range of complicated and complicating relationships in which deliberate timing and accumulated leverage mean everything.

Thus we have highlighted how the Tanzanian context differs significantly from other national contexts described in this volume, where 'choice' policies have moved to the forefront of national and local conversations. Before concluding, we would like to offer some preliminary thoughts as to why this might appear to be the case.

We propose that 'choice' policies hold currency especially in contexts where people can draw on notions of 'universal rights' to make claims on unequally distributed and actively contested public resources for education. That is, 'a right to education' is most significant where there exists a reasonable capacity to actualize that right (i.e. that potential openings in schools and pupils can approximate a one-to-one relation to each other). Likewise, the 'right to choice' becomes important where the right to education is generally acknowledged but there is concern or complaint about significant heterogeneity in the quality and kind of education available. So despite the fact that heterogeneity certainly exists in Tanzania, and we see some Tanzanians exercising their privilege of choosing from the several different kinds of schooling to which they have access, the majority of Tanzanians still have *no* access to opportunities for secondary education. There are, at present, too few schools, and too few teachers. 'Choice' therefore holds little social or political currency as a means of mobilizing sympathy or support for access to education in general, much less access to a specific kind or quality of education in particular. The cultivation of relationships, on the contrary – with neighbors, extended family, patrons, and God – provides a powerful social narrative and political mechanism for accessing scarce opportunities for educational advancement.

Notes

[1] To ensure confidentiality, all names of people and places are pseudonyms. When necessary, some aspects of identity and location have also been changed.

[2] Our implicit comparative framework is 'choice programming' in the United States. See, for instance, http://www.ed.gov/parents/schools/find/choose/index.html, where 'choice' is conceptualized as a free-for-all opportunity for parents – even though 'choice' in this context is highly constrained by parents' knowledge of how to navigate the system, by spaces available in various schools, and ultimately by household location.

[3] In January 2007, the Tanzanian Government mandated a rapid expansion of secondary education at the ward level. As this book went to press, makeshift secondary schools opened around the country. The long-term implications of this rapid growth for debates about 'choice' remain to be seen.

[4] Since most secondary school students in and from Kilimanjaro are enrolled in one or another form of private schools, and not in government secondary schools, we do not focus on government schools here. The proportion enrolled in private schools is approximately two-thirds of the total student population (Municipal Education Office personnel, personal communication, June 2002).

References

Bagley, C. (2006) School Choice and Competition: a public-market in education revisited, *Oxford Review of Education*, 32(3), 347-362. http://dx.doi.org/10.1080/03054980600775656

Buchert, L. (1994) *Education in the development of Tanzania: 1919-1990*. London: James Curry.

E.G. West Centre (2007) Private Schools Serving the Educational Needs of the Poor: a global research and dissemination project. http://www.ncl.ac.uk/egwest/research/privateschools.html (accessed 24 March 2007).

Good, T.L. & Braden, J.S. (2000) *The Great School Debate: choice, vouchers, and charters*. Mahwah: Lawrence Erlbaum Associates.

Guyer, J. (1995) Wealth in People as Wealth in Knowledge, *Journal of African History*, 36(1), 91-120.

Hoxby, C.M. (1998) Analyzing School Choice Reforms that Use America's Traditional Forms of Parental Choice, in P.E. Peterson & B.C. Hassel (Eds) *Learning from School Choice*, 33-156. Washington, DC: Brookings Institution Press.

Jansen, J.D. (2005) Targeting Education: the politics of performance and the prospects of 'Education for All', *International Journal of Educational Development*, 25(4), 368-380. http://dx.doi.org/10.1016/j.ijedudev.2005.04.009

Jellicoe, M. (1978) *The Long Path: a case study of social change in Wahi, Singida District, Tanzania*. Nairobi: East African Publishing House.

Lawrence, C.R. III. (2005) Forbidden Conversations: on race, privacy, and community (a continuing conversation with John Ely on racism and democracy), *Yale Law Journal*, 114(6), 1353-1403.

Lockheed, M. & Jimenez, E. (1994) *Public and Private Secondary Schools in Developing Countries: what are the differences and why do they persist?* The World Bank: ESP Discussion Paper Series, No. 33. Washington, DC: World Bank.

Ministry of Education and Culture (1996) *Basic Education Statistics in Tanzania (BEST): 1994 regional data*. Dar es Salaam: United Republic of Tanzania.

Ministry of Education and Culture (1999) *Basic Education Statistics in Tanzania (BEST): 1994-1998 national data*. Dar es Salaam: United Republic of Tanzania.

Olson, H.S. (1964) Rimi Proverbs, *Tanganyika Notes and* Records, 62. Dar es Salaam.

Rajani, R. (2006) *More than Classrooms: statement on expanding secondary education*. Dar es Salaam: Hakielimu. www.hakielimu.org

Sanders, T. (2003) Invisible Hands and Visible Goods: revealed and concealed economies in millennial Tanzania, in Harry G. West & Todd Sanders (Eds) *Transparencies and Conspiracy: ethnographies of suspicion in the new world order*. Durham, NC: Duke University Press.

Serpell, R. (1993) *The Significance of Schooling: life journeys in an African society*. Cambridge: Cambridge University Press.

Smith, A. (1904) *An Inquiry into the Nature and Causes of the Wealth of Nations*, ed. Edwin Cannan (5th edn). London: Methuen.

Stambach, A. (1998) Education, Mobility, and Money: comparative reflections on the meaning of investment, *Advances in Educational Policy: perspectives on the social functions of schools*, 4, 3-18.

Stambach, A. & Becker, N.C. (2006) Finding the Old in the New: on race and class in U.S. Charter School debates, *Race, Ethnicity and Education*, 9(2), 159-182. http://dx.doi.org/10.1080/13613320600696730

Stambach, A. & David, M. (2005) Feminist Theory and Education Policy: how gender is 'involved' in family school choice debates, *Signs: Journal of Women in Culture and Society*, 30(1), 1633-1658. http://dx.doi.org/10.1086/382633

The African (2003) Singida Vows to Improve Education, 20 January.

Tooley, J. & Dixon, P. (2002) The Private Sector Serving the Educational Needs of the Poor: a case study from India. http://www.cfbt.com/cfbt/web.nsf/ID/502C36EC884C45DA80256D3A0054016F?OpenDocument

United Nations Development Program (2005) *Human Development Report 2005*. http://hdr.undp.org/statistics/data/countries.cfm?c=TZA

United Republic of Tanzania (1995) *Education and Training Policy*. Dar Es Salaam: United Republic of Tanzania.

United Republic of Tanzania (2001) *Primary Education Development Plan*. Dar es Salaam: Ministry of Education and Culture.

United Republic of Tanzania (2005) *Secondary Education Development Plan*. Dar es Salaam: Ministry of Education and Culture.

West, A. (2006) School Choice, Equity, and Social Justice: the case for more control, *British Journal of Educational Studies*, 54(1), 15-33. http://dx.doi.org/10.1111/j.1467-8527.2006.00334.x

CHAPTER 9

Competition, Audit, Scientism and School Non-Choice in Rural China[1]

ANDREW KIPNIS

SUMMARY The promotion of school choice has often been interpreted as part of the worldwide spread of neo-liberal governmentality. School choice, in this vision, is seen as a measure to encourage competition and thus effect the efficient production of atomized, neo-liberal subjects. School choice is imagined as enforcing market discipline on the providers of educational services, providing a neo-liberal form of audit and accountability. This chapter describes in detail the policies of one county in rural China with regard to (mostly preventing) school choice while promoting competitive exercises (between students as individuals, classes of students, teachers, schools, principals and school districts) in the extreme and conducting scientistic 'quality' audits. The resulting combination of governing techniques can be said to have a coherent logic of sorts, but it is not neo-liberal. In addition to providing a case study from a Chinese context, by a careful questioning of what forms of education policy, audit culture, and competition deserve to be labelled neo-liberal, this chapter suggests that great care must be taken in using that term.

In Western academia, the promotion of school choice has often been interpreted as part of the worldwide spread of neo-liberalism (e.g. Klees, 2002; Hursh, 2005). School choice, in this vision, is seen as a measure to encourage competition between schools and teachers as well as students and thus effect the efficient production of atomised, neo-liberal subjects. School choice is imagined as enforcing market discipline on the providers of educational services, serving to break teacher unions and provide a neo-liberal form of audit and accountability. Many of these same critics see competitive regimes of testing, as well as the introduction of new practices of audit and accountability in the evaluation of teachers and university academics, as part of the same mode of neo-liberal governance (e.g. Shore & Wright, 2000). While I share in the desires of these scholars to criticize certain versions of neo-liberal ideology, I am less confident than these scholars about depicting the variety of school reforms that include school choice, encouraging competitive regimes of testing and implementing new regimes of audit and accountability as a single neo-liberal whole.

In this chapter I detail the educational policies of Zouping – a rural but rapidly industrializing county in Shandong province, China – with regard to (mostly preventing) school choice while promoting competitive exercises (between students as individuals, classes of students, teachers, schools, principals and school districts) to an extreme degree and conducting 'quality' audits in a manner that could be described as absurd and scientistic. The resulting combination of governing techniques has a coherent logic of sorts, but does not constitute a holistic frame of government that may be called 'neo-liberal.' While some may dismiss this exercise as simply a case study that demonstrates how (one county) in China is not neo-liberal, I believe that my critique is more significant than that. By a careful questioning of what forms of education policy, what forms of audit culture, and what forms of competition deserve to be labelled neo-liberal, I implicitly critique sloppy uses of the application of the word neo-liberal as an explanatory trope in comparative discussions of governing.

Neo-liberalism is a slippery term, and elsewhere I have published a longer discussion of the many ways in which 'neo-liberalism' is used as a theoretical trope, especially in anthropology (Kipnis, 2007). The critique developed in this chapter applies primarily to Marxian critiques of neo-liberalism by education researchers, especially as articulated by David Hursh.

Even Hursh agrees that there are many 'contradictions' in what he depicts as neo-liberal education policies:

> The first neo-liberal policy contradiction is between the notion that markets are self-regulating and the reality that they require significant governmental intervention in the everyday life of teachers and students in the forms of standards, testing and reporting. The second contradiction is between desiring competitive markets to promote innovation and diversity while constraining innovation by curriculum standards: in England by a national curriculum and high-stakes standardized tests. Third, markets are meant to promote competitive individualism; however, some governments ... have realized that individualism can be carried to an extreme. Lastly, while the reforms are promoted as guaranteeing a quality education for all ... the culture of testing and choice is leading to increasing disparity between schools. (Hursh, 2005, p. 11)

Many of these contradictions are apparent in Zouping as well, but the explicit forms of ideological justification are rather different from those described by Hursh. Key ideological notions in contemporary China relate primarily to raising the 'quality' (*suzhi*) of the population rather than promoting 'freedom' or 'individualism' through choice, or self-regulating markets (for more on quality, see Kipnis, 2006a). The Chinese Communist Party-led government proudly proclaims the importance of its own governmental leadership rather than asserting that he who governs least governs best. Nonetheless, tensions over what constitutes 'quality' and how to measure and promote it lead to dilemmas that are not so different from those that Hursh describes.

Zouping's Education System

It would be simplistic to think of Zouping as representing all of China, as there is no single place that could do this. On the other hand, it would be equally simplistic to think of Zouping as an island that has no relation to social dynamics of education and school choice in other parts of China.

Figure 1. Maps of China and Shandong.

Where possible, I will attempt to specify the geographic scope of the governing dynamics described in this chapter, but I begin from a general overview of socio-economic conditions in Zouping.

Until 1995, in terms of economic development, Zouping could be considered a relatively middling rural county in China. In that year, however, a highway constructed from Jinan, the capital of Shandong province, to the port city of Qingdao provided Zouping with a direct transportation link to the export markets of South Korea and Japan. This access, along with the expansion of the Weiqiao Textile Group, which is now the largest cloth producer in the world, has spurred extremely rapid economic growth. In 2005 Zouping was for the first time named one of the 100 most economically developed counties in China (there are roughly 2000 rural counties in China). In 2005 the average annual income for a working adult amounted to approximately US$1250. Clearly, both the county government and individual households in Zouping have more to spend on education than in most rural areas. Nevertheless, educational spending patterns in Zouping are representative of relatively well-off rural counties on China's eastern seaboard where perhaps 100 million people live. Moreover, educational conditions there are also indicative of the hopes and desires of at least the local leaders in the majority of China's rural counties as well as the direction in which many other economically average and above average counties might head if economic growth in China continues at its current rapid pace.

Though the majority of Zouping's (roughly 700,000) people still live in rural villages, the county seat has grown from a small town to a mid-sized city of roughly 250,000 people. All of Zouping's villages now have a paved road that links them to the county seat and the other more minor towns scattered throughout the county. The growing economy of the county seat is attracting migrants from outside of Zouping and, as in many places where economic in-migration occurs, questions about who will pay for the education of migrant children have been raised. Unlike the situations in China's large cities such as Beijing and Shanghai, where children of migrant workers feel too estranged from local society to attend local schools even when there are no economic barriers (Woronov, 2002; Froissart, 2003), in Zouping the children of migrant workers are being successfully integrated into local schools. Before 2005, these children attended local schools, but their households had to pay extra fees. In 2005, following pressure from the central government, these charges were waived.

As in most of China, since the late 1980s Zouping has been consolidating schools both because the birth control policy has led to a decline in the number of school-aged children and because of the perceived abilities of large schools to provide better facilities and instruction. This consolidation has involved turning the majority of junior middle and senior middle schools into boarding schools and bussing children to primary schools outside of their home villages. At the end of the 1980s, the county administrated over 700 primary schools and 70 junior middle schools. This amounted to a primary school in almost every village (a few neighbouring villages shared primaries) and a junior middle school for every 10 primary schools. By mid-2006 there were only 63 primary schools and 20 junior middle schools. Now most rural primary schools serve between 20 and 40 villages each, averaging 1500 students over six grades (for more detail, see Kipnis, 2006b).

As in all of China, nine years of education (years 1-9) are compulsory. Furthermore, as is the case in many parts of China, the vast majority of Zouping's children (over 95%) attend school for at least that long. Not surprisingly, in the poorer parts of China higher proportions of students fail to complete the compulsory nine years. In Zouping a small but significant percentage of students drop out of school in year eight or nine, not so much for economic reasons but because they intensely dislike the highly competitive examination-oriented pressure (Kipnis, 2006b).

Annual school fees for the compulsory primary and junior middle school years have ranged between US$30 and US$120 over the past few years, not including food for boarders. In addition, over 90% of Zouping children now attend three years of pre-school, even though fees for this non-compulsory schooling are somewhat higher, ranging from US$250 to US$1200 per year. The majority also attend some form of senior middle school, years 10-12, with nearly half of junior middle school graduates attending one of the two 'elite' academic senior middle schools, another quarter attending one of the two non-elite academic senior middle schools and close to 15% attending some form of vocational school. Annual fees for senior middle school vary, but begin at US$400, not including room and board. Almost half of those who graduate from an academic senior middle school will move on to some form of tertiary education, with slightly more than half of these attending a regular university. University fees in China are very high, with even inexpensive universities charging annual tuition fees of US$1500.

Zouping children are supposed to, and generally do, attend primary and junior middle school according to the district in which they live. At the end of junior middle school, all students take a standardized examination that determines whether or not they are offered a place in one of the two elite academic senior middle schools. Students who pass the cut-off score on this examination are then assigned a place at one of these two schools. The other students may either pay an extra fee to attend one of the elite schools (if their scores were reasonably close to the cut-off), or choose among the remaining two academic senior middle schools and the vocational senior middle school. For pre-school, most village children will attend the public pre-school in their district. For those who live in the county seat, there are a variety of public and private pre-schools from which to choose, and this is perhaps the only level of schooling that offers parents a significant 'choice'. There is also one private, combined primary/junior middle school in the county seat and a second quasi-private (state-owned but privately run) junior middle school. These are boarding schools that attract students from all over the county and beyond.

I have been conducting research in Zouping since 1987. Since 1999, my research has focused on processes of education reform, and in 2005 and 2006 I spent nearly six months conducting fieldwork on this topic. During this time, I spent two months gaining an overview of the county education system by interviewing officials in the county education bureau (*jiaowei*), visiting a wide variety of schools, providing oral English classes to local English teachers and interviewing these same teachers. I then selected three primary schools, one in the county seat that teaches children from urban households, one in a relatively impoverished rural township that teaches children from more than 25 surrounding villages, and one on the fringes of the county seat that teaches the children of suburban villagers and migrant workers.[2] At each school I spent two weeks following one year six class and two weeks conducting household interviews with the families of the students in that class during the evenings and spending time in the year six teachers' office during the day. In all, I conducted over 100 household interviews. As the classes that I observed were constructed to have equal numbers of above and below average students, the sample of households I interviewed was relatively representative of Zouping households with a child in year six.

School (Non)Choice in Zouping

The phrase for school choice in Chinese, *zexiao* – more literally the selecting of schools – is not a particularly positive one. In Zouping I have never heard the term associated with a discourse of freedom or freedom of choice. Often it is written of or discussed as a form of corruption – parents breaking rules or bribing officials in order to get their child admitted to a school that they imagine is better than one that their child would otherwise attend. Other times it is depicted as an economic necessity (Xinhua, 2006; Wen, 2006). In order to fund new schools or equipment, some schools are allowed to accept children from outside of their districts, and charge a fee. In some periods, at certain Zouping schools, this has been carried out in a perfectly legal manner. With permission from the county education bureau, a given school sets a 'school selecting fee' (*zexiao fei*). Students from outside the district (or under the examination cut-off score) who meet certain criteria and whose parents are willing to pay the fee may attend that school. These fees have ranged from US$150 per year at public primary schools to a one-off fee of US$2000 for senior middle school students choosing to attend one of the elite academic schools without having achieved the examination cut-off score. At times, the fees in such cases have varied according to the number of points by which the cut-off score was missed. As described above, until 2005, the children of migrant workers were often treated like children whose parents were choosing a school outside their home district and, thus, also paid the annual school selecting fee.

Over the past 10 years policies towards school selection have varied somewhat, but exceptions to the general limitations on school choice have had mostly to do with desires to increase school funding and investment. In 2001, the county education bureau decided to encourage private investment in schools, and the county's only private school, the Bilingual Academy (*Shuangyu Xueyuan*), a co-educational school for year one to nine students, was built. The principal of this school argues that his school offers Zouping parents another choice for their education, but this offer of 'choice' must be considered in context of the enforced lack of choice for the majority. In general, parents cannot arrange for their children to attend school outside of their assigned district, so those who choose the Bilingual Academy are usually relatively wealthy families who happen to live in one of the less well-off school districts outside the county seat. The Bilingual Academy's school building was built on loans, and the state-regulated annual payments of US$700 for each student are barely enough to cover salaries, operating costs and loan repayments on the building. Nevertheless, by teaching some of the county's wealthier students at no cost to the county, the school can be said to be reducing fiscal pressures on the county education budget.

Figure 2. Zouping's Number One Senior Middle School.

The other quasi-private school in the county was opened in 2003. In that year, the county completed construction on a new campus for the county's Number One senior middle school. This new campus is truly spectacular, with facilities better than any I have seen at any Australian senior middle school. The cost of construction was roughly US$30 million, most of which the county government borrowed. To help repay the loan, the county decided to turn the old campus into a quasi-private junior middle school, now called the Old Number One junior middle school. Though run by the state, this junior middle school charges tuition at the state-regulated private rate (US$700 per year) and attracts students from all over the county and beyond. It sells itself by offering its graduates a 50-point bonus on the entrance examination for senior middle school (valid only for attendance at the new Number One senior middle school) and by claiming to have superior teaching staff.

The county government's rather cynical and mercenary attitude towards school choice is also evident in the manner in which it assigns senior middle school places for the county's best students. As described above, those who rank in the top 30% on the senior middle school entrance examination at their own junior middle school are assigned a place at either the Number One or the Number Two senior middle school. Despite the massive investment in the Number One school, the county decided it wanted two excellent senior middle schools but feared that if all of the top scoring students were given a choice then they would all go to the Number One school. Therefore, in addition to giving the Number Two school some new facilities and ensuring that it had its share of excellent teachers, the county government assigns half of the top scoring students to it. Most of the students allocated to the Number Two school go there, and the Number Two school has proven itself competitive with the Number One school in terms of the scores of its graduates on the university entrance examinations.

In addition to students assigned to the two elite senior middle schools, who account for roughly half of the students attending them, these two schools attempt to earn money by selling the rest of their places to students who pay a special one-time entry fee above the standard tuition rates. Because of its exceptional facilities, the Number One school is more successful in marketing itself to students from outside the county. But both schools are able to raise significant funds by offering places to Zouping students who just missed the cut-off scores. In short, school choice is something that the Zouping government deliberately limits, allowing it to happen only occasionally and only under circumstances in which the government is desperate for funds.

Even to the extent that there are some options for choosing schools in Zouping, the overwhelming similarity of the schools limits the significance of this choice. The type of educational rhetoric that suggests that different types of children can benefit from different types of education can be found in China. Some educators promote 'child-centred' education over 'teacher-centred' education for this reason, and efforts are made to create a well-rounded curriculum that exposes children to a diversity of activities in the hope that all children can discover their personal niche (Liu et al, 1997; Kipnis, 2001b). In Zouping, however, more emphasis is placed on 'standardization' (*guifanhua*). The county education bureau conducts standardized tests for every subject at every grade level at every school twice a year. Textbooks are standardized, teacher training is standardized and even particular lesson plans are standardized. To further standardization, the county has developed an education intranet to which all schools are wired. A teacher whose students do well on standardized tests will be required to share his or her lesson plans and teaching tips and other teachers will be pressured to adopt them.

The examination-oriented competitiveness of the Chinese education system is central to this process of limiting choice. As described above, I conducted 103 household interviews with a relatively random selection of Zouping year six students. Every single parent in these 103 households hoped that their child will one day attend university. From the point of view of Zouping parents, the purpose of school, even at the primary and junior middle levels, is to lay the basis for eventual success in the university entrance examination. It is only at the senior middle level, where some students have clearly demonstrated their inability to cope with China's examination mania, that perhaps 20% of students either drop out or are channelled into more vocational forms of training. As a result of this exam mania, the curriculum of all the schools that Zouping parents might choose among is basically the same. Even the 'Bilingual Academy' follows the same curriculum as the public primary and junior middle schools. Bilingual Academy teachers of subjects like mathematics and geography and physical education are simply encouraged to use the occasional English language word in their lectures.

From a parent's perspective, choice is mainly about whether they believe that teachers at one school might be more effective in teaching the mandated curriculum in the mandated way than teachers at another school. As I heard over and over again from parents who were thinking of paying money to send their child to either the Bilingual Academy or the Old Number One junior middle school, the level of teaching competence was the major concern. They believed the marketing lines about teacher superiority that these schools articulated. While I have no firm measure of teacher quality, in my observations of classrooms in a wide variety of schools, I could not detect any significant differences between schools. Parents who told me that teacher quality was better at a given school could never offer concrete evidence, even when pressed. While some school principals argued that the training at the normal schools had become more 'scientific' over recent years and, consequently that their recently hired, younger teachers were better than those at other schools, my ethnographic observations did not seem to support the principals' faith in scientific progress.

Finally, the choices available to the students within a given school are also quite limited. Even at the senior middle school, choices are limited to those related to university entrance examinations. As there are different entrance exams for science and humanities, students must choose, at the beginning of year ten, whether they wish to specialize in humanities or sciences. In addition, a few more specialized university courses exist for students who excel in music, art, or sport. Consequently, all of the senior middle schools offer specialized courses for students with talent in these areas. But beyond the choice of which type of university entrance examination a given student wishes to prepare for, students have no choices to make. There is simply no time for after-school activities or student activity groups. Once the choice of a particular course has been made, all of a given student's activities for the next three years will be the same as his or her classmates.

In short, even to the extent that there are some options for those Zouping parents wealthy enough to afford private school tuition or a place at a senior middle school for a relatively low testing student, these options do not offer a significant 'choice' with regard to the content of the school curriculum or even the methods by which that curriculum is taught. Once the senior middle school level is reached, students may choose the course they will take, but very little other than that. Particularly from an American perspective, the range of 'choice' seems very limited indeed (see Kipnis, 2001a).

Competitive Egalitarianism

In analyses of school choice in other parts of the world, some analysts describe it as going together with ideologies of competition and the promotion of a *de facto* social inequality (e.g. Klees, 2002). In Zouping anyway, such an analysis could not work. Competition is encouraged without choice, and egalitarian policies are promulgated in order to increase the ferocity of the competition.

The county education bureau has taken many measures to promote competition by socially engineering a more level playing field. As county education officials rightly point out, a competition between vastly unequal parties is not really a competition at all. For a competition to have the effect of pushing all of the participants to work as hard as possible, each participant must have the feeling that an increase in effort could well make the difference between winning and losing. Several examples can illustrate the education bureau's strategy in this regard. As described above, after investing heavily in a new campus for the Number One school, the bureau then granted the Number Two school a fair share of the best teachers and students. The bureau thereby ensured that the Number One school would have a significant competitor within the county. The county education bureau compares the two schools in every possible way: the number and percentage of graduates who enter university, the number and percentage of graduates who enter top universities, the average test scores of students at every level on standardized examinations, the number of students who win science fairs, Math Olympics, essay writing contests, debates, oral English competitions, and so on.

To promote competition among teachers within a given junior middle or primary school, the county school board insists that streaming of students by ability is not permissible. Though the county board experimented with streaming in the late 1990s, it did not like the fact that streaming made classes of students incomparable. Since 2000, every class in the same grade at every school has had the same number of students who in the previous year did well on standardized exams and the same number of students who did poorly on standardized exams (so called 'late developing students' *houjin sheng*). Teachers can then be forced to compete with one another not just in terms of the average scores of the students in their class, but also the rate at which they have enabled the 'advanced' students to excel even further and the rate at which they have enabled the late developers to catch up with the rest of the class.

Figure 3. Flag-raising ceremony at rural primary school.

This competition among teachers naturally extends to the students as well. In Zouping class sizes can be quite large (at many schools averaging roughly 60 pupils per class), and a given class will stay together for an entire year, in the same classroom, while the teachers of different subjects rotate in and out of the single room (with the exception of classes like science, which require the students to move as a group to a specialized classroom). This structure allows the schools to promote group bonding among members of a given class. The boot-camp-like, seven-day-a-week schedules at middle schools further this bonding (see appendix), as do the huge variety of inter-class competitions that every school organizes. Classes compete in examination scores, in all variety of athletic competition, in keeping their classrooms neat, in finishing assigned chores like cleaning the bathrooms and hallways, in school spirit, in hygiene, in helping old people, and so on. Scores in competitions are posted in central locations for all to examine, and winners or high scorers are announced at weekly Monday morning flag-raising ceremonies.

The county education bureau also takes measures to ensure that there is a relatively equal playing field and ferocious competition on the senior middle school entrance examination. During the early 1990s, some junior middle schools were outperforming others on this examination and the county education bureau feared that some schools were likely to become despondent: sites of high drop-out rates and few hopes of attending a good senior middle school, let alone university. To remedy this situation, the county education bureau shifted from an examination system to an exam and quota system. Every junior middle school was assigned a quota of places, which is now roughly equivalent to 30% of the graduating class, at the elite senior middle schools. The standardized senior middle school entrance examination is then used to select which students at a given school get that school's quota places (Kipnis, 2001b). In effect, despite taking a county-wide exam, students are mostly competing only with students from their own junior middle school. A few places are reserved for the top testing students in the county who do not secure one of their school's quota places. In this way, the county maintains an incentive for schools as a whole to outperform schools from other districts, while at the same time ensuring that no school falls so far behind that its students feel there is nothing to be gained by studying hard for examinations.

The county education bureau has also taken steps to improve the quality of the education system in the townships that were doing poorly on the senior middle school entrance examination. In 2003 they began paying teacher salaries out of the county's budget rather than the townships' budgets. This helped ensure that the wealthier townships would not be able to pay higher salaries for the same grade of teacher. In 2004 they began paying higher salaries to teachers who agreed to work in the poorer and more remote townships.

The push for examination competitiveness especially influences the private schools, whose reputations and ability to attract tuition paying students rest on the collective examination results of their students. The administrators of the Old Number One junior middle school at one point feared that because of the policy of offering a 50-point bonus on the senior middle school entrance examination, the exam competitiveness of its students would drop. To prevent such a situation from emerging, the school instituted a sliding rate of tuition fees based on (initially) the school's own entrance examination and then on the county-wide standardized examinations that are conducted each semester. In any given semester, of the roughly 560 students at a given grade level, the 50 top-scoring students will pay no tuition fees, students 51-100 will pay 40% of the full tuition fees, students 101-150 will pay 60% of the full tuition fees and students 151-200 pay 80% of the full tuition fees. This information is posted publicly on school bulletin boards and reprinted in newspaper advertisements.

Finally, because of all of the examination pressure in their education system, the county education bureau fears that some schools might be tempted to skimp on subjects that are not emphasized in the standardized exams. To counter this tendency, the bureau runs a wide series of competitions among schools on aspects of the curriculum not covered by examinations. These include, among other things, athletics, art and music, oral English, and calligraphy.

A Culture of Scientistic Audit

Scholars often criticize practices of accountability and audit that are used to measure the performance of teachers, schools and principals for their links to ideologies of neo-liberalism (e.g. Shore & Wright, 2000). In Zouping there is an especially thoroughgoing series of auditing practices at public schools, perhaps because they are not subject to the pressures of parental choice. While these audit practices may well be worthy of academic criticism, whether they may be considered neo-liberal is open to debate.

Zouping teachers often complained to me about the never-ending series of competitions and evaluations (*pingbi*) to which their performance is subject. Teachers are not just evaluated in terms of the examination scores of their students, in addition their classes may be observed by personnel from the county education bureau at any moment. All teachers must have their classes observed several times a year by the senior teachers and deans of education at their schools. Teachers were further rewarded if their students did well in various non-exam competitions such as in sport, music, art, and debating.

Teaching loads at Zouping schools are surprisingly light. For example, an average primary school teacher might teach thirteen 40-minute periods a week. However, even primary teachers are expected to spend over 45 hours a week at the school and to do some work during school holidays. Teachers are encouraged to write articles on teaching methods for education journals and are rewarded for publishing. They are also expected to enter contests in their specialty areas. English teachers are expected to enter county and prefecture wide oral English contests, Chinese and social science teachers are expected to enter essay writing contests, usually on politically acceptable topics like 'Why there could be no new China without the Communist Party'. There are also calligraphy contests where teachers copy model essays in their best handwriting.

Teachers are also supposed to help develop new lesson plans and contribute to the life of the school. They spend their non-teaching time in large, group offices with teachers of similar subjects or of the same grade level. At one school I visited, all of the teachers were required, via a secret ballot, to rank the contributions to pedagogy and school life of all the other teachers in their office. This happened every semester and no two teachers could be ranked equally.

In addition to the complex and multilayered practices of accountability that teachers must face, education bureaus at various levels of government undertake a ranking of schools as a whole. The rewards for principals, and a few other high-level administrators, are determined through these rankings. I was present at one primary school when a delegation from the prefectural education bureau, which is the level above the county, came to evaluate whether the school deserved to be ranked among the 10 best schools in the prefecture. If the school was selected, the principal would receive a bonus equivalent to an extra month's salary and the school would gain considerable public recognition. Though many factors, such as test scores, had gone into drawing up a shortlist of finalists for this competition, the final evaluation was determined by this inspection tour. The principal thus prepared hard to receive the delegation.

On the morning of the visit the students were taken out of their regular classes and placed into a wide variety of activity rooms for the delegation to observe. The best basketball players were playing basketball, the best ping pong players were playing ping pong, the best Chinese chess players were in the Chinese chess room, a troupe of dancers dressed in tights and tutus was in the dance hall. The school band was playing in the music hall, the computer room was full of students practising the use of PowerPoint, and so on. As some schools had been publicly accused of buying fancy equipment for show, but never actually using it because of the time spent preparing for examinations, the point of these activities was not only to show off the school's excellent facilities, but also to demonstrate that these facilities were actually put to use. A group of students was also selected to greet the delegation when it arrived and an articulate year six student was selected to give a welcome speech, which she had memorized. Brochures and other materials describing the school and the accomplishments of its students and teachers were laid out on tables in front of the school along with bottles of mineral water to hand out to the delegation.

At 9.30 a.m. a convoy of six large black cars and a tour bus pulled up to the school and 70 men and women from the prefectural evaluation team poured out. The students passed out water and brochures. The principal first gave a short speech. I had been asked by the principal to say a few words myself (and was coached on which official phrases to use) and delivered a short speech describing how 'advanced' the principal's management methods were. Finally, the selected year six student gave her speech. The evaluation team then toured the facilities and observed the students in their various activities for roughly 40 minutes before reboarding their vehicles and heading off to the next shortlisted school.

Afterwards, I learned that the principal had three staff members working full-time on preparing for the visits of various audit conducting government officials and that the school had spent over US$1400 on brochure printing and mineral water purchase in preparation for this particular audit. In this case the efforts were worth it as the school was selected as one of the prefecture's 10 best schools for the year.

As in many Western nations, in China I have spoken to teachers and academics from all levels (primary school through university) who express dissatisfaction with the regimes of evaluation that they face. But I have not heard a critique that links these audit cultures to ideologies of neo-liberalism. In fact, the few Chinese academic essays I have read on the topic point in exactly the opposite direction. They compare the attempt to produce examination scores for all measure of human attributes, or, in the absence of exams, to devise other techniques for quantifying performance and ranking teachers, as well as the resulting counter-strategies of teachers, academics and students to rank highly in these various measured criteria, with the ritual of fulfilling production quotas in the old socialist planned economy (Jiang, 2006). Indeed, as Lampland (1995) notes, socialist planned economies and their ritualistic fulfilling of production quotas can lead to a form of selfish, calculating individualism even more extreme than that apparent in 'capitalist' nations. Under socialist economic regimes, the quality or marketability of goods counted for nothing, all that mattered was ritualistically announcing that the production quota had been met and bluffing one's superiors into believing that one had done so. The essays by Chinese critics of academic audit culture critique the mentality that produces these systems of governmental evaluation as a legacy of socialist thinking, and draw upon the critiques of scientism by that arch neo-liberal thinker Friederich von Hayek (1979). In short, for these critics of the economistic cultures of evaluation and audit that seem to be emerging in educational institutions all over the globe, what is needed is not a critique of neo-liberalism, but a neo-liberal critique! Regardless of the language used for criticism, perhaps all can agree that rigidly applied attempts to provide quantifiable measures for such inherently unquantifiable ideals as clear thinking, innovative teaching and artistic creativity can only lead to the destruction of the various capacities that are so measured.

Conclusion

Some of the contradictions in recent Western education policies described by Hursh at the beginning of this chapter are also evident in Zouping. While there exists rhetoric extolling the benefits of diversity, efforts guided by this rhetoric are overshadowed by the drive for standardization and the overwhelming exam culture. While the exam culture is extremely competitive, producing clear winners and losers, the county education bureau regularly intervenes in order to level the playing field.

In contrast to Hursh's discussion, there is little neo-liberalism of the sort that claims markets to be self-regulating or which argues that government action can produce nothing positive. There is, however, quite clearly a promotion of the notion that competition is to be valued for the way that it disciplines students, teachers, classes and schools as a whole. For some analysts, this rhetoric may count as a neo-liberalism of a sort, but I see it more as a value on discipline for its own sake. For one, it might be argued that this discipline does not produce the 'responsibilitized, entrepreneurial subject/citizens' so central to neo-liberal ideologies. If anything, such a system could be seen as producing graduates who desire permanent jobs in government offices. More important, however, is to see how this discipline constitutes an end in itself. The contradiction of simultaneously enacting competition and continually levelling out the playing field can be explained in this way. Abject losers become despondent while constant winners become complacent. To enact a discipline-producing competition rather than a despondency and complacency producing competition, constant government intervention is necessary. School choice itself has little place in this value structure. As in many other places, reducing government outlays on education is desired and some private education and 'choice' is allowed as a means to this end. But little value is placed on the availability of choice in itself.

In sum, while there are elements of the Zouping education system that may be compared to aspects of education under 'neo-liberal regimes', I doubt that analyses of neo-liberalism can explain much about what is happening in Zouping. The social and political factors behind the shape of Zouping's school system must be sought elsewhere.

Notes

[1] The research upon which this chapter is based was funded by an Australian Research Council Discovery Grant, no. DP0556422. Thanks to all those in China who assisted with my research and to Martin Forsey for useful suggestions during the rewriting process

[2] The term 'suburban villagers' refers to people who live in villages that were absorbed by the urban area of the county seat as it has expanded over the past two decades. These people have a distinct set of welfare rights that reflect the fact that their land was taken over by the city without receiving urban

household registrations (see Solinger, 1999; Kipnis, 2004). They usually live together in a single urban housing compound that was granted to a particular village.

References

Froissart, Chloe (2003) The Hazards of the Right to Education, *China Perspectives*, 48, 21-36.

Hayek, Friederich von (1979) *The Political Order of a Free People*. London: Routeledge & Kegan Paul.

Hursh, David (2005) Neo-liberalism, Markets and Accountability: transforming education and undermining democracy in the United States and England, *Policy Futures in Education*, 3(1), 3-15. http://dx.doi.org/10.2304/pfie.2005.3.1.6

Jiang, Xiaoyuan (2006) Women Yao Xujiade Xueshu Fanrong Gan Shenmene? Cong Weikexuezhuyi Dao Xueshulianghua Kaohe. http://www.acriticism.com/article.asp?Newsid=7973&type=1008

Kipnis, Andrew B. (2001a) Articulating School Countercultures, *Anthropology and Education Quarterly*, 32(4), 472-492. http://dx.doi.org/10.1525/aeq.2001.32.4.472

Kipnis, Andrew B. (2001b) The Disturbing Educational Discipline of 'Peasants', *The China Journal*, 46, 1-24. http://dx.doi.org/10.2307/3182305

Kipnis, Andrew B. (2004) Anthropology and the Theorization of Citizenship, *The Asia Pacific Journal of Anthropology*, 5(3), 257-278. http://dx.doi.org/10.1080/1444221042000299592

Kipnis, Andrew B. (2006a) Suzhi: a keyword approach, *The China Quarterly*, 186, 295-313. http://dx.doi.org/10.1017/S0305741006000166

Kipnis, Andrew B. (2006b) School Consolidation in Rural China, *Development Bulletin*, 70, 123-125.

Kipnis, Andrew B. (2007) Neoliberalism Reified: suzhi discourse and tropes of neoliberalism in the PRC, *Journal of the Royal Anthropological Institute*, 13(2), 383-399. http://dx.doi.org/10.1111/j.1467-9655.2007.00432.x

Klees, Steven (2002) Privatization and Neo-liberalism: ideology and evidence in rhetorical reforms, *Current Issues in Comparative Education*, 1(2), 19-26.

Lampland, Martha (1995) *The Object of Labor: commodification in socialist Hungary*. Chicago: University of Chicago Press.

Liu, Linping (Ed.) (1997) *Ai de Wuqu: Zhongxiao Xuesheng Chengzhang Wenti Bei Wanglu*. Beijing: Zhongguo Renshi Chubanshe.

Shore, Cris & Wright, Susan (2000) Coercive Accountability: the rise of audit culture in higher education, in M. Strathern (Ed.) *Audit Cultures: anthropological studies in accountability, ethics, and the academy*. London: Routledge.

Solinger, Dorothy J. (1999) *Contesting Citizenship in Urban China: peasant migrants, the state, and the logic of the market*. Berkeley: University of California Press.

Wen, Tao (2006) Zexiaosheng Bu Xiangshou Zhibiaosheng Daiyu, *Qilu Wanbao* [Shandong Evening News], 28 April.

Woronov, Terry (2002) Transforming the Future: 'quality' children for the Chinese Nation. PhD, University of Chicago.

Xinhua She (2006) Guifan Zhongxiaoxue Shoufei Jushouwei, *Qilu Wanbao* [Shandong Evening News], 12 May.

APPENDIX
Junior Middle School Daily Schedule (Summer)

The senior middle school schedule is much the same except that there is a fourth study hall in the evening (and a correspondingly later lights out). During the winter, noon-time rest is replaced with a slightly longer evening rest.

6.00 a.m.:	wake up bell.
6.10-6.30:	morning chore – students from a single dormitory room share a communal cleaning chore, such as cleaning particular halls or bathrooms.
6.30-7.00:	breakfast.
7.00-7.05:	prepare for class – students must be seated at their desk and quiet, should be focusing their minds on the upcoming morning read.
7.05-7.30:	morning reading period – students memorize (by chanting aloud) a text assigned by either their Chinese or English teacher.
7.40-8.25:	class period one – a class of students generally stays in the same classroom all day, while the teachers of differing subjects rotate in and out. Students talk freely to each other during the 10 minutes between classes. One minute before the next period is to begin, a bell rings and students return to their desks and become quiet.
8.35-9.20:	class period two.
9.20-9.50:	between class exercise – students go down to the schoolyard, line up in evenly spaced rows and columns and do exercises, in unison, to a broadcasted recording that is the same every day. In 1999, these were military drills, but in 2006 they switched to an aerobics dance routine that was done to an up-tempo version of the American folk song 'Oh Suzanna'.
9.50-10.35:	class period three.
10.45-11.30:	class period four.
11.30-12.15:	lunch.
12.15-13.40:	rest – many Zouping residents customarily take a short nap after lunch during the summer. Students must be on their beds and quiet, but they can read instead of sleeping if

	they wish.
13.50-14.00:	prepare for class – in desks and quiet, focusing mind on upcoming class.
14.00-14.45:	class period five.
14.45-15.00:	eye exercises – to prevent nearsightedness, educational authorities designed a routine involving massaging the areas around the eyes. The students do these exercises at their desks, in unison, to a pre-recorded broadcast.
15.00-15.45:	class period six.
15.55-16.40:	class period seven.
16.40-17.20:	activity period – some form of sport, music or artistic activity done under the supervision and direction of teachers.
17.20-18.00:	dinner.
18.10-18.30:	evening discussion – students return to desks and meet with their head teacher and discuss either a news story or issues arising in school life.
18.30-19.15:	study hall one – students do homework quietly at their desks.
19.25-20.10:	study hall two.
20.20-21.15:	study hall three.
21.40:	lights out.

CHAPTER 10

School Choice in India: disadvantaged groups and low-fee private schools

PRACHI SRIVASTAVA

SUMMARY Increased marketisation and privatisation of schooling in economically developing countries have led to the emergence of private schooling for socio-economically disadvantaged groups. The 'low-fee private' sector in India is one example of a private schooling sector that is targeted to and financed by fees from lower income households that have traditionally had low participation in formal schooling. Thus, the emergence of the low-fee private sector marks the need to examine changing school choice behaviours of disadvantaged groups. Dominant middle-class hegemonic discourse in India and the wider literature has characterised these groups as 'vulnerable' and 'likely to be duped' or as 'irresponsible', ignorant of the benefits of schooling, and unwilling to send their children to school due to limited resources. To arrive at a more nuanced understanding, this chapter, based on a study of low-fee private schooling in Lucknow District, Uttar Pradesh, presents a model explaining the school choice processes of one group of disadvantaged households accessing the low-fee private sector. Challenging traditional assumptions, results indicate that households in the study made active choices about their children's schooling through a complex process that involved analysing competing school sectors, incorporating their beliefs about education, analysing local school markets, and managing particular constraints.

Setting the Scene

Reported deterioration in the quality of public schooling in many economically developing countries has resulted in increased private provision (De et al, 2002a; Harlech-Jones et al, 2005; Tooley & Dixon, 2005; Glick & Sahn, 2006). Especially striking is that increasing marketisation and privatisation are not limited to changes in schooling provision for middle or elite classes, but in many nations they are leading to the emergence of private schools of various forms for lower income groups (e.g. Alderman et al, 2001; Bangay, 2005, 2007; Rose, 2005; Rose & Adelabu, 2007; Tooley & Dixon, 2007a; Srivastava, 2007a). The mushrooming of what have been termed here '*low-fee private*' (LFP) schools in India for socially and economically disadvantaged groups is one such phenomenon.

While the heterogeneity of private schooling in India has been noted (Majumdar & Vaidyanathan, 1995; Tilak & Sudarshan, 2001; De et al, 2002b; Tooley & Dixon, 2005; Mehrotra & Panchamukhi, 2007), there is a dearth of research on the schooling choices of disadvantaged groups, and specifically of those who access the LFP sector. As a private sector targeted to groups with traditionally low participation in schooling, the significance of the LFP sector is crucial in understanding the schooling choices of those who have been marginalised in dominant educational research, and who are operating within a changing context of increased private schooling provision. This chapter takes its cue from Stromquist's (1999) call for in-depth analyses of how schooling decisions are made within households, since they are the primary sites affecting educational access.

Critics of dominant Indian education discourse contend that prevailing middle-class hegemony presents disadvantaged groups as unaware of the benefits of schooling and favouring child labour (Balagopalan, 2004). Such rhetoric portrays these groups as 'vulnerable' and likely to be 'duped' by LFP schools (Singh, 1995), or as 'irresponsible' (e.g. Government of India, 2002, p. 86; Banerji, 2003). From this perspective, disadvantaged groups are characterised as disinterested in schooling, ignorant of its benefits and, when faced with limited resources, unwilling to send their children to school. Undoubtedly, the views and motivations of the heterogeneous group of parents that fall within the construct of 'socially/economically disadvantaged' will not be so stark. The discussion merits a more nuanced understanding of their school choice processes within an increasingly privatised schooling context.

Within this context, the purpose of this chapter is to present a model explaining the school choice processes of one group of disadvantaged households accessing the LFP sector, in a qualitative study on Lucknow District, Uttar Pradesh. In line with analyses on poorer parents in economically developing countries that question assumptions of 'false consciousness' in school choice (Maile, 2004; Woolman & Fleisch, 2006), or that 'poverty creates a dependent class that is entirely reactive and cannot make decisions' about schooling (Woolman & Fleisch, 2006, p. 53), this model presents households in the study as engaging in 'active choice'.

Active choice is seen as the deliberated action of households in making concerted choices about their children's schooling through a complex process. For households in the study, the process involved assessing competing school sectors (mainly the state and LFP), and analysing particular household circumstances and local school markets through a systemic set of values, beliefs, and 'mental models' (North, 1990) about education and their schooling options. Following a presentation of the research context and strategy, the chapter reframes the context for LFP school choice in India, highlights some gaps in the literature relevant to analysing school choice in economically developing countries, presents the school choice model for households in the study, and draws out some potential implications of increased choice in a privatised arena.

Research Context

There are three main types of formal provision in India: government (typically referred to as schools operated by state Departments of Education); private aided (schools that are privately managed but publicly financed through state grants-in-aid); and private unaided (independently managed and financed) (see Kingdon, 1996; Panchamukhi & Mehrotra, 2005; Srivastava, 2007b). Private unaided schools can be recognised or unrecognised, and form a highly heterogeneous group of schools occupying all fee levels from elite, high-fee schools to modest, low-fee schools such as those introduced in this study.

In addition to the well-documented lack of data on unrecognised private unaided schools (Kingdon, 1996; Tooley & Dixon, 2007b), researching LFP schools was not easy since the LFP sector is not officially defined by the state and, at the time of the study, had not been operationally defined by researchers. Thus, for the purposes of this study, the LFP sector was defined as occupying a part (often unrecognised) of the private unaided sector. LFP schools were further defined as those that saw themselves targeting disadvantaged groups, were entirely self-financing through tuition fees, and charged a monthly tuition fee not exceeding about one day's earnings of a daily wage labourer at the primary and junior levels, and two days' earnings at the secondary levels.

Uttar Pradesh is officially classed as one of the most 'educationally backward' states in India. With a literacy rate of 57.4%, it is placed thirty-first of 35 states and territories on this measure (Government of India, 2001). According to the latest District Information System for Education (DISE) data, in 2005, 78.35% of all recognised schools in Uttar Pradesh were run by the state Department of Education; 4.38% were private aided; and 14.18% were private unaided (Mehta, 2006, pp. 212-217). There was a 4.06% increase in the proportion of recognised private unaided schools in Uttar Pradesh since the first DISE report on 2003 data (Mehta, 2004). This is contra-intuitive given the State and Central Government's commitment to free education for all (Srivastava, 2007b). Since unrecognised schools are excluded in DISE and other education data sets, the true number of private unaided schools in Uttar Pradesh is likely to be higher. Available data do not disaggregate schools by fee level and official government lists do not include unrecognised schools; therefore, the exact number of LFP schools is unknown. However, there is general agreement among officials that the number has increased many-fold over the last decade or so.

Research Strategy

Data collection roughly spanned one school-year, and was conducted from July 2002 to April 2003. Household-level results presented here are part of a larger household, school, and state level case study on LFP schooling in Lucknow District (Srivastava, 2006, 2007a, 2008a). Data collection methods and sources of evidence specific to the household level are presented below, the methodologies for which are further documented in Srivastava (2006, 2008a, b).

Focus Schools

One urban (Taj Nagar Inter-College) and one rural (Siyapur School) school [1] were chosen from the 10 case study schools (five urban and five rural) for more concentrated ethnographic-style study. Focus schools were chosen on the basis that they were deemed to be the best competitors of each group, having secured the largest enrolments in their areas (Taj Nagar with 1089 and Siyapur with 258), and facing direct competition from multiple LFP and state schools in their immediate vicinity. At the household level, the rationale was that focus schools would provide a pool of household interviewees who could best articulate their decisions about private schooling, perceptions of their chosen school, and why that school was chosen over competing ones. Like the other case study schools, Siyapur and Taj Nagar were Hindi medium, though they taught English from kindergarten. Elementary school fees at Siyapur were Rs. 40 per month for primary (Classes 1 to 5) and Rs. 50 a month for junior (Class 6 to 8). At Taj Nagar the monthly fees were Rs. 55 for primary and Rs. 80 for junior.[2]

Data Collection

Data presented in this chapter were mainly collected through semi-structured interviews with 60 parents or close family members, with 30 coming from each focus school. Household interviews, which took 30-45 minutes, were conducted by the researcher in Hindi on school premises in a private area. The interview schedule comprised questions on household socio-economic background, family composition, educational profiles, factors influencing choice and decision-making processes regarding private schooling, perceptions about chosen schools, and the level of school-responsiveness and parental 'voice' at the school. Questions on household and educational profiles were structured, which allowed the collection of quantitative data about participants. As the sample was not representative, these data were not intended to be generalised but to better contextualise interviewees' responses as a group and identify schooling patterns within it.

The 10 formal school interviews with case study school owners/principals of relevance here were the second of three sets of interviews with each school. The interviews of interest addressed schools' assessments of the educational needs of their target group, strategies for responsiveness, and parental participation (school strategies; perceptions of involvement). They were conducted in Hindi by the researcher on school premises and averaged 60 minutes. Numerous informal interviews were conducted throughout the 10-month period with owners/principals to follow up on observation events or formal interviews, and in an atmosphere where they were more comfortable in giving details on privileged or sensitive information (e.g. school income).

A significant aspect of the data collection involved school-based observations of parent–owner/principal interactions over the 10-month period. These observations were primarily conducted at focus schools in the principal's office during the break between shifts at Taj Nagar, and near the end of the school day at Siyapur. Student records and documents on information dissemination to parents were also analysed. These included attendance and enrolment records, letters or notices to parents, and school diaries.

Household Profiles

Profiles of the participating households are presented in Table I in an attempt to understand where they placed in relation to different forms of (dis)advantage: caste, income, occupation, and education level. The majority of households fell under at least one (but generally multiple) forms of (dis)advantage, as well as within Taj Nagar's and Siyapur's intended target group.

Caste	55% belonged to Other Backward or Scheduled Caste groups (defined as among the lowest official caste groups in India)
Household income	80% earned below the minimum annual taxable income of Rs. 50,000; mean maximum rural income: Rs. 26,018 (excluding outlier); mean maximum urban income: Rs. 41,768
Parents' occupation	84% fathers: manual labour, small farming, or low skilled jobs; 83% mothers: housewives (of those who worked all but three engaged in domestic or manual labour)
Parents' educational level	51% of parents either had no schooling or only some primary schooling; 58% of urban mothers and 53% of rural mothers had no schooling

Table I. Profiles of participating households.

Reframing School Choice for the Indian Context

There is a need to contextualise school markets (Waslander & Thrupp, 1997) and frame the overall institutional parameters within which choice is operating in India. Firstly, unlike the USA or United Kingdom, school choice as a 'policy that is designed to reduce the constraints that current school configurations place on schools and students' (Goldhaber, 1999, p. 16) is not applicable. This is because the system of catchments dictating public school allocation does not exist in principle. However, it may be that most parents who send their children to state schools do so based on their proximity. According to most state and central government regulations, government schools are not to deny admission to any child who wishes to be enrolled.[3] Therefore parents should have a choice between state government schools, but only if they exist in their local area.

Secondly, similar to the USA and United Kingdom, privileged parents have long had the freedom to choose private schooling for their children (see Gewirtz et al, 1994; Goldhaber, 1999; Ball, 2003). However, the uptake of private schooling options by parents from lower middle-class and disadvantaged groups, changes that seem to be linked to an increase in the heterogeneity of private schooling provision by fee level (Tilak & Sudarshan, 2001; Srivastava, 2007a), marks the need to examine changing school choice behaviours in disadvantaged households.

Finally, increased choice for disadvantaged groups did not come from voucher programmes as in some countries (e.g. Chile) or the alleviation of catchment rules in others (e.g. USA or England), but from increased private provision. As Carnoy (2000) notes, 'When choice is about privatization, we need to know much more about how such an educational system would look' (p. 15). In effect, school choice in the Indian context must be analysed through a distinction of different choice systems.

Tooley (1997) distinguishes between two choice systems which are useful to work with. The first is annotated as '$choice_s$', and refers to the 'system where parental choice exists within heavy state regulations, funding, and school provision' such as the catchment restrictions used in England (p. 104). The second is '$choice_m$' or choice in the market – 'the market of the economists where the state is not the monopoly supplier and funder' (p. 110). Tooley further describes '$choice_m$' as choice between competing suppliers, with an opening of the supply side reducing state monopoly in supply and funding. According to results of this study, choice by disadvantaged groups accessing the LFP sector was enacted through $choice_m$. That is, LFP school choice is operating within a rapidly expanding array of private schools that are independent of state funding and management, and operate through their own informal set of rules and operational mechanisms (see Srivastava, 2008a). However, current understandings of school choice in India have not yet incorporated this changing context.

Mind the Gap: current understandings of school choice

Apart from studies on voucher programmes (McEwan & Carnoy, 2000; Mizala & Romaguera, 2000; Gauri & Vawda, 2004), less relevant to public/private sector school choice in the absence of government programmes or private subsidies, research on school choice in economically developing countries is limited (e.g. Glewwe & Jacoby, 1994; Alderman et al, 2001; Harlech-Jones et al, 2005; Glick & Sahn, 2006; Woolman & Fleisch, 2006), and even scarcer regarding the private sector in India. While some studies have contemplated the potential role of the private sector in meeting India's *Education for All* goals (Tilak & Sudarshan, 2001; De et al, 2002a; Mehrotra, 2006), a serious engagement with the concept of 'school choice' is lacking in the discourse. Clearly this study helps reconcile that gap.

In its starkest form, choice in the context of individualism and liberal market reforms is based on an extension of the concept of *Homo economicus*, conceiving of the parent as a rational thinking individual operating in an 'open' education system for self-interest. In their critique, David et al (1997) argue that from this perspective choice can be thought to involve various rational stages which are applied to the selection of a school:

> (1) possibilities are identified and separated out as 'different' and distinctive from one another;
> (2) information is acquired about each different option so that they can be evaluated one against another, and against previously held criteria; and
> (3) this rational appraisal leads to the selection of one option as the 'choice'. (p. 399)

Of course, choice is a much more complicated process. Studies in the USA and the United Kingdom have examined complications in choice making arising from issues such as incomplete information (e.g. Schneider et al, 2000; Schneider & Buckley, 2002); confounding race and class factors (e.g. Gewirtz et al, 1994; Wells & Serna, 1996; Henig et al, 1999; Tedin & Weihr, 2004); and different political contexts and choice programmes (Whitty et al, 1998; Fusarelli, 2003; Belfield & Levin, 2005). However, the current predominant analysis of household decision-making processes and schooling choices of disadvantaged parents in economically developing countries lacks serious engagement of these and other potentially relevant issues.

For instance, a much-cited study on school choice in Ghana (Glewwe & Jacoby, 1994) showed that higher quality schools (regarding certain school characteristics) were attractive to parents. The researchers reported that repairing leaking classrooms produced the greatest increase in test scores, but investing in school libraries or reducing travel time by building more schools yielded only modest increases. They explained this seemingly contra-intuitive result by stating that 'If parents choose schools based on their attributes, then these attributes are endogenous in an educational production function; any positive choice association between school quality and cognitive skills ... may simply be due to the fact that more motivated students go to better schools' (Glewwe & Jacoby, 1994, p. 844). However, as Lloyd et al (2000, p. 113) astutely observe, such analyses ignore the aspects of schooling that encourage initial enrolment and retention.

Households in this study chose LFP schools partly on their assessments of what constituted 'good schools' using indicators which were sometimes contrary to accepted educational research (see Srivastava, 2006). For example, large class sizes in LFP schools were often cited as an indicator of good schooling because, to these households, they indicated school popularity. Parents interpreted this as a sign that schooling must be 'good', which encouraged both initial enrolment and retention in a particular LFP school. Thus, it could be that in the Ghanaian case above, fixing a leaking roof had more impact on achievement not (only) because more motivated students went to better schools, but because it motivated greater retention or enrolment by targeting a measure of quality in that school type that parents perceived to be important. Such examples may point to the endogenous nature of school choice, not only in achievement, but on initial enrolment and retention related to perceived quality.

In Alderman et al's (2001) study on public/private schooling choices of low-income households in Pakistan, 37% of children were enrolled in private schools among families in the lowest income bracket (less than Rs. 2000/month) surveyed in Lahore. Of all children in that income bracket, a slightly higher proportion of girls was enrolled in private schools (37%) compared to boys (35%). Alderman et al contend that schooling choices of poor parents are affected by fee level, school proximity, and quality. However, they do not examine the process households followed to arrive at their findings, or how parents maintained or later changed that choice. Similarly, in their study on Madagascar, Glick & Sahn (2006) found that school choice was related to quality and negatively to multi-grade teaching and poor facilities, but there was no analysis of household choice processes. Although such studies provide a useful starting point for outlining potential factors influencing resulting school choices, they fall short of analysing the *processes* through which schooling decisions are made within households.

Mental Models and Choice Making

Apple (2004, p. 396) reminds us that the focus on school choice should be more comprehensive, to include 'a *systemic quality*, a set of values, skills, dispositions, and propensities'. The focus on a systemic set of attitudinal factors that influence choice making reframes traditional school choice analyses to include sociocultural factors alongside economic concerns. As Dehsi (2001, p. 14) notes regarding choice in India:

> The individual's socialization process, social structure in which he/she is embedded, norms and values he/she inherits influence his/her world view and the way he/she interprets his/her

> environment and evaluates opportunities ... theory has to be modified to take account of the societized behaviour of individuals.

In other words, individuals' choices are guided and structured by mental constructs reflective of their 'perceptions of the world and the way it 'works'' (North, 1992, p. 4). Approaching the analysis of the schooling choices of disadvantaged groups in this manner necessarily enables the conception of disadvantaged groups accessing the LFP sector as potentially active agents in their children's schooling rather than as passive bystanders.

The concept of 'mental models' from new institutional theory may help to move our thinking forward. North (1990, p. 20) defines mental models as the 'pre-existing mental constructs through which they [actors] understand the environment and solve the problems they confront', and which are essential to choice-making behaviour. They help actors 'decipher the environment' and assume importance when choices are considered risky or where individuals have incomplete information. Mental models are partly acquired through local experience and learning, and partly through intergenerational transfers of values and beliefs. Change to existing mental models comes when they cannot explain unexpected or inconsistent outcomes, or when the greater institutional context changes.[4] Of relevance to our discussion are the changing context for the provision of schooling for disadvantaged groups through the relatively rapid expansion of the LFP sector in general and the specificities of local schooling markets available to households in the study. The underlying perceptions, values, and beliefs encapsulated in actors' mental models are of interest in understanding their resulting schooling choices.

The mental models of parents in the study were tied to their beliefs and values about education, perceptions of the different school sectors accessible to them, aspirations for their children's futures, and economic concerns (see Srivastava, 2006). Their choice processes were also related to the particular socio-economic positions that participating households occupied in relation to local school markets. Households in the study viewed the schooling arena as highly marketised, one where every social group 'has its place', and saw the LFP sector targeted to them (Srivastava, 2007a). In fact, though not intended to be generalised, certain choices they made (e.g. the equal likelihood of sending a daughter or a son to an LFP school) were contra-intuitive and contrary to the literature on private schooling in India (see Srivastava [2006] for further elaboration). Finally, though deeply considered and systematic, results indicate that the school choice process of households in the study was not ordered or linear and, very often, the resulting choice of school was not seen as the 'best' or a permanent choice, but a workable proposition at that moment in time. An in-depth examination of their processes follows a brief presentation of household schooling patterns.

The LFP Sector and School Choice

Household Schooling Patterns

The majority (88%) of the 181 school-aged children in participating households were sent to focus and other LFP schools. The remaining school-aged children went to state (8%) and religious (1%) schools, while 3% were out of school. The most popular choice for households in the study was LFP focus schools, which is undoubtedly related to the fact that all interviewees were from the focus schools themselves. However, what was surprising was the *extent* to which focus schools were accessed.

Given their limited financial resources and low educational status, the assumption was that households in the study would be selective and access the private sector for one child (probably male) (e.g. Probe Team, 1999; Tilak & Sudarshan, 2001; De et al, 2002a). However, households in the study chose LFP focus schools for almost all (83%) of their school-aged children, urban households sending 2.35 and rural households sending 2.6 school-aged children to their respective focus schools. Furthermore, they were just as likely to send their daughters to LFP schools as their sons (Srivastava, 2006). Though not a representative sample and not intended to be generalised, given that this was one of the first studies expressly examining LFP school choice processes of disadvantaged groups in India, the results of this study challenge prevailing views and provide a different empirical context from which to examine the school choice processes of households in this study.

For participants, choosing the LFP sector was a dynamic and multifaceted process and not the automatic result of choosing between available state and LFP schools. It was particularly significant given households' very limited finances, and parents' low education levels and relative inexperience with formal schooling. There were prerequisites for LFP school choice, or certain necessary conditions that had to exist for households in the study to make the initial choice to school their children. Similar to other studies (Karlekar, 2000; Harlech-Jones et al, 2005; Woolman & Fleisch, 2006), the prerequisites pointed to barriers that may have traditionally blocked disadvantaged households from accessing schooling at all. These are discussed elsewhere in depth (Srivastava, 2006) but can be broadly categorised as: (a) infrastructure (mixed pool of school types and safe access to school), and (b) prioritising education (ability to prioritise due to factors such as decreased family size and increased financial resources; and mental model shifts prompted by peer influence and broad-based social and economic changes).

Having made the prerequisite choice to send their children to school, there were two interrelated levels of choice for the purposes of the study: (1) a macro-level choice of school type: the choice between different sectors (most commonly, state and LFP) and (2) a micro-level choice of specific school: the choice between competing schools in local school markets. The process was structured by the *macro-level attitudinal factors*, 'perceptions about state and private sectors' and 'beliefs about education and LFP schooling', and the *micro-level contextual factors*, 'information about local school characteristics' and 'constraints' (see Figure 1). Choosing one sector over the other at a macro level did not necessarily exclude selecting a school from the other, given micro-level assessments of local school markets or constraints. For example, a minority of 13 households simultaneously accessed LFP schools and state, religious, or no schools for some of their school-aged children. In effect, the macro level almost acted as an umbrella under which households took stock of their specifric circumstances, contexts and needs.

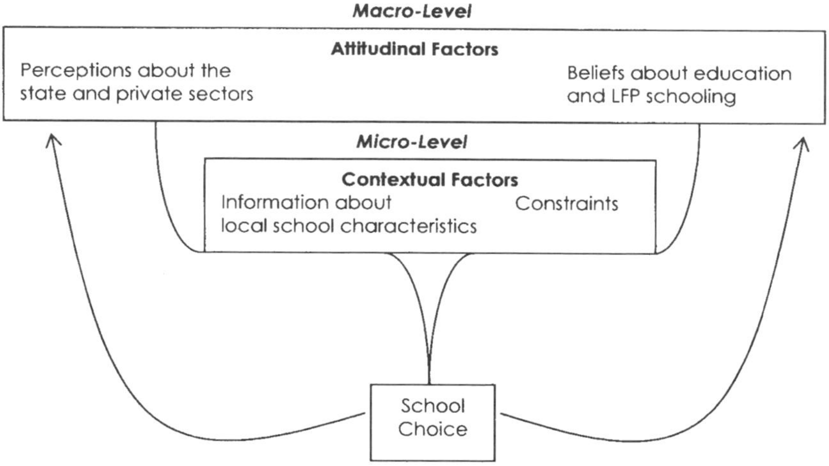

Note: The model outlines the process employed by households guiding their choice of LFP focus schools, and not previous or subsequent choices.

Figure 1. Attitudinal and contextual factors of household LFP school choice process.

Macro-level Attitudinal Factors

Perceptions about the state and private sectors. Participants held firm macro-level perceptions about state and private sectors, which were applied to their local contexts in choosing a school. Similar to other studies on India (Probe Team, 1999; Govinda, 2002; Jeffery et al, 2005), they generally viewed both sectors as binary opposites, with all private schooling types offering a better quality (however defined) of schooling. One rural father stressed:

> The difference between here [the private sector] and there [the state sector] is like that between the ground and the sky. (Ram Dev)[5]

Similar to Ram Dev, many parents asserted that there was 'something' inherently different about private sectors that the state sector simply could not match. This somewhat intangible set of qualities was a combination of parents sensing a more conducive climate for schooling and more educational activities in private schools. Household interviewees perceived differences between the state and private sectors as deficiencies in the former. They perceived these deficiencies mostly due to the general discourse on schooling in their local communities, and in some cases, through personal experience of both sectors.

Deficiencies in the state sector were attributed to a number of school-related factors, such as: lack of adequate school facilities; short-staffing of teachers; unsanctioned school closures and irregular school staff attendance; inadequate or infrequent monitoring or school inspections; lack of strict disciplinary procedures for children; an unsupportive and non-responsive school environment for parents; and unreliable teachers and unsatisfactory teaching practices. There is converging evidence in existing literature on many of these points (e.g. Probe Team, 1999; Jabbi & Rajyalaskshmi, 2001; Nambissan & Sedwal, 2002; Balagopalan & Subrahamanian, 2003).

Household perceptions about differences between the state and LFP sectors were most deeply ascribed to the attitudes and work practices of teachers, which were largely conceived as negligent and dubious. Many viewed state teachers and their teaching practices with disdain. In more extreme cases, some households expressed a heightened lack of confidence in the state sector, dismissing it as being gravely malfunctioning and corrupt. Among this group, parents (and LFP owners) made allegations that state inspectors did not make regular inspections or accepted *ghoos* (bribes) to pass malfunctioning schools (Tooley & Dixon, 2005; Srivastava, 2007a). Nonetheless, teachers were blamed as the main culprits, seen as manipulating the state sector by resorting to questionable practices such as transferring from remote postings for personal motives. As one urban father, Alok Kumar, put it:

> *A.K.* There's nothing but deceit and disloyalty in state schools. People sit at home and accumulate their pensions. They don't want to teach. Teachers get their postings transferred locally [from rural schools]. They do their household chores ... farming and agriculture or business, they do everything. They have no interest in teaching. So two or four children from the local area go just to hang out, they're not the studying type ... what difference does it make? Instead of playing at home they go and play at school.
> *Interviewer*: And here in the city, what's the situation in the state schools?
> *A.K.* I've never seen them. Nor do I have any power to go and visit them. I think that it'll be approximately the same type of environment here as well.

Such perceptions about the state sector were deep-rooted and, as was the case with Alok Kumar, they were held even if they were not validated in local contexts. In contrast, the LFP sector was generally perceived as being efficient and successful in delivering a satisfactory standard of schooling, mainly because for many, fee charging was seen as a prerequisite for 'good' schooling.

When commenting on the LFP sector parents felt that they generally had better school facilities, adhered more strictly to school calendars and daily timetables, attracted a higher class of clientele, and showed higher levels of school responsiveness to specific needs. They were also said to have more interested and capable teachers, an environment more conducive to learning, a better quality of schooling and more effective school management. Positive perceptions about the LFP sector were related to a feeling that there was some guarantee on the quality of schooling delivered, simply because households paid a fee (no matter how low) which contributed to the school's very existence. Some parents felt that paying a fee gave them a right to test the claims made by their chosen LFP school, contrary to the state sector.

Beliefs about education and LFP schooling. The second attitudinal factor was concerning households' general beliefs about the necessity of formal education and its role in their children's futures. Most households felt that traditional trades were no longer sustainable, and thus required their children to seek formal education for employment in different sectors. Regarding the state and LFP sectors, these beliefs were most expressly attached to the latter, where parents perceived that the type of education required in India's changing socio-economic context was available. This was despite their lack of knowledge about the curriculum and in spite of LFP schools in the study rigidly following the same curriculum delivered in state schools (see also De et al, 2002b).

Nonetheless, LFP schooling was seen as an essential commodity to acquire a place in the new labour market. However, households felt that although education was necessary, it would not guarantee a job. Some attributed that to fate, while others felt that nepotism or institutionalised corruption stood in the way:

> There's no guarantee at all [that they'll find a job] ... even those who've passed intermediate [grade 12] roam around empty-handed. But having been educated they can start their own business or trade. It's common practice to give a Rs. 150,000 bribe to get a job somewhere ... even as a bank manager or teacher. (Brij Bihari, rural father)

Some households felt that the benefits of education were curbed after students reached the level of junior or high school. For them, the decision to access secondary or post-secondary education for their children was pre-empted from the outset, in favour of setting up small trades. Similar to Jeffery et al's (2005) account of privatisation in Uttar Pradesh, this sub-group of households saw the LFP sector as a commodity, but accessed it for a specific purpose: to educate their children to an adequate standard in the '3 Rs' so that they might be self-sufficient in the future.

Beliefs about LFP schooling contributing to self-sufficiency were stressed by parents who claimed that their own lack of education underscored the importance of schooling their children. They specifically conceptualised LFP schooling as promoting self-sufficiency and raising their children's socio-economic status, as well as negotiating barriers in everyday life and fostering independence, particularly for their daughters. Similar to other studies (e.g. Jeffery, 2005; Page, 2005), while many parents acknowledged that girls' education was important for employability, the changing 'marriage market' held relatively more importance (Srivastava, 2006). Parents believed that accessing the LFP sector for their daughters would increase social mobility by attracting better marriage proposals. In some households, the need for girls' education was contested and choosing the LFP sector was the result of continuous advocacy. As is clear, macro-level factors were applied to households' specific contexts, and were mediated by the micro-level contextual factors such as 'information about local school characteristics' and the constraints associated with choosing local LFP focus schools.

Micro-level Contextual Factors

Information about local school characteristics. LFP focus schools were not chosen by default. There was an adequately sized pool of potentially accessible state and LFP schools for rural and urban households to choose from.[6] Choosing a specific school partly relied on gathering information about potential schools' different characteristics, such as: fee structure, fee management practices, teachers' attendance rate, school facilities, school environment, children's results, and medium of instruction. Parents gathered this information to make a judgement on the relative quality of different local schools according to their own indicators and mental models.

Their primary and overwhelming sources of information were other parents in the neighbourhood or village, family members, and close friends who were considered trustworthy and reasonably informed. The information was largely comprised of their sources' experiences of and general perceptions about focus schools compared with other local schools. Except for a small minority of households that visited focus schools prior to enrolling their children, or who had some direct knowledge by having previously accessed them, most gained something similar to 'hot knowledge' (Ball & Vincent, 1998; Ball, 2003) by speaking to other parents.

Surprisingly, even though the context and socio-economic status of households in this study were vastly different from middle-class parents in England, parents seemed to engage in similar behaviour of 'chattering' about schools (Ball, 2003). Households in the study engaged in dynamic conversation about local schools, actively sought information about them, and called on each other for insider knowledge. Once the information was collected, it was matched against similar information about other local state and LFP schools and linked back to attitudinal factors. In light of the information, they conducted a sort of cost–benefit analysis on the perceived quality of local schools. For example, even though state schools had the lowest tuition fees and despite their incentives (free textbooks, 3 kg wheat per month/child, and scholarships), households did not feel that these benefits outweighed the costs of what was thought to be an inferior quality of schooling.

Generally, the level of 'goodness' of different school types was perceived to increase as fee levels and English instruction increased, highlighting the marketised nature of local school arenas. For example, Hindi-medium LFP schools were perceived to be better than state schools, medium-fee English private schools better than Hindi-medium LFP schools, and high-fee English private schools were perceived as the best. Thus, most chose LFP focus schools not because they were perceived as the 'best' overall choice, but because they were the most workable and accessible to households in the study. Nonetheless, most households felt that given their budget and available information on the quality of different schools according to their conceptions of 'good' schooling, the focus schools were the best 'value for money'.

Generally, household conceptions of what constituted a 'good school' and 'good schooling' at the macro-level held for the micro-level. The relative 'goodness' of focus schools was related to certain household-articulated indicators, such as: school popularity indicated by large class sizes and high instances of enrolment from local families; children's views on their degree of happiness; the practice of fee charging; English instruction (as a subject even if not English-medium); high promotion rates; good pass rates on school tests and Board examinations; regular teachers' attendance; teachers paying attention to children in class; strict discipline practices; and local parents' opinions.

Valuing large class sizes may partially explain why Taj Nagar's reputation grew as a 'good school' despite the fact that until 2001, when the school's facilities were extended, average class sizes were 60-70 in cramped conditions. In fact, the owner explained that increased revenues due to jumps in enrolment and increased popularity during this time enabled expansion. In Taj Nagar's experience, stifling conditions and large class sizes prompted even more parents to access it.

High promotion rates were also an important consideration, since households reported that these were the only check they had on the schooling delivered. However, other than students who took Board examinations, all other assessment was school based and there were no external criterion-based assessments that could confirm students' performance. Nonetheless, households did not question whether high promotion rates resulted from student mastery of key concepts or lenient grading criteria. In fact, some case study schools stated that they adopted lenient promotion policies since lower promotion rates would indicate low learning levels, which would be interpreted by current and potential clients as low quality, and adversely affect popularity.

Constraints

Unsurprisingly, practical constraints affected households' choice of school. While financial constraints were the most acute and pervasive, there were other issues (see Table II). For example, contrary to assumptions about many economically developing countries, that children do not wield much voice in the choice of school (Maile, 2004), some parents commented that their children had considerable say. This finding is similar to research on working-class families in England (Carroll & Walford, 1997). A minority of parents accessing the rural focus school stated that the choice was influenced by a sense of obligation to the owner because of a long-standing personal relationship. Other parents felt that while they may have liked to choose another school, they were familiar with focus school practices and were confident that any additional or 'hidden' costs were minimal.

Constraint	Participant articulations
Financial	Household income inadequate to meet high schooling costs given low income levels, family size, and competing needs
Location of school	Certain 'ideal' schools too far, which would add to daily transport costs; distance of school too great to be deemed as a safe choice for children to navigate alone (more acute in rural group)
Personal relationship with principal	A sense of obligation to choose a school because of personal relationships with the principal and school management
Additional school expenses	Too many 'hidden' costs of schooling: registration fees, exam fees, books and school supplies, school activity fees, uniforms, private tuition
Child's choice	Household compliance with child's wish not to attend a particular school
Fee amounts and collection practices	Higher fees, fewer concessions, and inflexible fee collection practices at 'ideal choice'

Table II. Constraints influencing LFP school choice.

Nonetheless, parents explained that monetary resources were the primary constraint and a determining factor in deciding which local school to access. Households reported that they tried to find a local school that matched as many desired school characteristics as possible, which links back to their perceptions about the state and LFP sectors, within their limited budget. For example, most of the 13 households that simultaneously accessed LFP focus schools in combination with other school types reported that this arose because financial constraints did not enable them to choose LFP schools for all of their children. In such cases, households opted for state schools based on the presumed aptitude of their children. Others, particularly Muslim families, chose lower fee religious schools (*madrasas*).

While most parents were satisfied with their choice of LFP focus school for the time being, some were concerned that a combination of constraints conspired, restricting their choice from some 'ideal' school. Specifically, even though parents identified elite private schools as being the 'best', the ideal school was typically articulated as being a medium-fee, urban, English-medium school. In line with their class-oriented constructed typology of the schooling market (see Srivastava, 2007a), most parents in the study felt that the highest fee elite schools were beyond their social positioning. In any case, given the higher tuition fee amounts and inflexible fee collection practices, additional expenses associated with such things as extra-curricular activities, extra courses and uniforms, as well as the location of medium-fee and high-fee schools in urban areas (acute for rural parents), LFP focus schools represented a viable option for households in the study. In their assessment, these schools had many desirable characteristics as compared to state schools and allowed them to manage their constraints.

Understanding the Implications of LFP School Choice in a Privatised Sector

The rapid emergence of the LFP sector, and, more so, the relative confidence of some disadvantaged groups in private over public providers to meet their basic educational needs, signals a need to examine the implications of LFP school choice. As was apparent from the results, households in the study actively engaged with the privatised schooling market and made concerted choices about their children's schooling. Four main insights must be highlighted from the results of this research.

First, without exception, households in this study placed greater value on the LFP sector than the state, and chose it for almost all of their children. By and large, their mental models discretely attached better employment opportunities, marriage prospects, and chances for social mobility, along with prestige to the LFP sector. This is in line with the views of disadvantaged parents in other research on private schooling in rural and urban areas, including slums (Banerji, 2000; De et al, 2002b). The mental models of households in the study seem to be in line with general perceptions about the relative quality of private and government sectors, that see 'government schools ... as of especially poor quality in comparison with their private counterparts ... with little exception' (Govinda, 2002, p. 11).

Secondly, 'choice' and 'quality' were conceptualised as operating in highly marketised and privatised schooling arenas. This is particularly contra-intuitive if we are to believe India's official policy and programmatic discourse on Education for All, as households in the study would constitute part of the group that the State has officially taken the greatest responsibility for. Households constructed a highly segmented class-oriented schooling market, where quality increased with fees. They expressly distanced themselves from the state sector, relegating it to the most educationally unaware and disadvantaged, and also felt that they could not access the high-fee sector even if they had the means because of their social positioning.

Similar to reports of the increased segregation and 'dalitisation' of government schools (Nambissan, 1996; Nambissan & Sedwal, 2002; Balagopalan & Subrahamanian, 2003; Karan & Pushpendra, 2006), this has implications for aggravating inequities among disadvantaged groups, and highlights the differential access that children have to schools of various quality (R. Srivastava, 2006). For example, even though households in the study sacrificed much to access LFP schools over what they termed were 'malfunctioning state schools', they felt that the best quality schools occupied the high-fee sector and would always be elusive. This further challenges the Government of India's vision of establishing a 'common school system' with the aim of providing a comparable education of adequate quality to all regardless of socio-economic background.

Thirdly, households in the study largely construed LFP schools as universally better than state schools, even if they did not provide 'good' quality in an objective sense. While teachers at LFP case study schools were rarely absent, taught every day, and schools had minimal closures, teaching practices were largely didactic and pedagogy was not innovative but rigidly followed the state curriculum. Furthermore, there are no data on the relative advantages, if any, LFP school completers experienced with regard to employment opportunities, even though this was often cited as a reason for choosing LFP schools. Thus, despite the Education for All rhetoric of providing access to meaningful education opportunities (Rao, 2000), the state sector has not managed to convince parents that it can do so. As a result, LFP schools have to perform only marginally better to be considered 'good', setting a very low baseline for the quality of the LFP sector as a whole.

Finally, the increased segmentation of the schooling market by social class diverts people with a stake in changing the system. Therefore, while the emergence of the LFP sector heralds an important change for the schooling choices of some disadvantaged groups, it also poses a paradox of further deteriorating quality for the state sector, because:

> While it is most clearly revealed in the private–public school case, one characteristic is crucial ... those customers who care most about the quality of the product and who, therefore, are those who would be the most active, reliable, and creative agents of voice are for that very reason also those who are apparently likely to exit first in case of deterioration. (Hirschman, 1970, p. 47)

According to Hirschman's typology, parents accessing the LFP sector would be classified as the quality-conscious 'alert clients' in relation to the competing state sector. This has fundamental implications for the future of children whose parents either cannot or do not access the LFP sector. For if the state sector is as malfunctioning as it is perceived and documented to be, and there is cream-skimming of clients even from among disadvantaged groups, the future of schooling for the most disadvantaged does not seem promising. From this perspective, while greater school choice through the LFP sector seems desirable for some disadvantaged groups who had little or no choice before, it may also be highly iniquitous if it has no recuperation effect for the state sector.

Notes

[1] All names are pseudonyms.

[2] At the time of data collection £1= approx. Rs. 80 and USD 1 = approx. Rs. 45. Fees quoted here constituted the schools' official monthly tuition fee, and the maximum they could charge. In practice, some parents 'fee bargained' and negotiated a lower amount, or 'fee jumped' and exited without paying the outstanding balance. In addition, LFP case study schools instituted fee concessions generally for families with multiple children enrolled (see Srivastava, 2007a)

[3] This does not hold for central government schools established for the children of government employees, or for government schools run by central departments for specific groups. For example, a small number of schools are run by the Department of Tribal Welfare (for tribal groups), the Ministry of Defence (*sainik* schools), and Ministry of Social Justice (for children with disabilities).

[4] Where institutions are understood as the 'humanly devised constraints that shape human interaction' (North, 1990, p. 1).

[5] All interview quotes are translated from the original in Hindi.

[6] Rural households had a total of six schools (three state and three LFP) they could choose from. Due to the large number of LFP schools in the vicinity of the focus school, the size of the urban school pool is indeterminate. However, the urban focus school received direct competition from four other LFP schools and two state schools on the same block.

References

Alderman, H., Orazem, P.F. & Paterno, E.M. (2001) School Quality, School Cost, and the Public/Private School Choices of Low-income Households in Pakistan, *Journal of Human Resources*, 36(2), 304-326. http://dx.doi.org/10.2307/3069661

Apple, M.W. (2004) Educational Reform and the Middle Class, *Educational Policy*, 18(2), 395-400. http://dx.doi.org/10.1177/0895904803262165

Balagopalan, S. (2004) Free and Compulsory Education Bill 2004, *Economic and Political Weekly*, 39(2), 7-13 August.

Balagopalan, S. & Subrahmanian, R. (2003) Dalit and Adivasi Children in Schools: some preliminary research themes and findings, *IDS Bulletin*, 34(1), 43-54.

Ball, S.J. (2003) *Class Strategies and the Education Market: the middle classes and social advantage*. London: RoutledgeFalmer.

Ball, S.J. & Vincent, C. (1998) 'I Heard it on the Grapevine': hot knowledge and school choice, *British Journal of Sociology of Education*, 19(3), 377-395. http://dx.doi.org/10.1080/0142569980190307

Bangay, C. (2005) Private Education: relevant or redundant? Private Education, Decentralisation and National Provision in Indonesia, *Compare*, 35(2), 167-179. http://dx.doi.org/10.1080/03057920500129742

Bangay, C. (2007) Cinderella or Ugly Sister? What Role for Non-state Education Provision in Developing Countries? in P. Srivastava & G. Walford (Eds) *Private Schooling in Less Economically Developed Countries: Asian and African perspectives*, 111-128. Oxford: Symposium Books.

Banerji, R. (2000) Poverty and Primary Schooling: field studies from Mumbai and Delhi, *Economic and Political Weekly*, 35(10), 4 March.

Banerji, R. (2003) Making the Grade: teach children the joy of learning, *The Times of India*, 14 July. http://timesofindia.indiatimes.com/articleshow/73693.cms (accessed 30 May 2006).

Belfield, C.R. & Levin, H.M. (2005) *Privatizing Educational Choice: consequences for parents, schools, and public policy*. Boulder: Paradigm.

Carnoy, M. (2000) School Choice?: or is it privatization? *Educational Researcher*, 29(7), 15-20.

Carroll, S. & Walford, G. (1997) The Child's Voice in School Choice, *Educational Management and Administration*, 25(2), 169-180.

David, M., Davies, J., Edwards, R., Reay, D. & Standing, K. (1997) Choice within Constraints: mothers and schooling. *Gender and Education*, 9(4), 397-410. http://dx.doi.org/10.1080/09540259721150

De, A., Majumdar, M., Samson, M. & Noronha, C. (2002a) Private Schools and Universal Elementary Education, in R. Govinda (Ed.) *India Education Report: a profile of basic education*, 131-150. New Delhi: Oxford University Press.

De, A., Noronha, C. & Samson., M. (2002b) Private Schools for Less Privileged: some insights from a case study, *Economic and Political Weekly*, 37(52), 5230-5236.

Dehsi, A.S. (2001) Expectations and Post-school Choice: some data from India. *Education & Training*, 43(1), 14-24. http://dx.doi.org/10.1108/EUM0000000005411

Fusarelli, L.D. (2003) *The Political Dynamics of School Choice: negotiating contested terrain*. New York: Palgrave Macmillan.

Gauri, V. & Vawda, A. (2004) Vouchers for Basic Education in Developing Economies: an accountability perspective, *World Bank Research Observer*, 19(2), 259-280. http://dx.doi.org/10.1093/wbro/lkh017

Gewirtz, S., Ball, S.J. & Bowe, R. (1994) Parents, Privilege and the Education Market-Place, *Research Papers in Education*, 9(1), 3-29. http://dx.doi.org/10.1080/0267152940090102

Glewwe, J. & Jacoby, H. (1994) Student Achievement and Schooling Choice in Low-income Countries: evidence from Ghana, *Journal of Human Resources*, 29(3), 843-864. http://dx.doi.org/10.2307/146255

Glick, P. & Sahn, D.E. (2006) The Demand for Primary Schooling in Madagascar: price, quality, and the choice between public and private providers, *Journal of Development Economics*, 79(1), 118-145. http://dx.doi.org/10.1016/j.jdeveco.2005.01.001

Goldhaber, D. (1999) School Choice: an examination of the empirical evidence on achievement, parental decision making, and equity, *Educational Researcher*, 28(9), 16-25.

Government of India (2001) State of Literacy, ch. 7, *Provisional Population Totals*. Census of India. India, Series 1, Paper 1 of 2001. Web edition. http://www.censusindia.net/results.html (accessed September 2003).

Government of India (2002) *Janshala: towards empowered community schools*. New Delhi: Department of Elementary Education and Literacy, Ministry of Human Resource Development. http://education.nic.in/Janshala/Contents.pdf (accessed 30 April 2005).

Govinda, R. (2002) Providing Education for All in India, in R. Govinda (Ed.) *India Education Report: a profile of basic education*, 1-20. New Delhi: Oxford University Press.

Harlech-Jones, B., Baig, M., Sajid, S. & ur-Rahman, S. (2005) Private Schooling in the Northern Areas of Pakistan, *International Journal of Educational Development*, 25(5), 557-568. http://dx.doi.org/10.1016/j.ijedudev.2005.03.002

Henig, J.R., Hula, R.C., Orr, M. & Pedescleaux, D.S. (1999) *The Color of School Reform: race, politics, and the challenge of urban education*. Princeton: Princeton University Press.

Hirschman, A.O. (1970) *Exit, Voice, and Loyalty: responses to decline in firms, organizations, and states*. Cambridge, MA: Harvard University Press.

Jabbi, M. & Rajyalakshmi, C. (2001) Education of Marginalised Social Groups in Bihar, in A. Vaidyanathan & P.R. Gopinathan Nair (Eds) *Elementary Education in Rural India: a grassroots view*, 395-458. New Delhi: Sage.

Jeffery, P. (2005) Introduction: hearts, minds and pockets, in P. Jeffery & R. Chopra (Eds) *Educational Regimes in Contemporary India*, 13-38. New Delhi: Sage.

Jeffery, R., Jeffery, P. & Jeffrey, C. (2005) Social Inequalities and the Privatisation of Secondary Schooling in North India, in P. Jeffery & R. Chopra (Eds) *Educational Regimes in Contemporary India*, 41-61. New Delhi: Sage.

Karan, A.K. & Pushpendra (2006) Bihar: including the excluded and addressing the failures of public provision in elementary education, in S. Mehrotra (Ed.) *The Economics of Elementary Education in India: the challenge of public finance, private provision and household costs*, 106-158. New Delhi: Sage.

Karlekar, M. (2000) Girls' Access to Schooling: an investment, in R. Wazir (Ed.) *The Gender Gap in Basic Education: NGOs as change agents*, 80-114. New Delhi: Sage.

Kingdon, G.G. (1996) Private Schooling in India: size, nature, and equity effects, *Economic and Political Weekly*, 31, 3306-3314.

Lloyd, C.B., Mensch, B. & Clark, W.H. (2000) The Effects of Primary School Quality on School Dropout Among Kenyan Girls and Boys, *Comparative Education Review*, 44(2), 113-147. http://dx.doi.org/10.1086/447600

Maile, S. (2004) School Choice in South Africa, *Education and Urban Society*, 37(1), 94-116. http://dx.doi.org/10.1177/0013124504268279

Majumdar, M. & Vaidyanathan, A. (1995) *The Role of Private Sector Education in India: current trends and new priorities*. Thiruvanthapuram, Kerala: Centre for Development Studies.

McEwan, P.J. & Carnoy, M. (2000) The Effectiveness and Efficiency of Private Schools in Chile's Voucher System, *Educational Evaluation and Policy Analysis*, 22(3), 213-241.

Mehrotra, S. (Ed.) (2006) *The Economics of Elementary Education in India: the challenge of public finance, private provision and household costs*. New Delhi: Sage.

Mehrotra, S. & Panchamukhi, P.R. (2007) Universalising Elementary Education in India: is the private sector the answer? in P. Srivastava & G. Walford (Eds) *Private Schooling in Less Economically Developed Countries: Asian and African perspectives*, 129-151. Oxford: Symposium Books.

Mehta, A.C. (2004) *Elementary Education in India: where do we stand?* analytical report 2003. New Delhi: Government of India and NIEPA. http://www.eduinfoindia.net/Report/ar2003/ar2003.pdf (accessed 23 August 2004).

Mehta, A.C. (2006) *Elementary Education in India: progress towards UEE.* Analytical report 2004-2005. New Delhi: NIEPA. http://www.dpepmis.org/Downloads/AnalyticalReport2005/AnalyticalReport2005.pdf (accessed 30 October 2006).

Mizala, A. & Romaguera, P. (2000) School Performance and Choice: the Chilean experience, *Journal of Human Resources*, 35(2), 392-417. http://dx.doi.org/10.2307/146331

Nambissan, G.B. (1996) Equity in Education? Schooling of Dalit Children in India, *Economic and Political Weekly*, 31(16/17), 1011-1024.

Nambissan, G.B. & Sedwal, M. (2002) Education for All: the situation of Dalit children in India, in R. Govinda (Ed.) *India Education Report: a profile of basic education*, 72-86. New Delhi: Oxford University Press.

North, D.C. (1990) *Institutions, Institutional Change and Economic Performance*. Cambridge: Cambridge University Press.

North, D.C. (1992) Institutions and Economic Theory, *American Economist*, 36(1), 3-6.

Page, E. (2005) Negotiation and Compromise: gender and government elementary education, in P. Jeffery & R. Chopra (Eds) *Educational Regimes in Contemporary India*, 178-196. New Delhi: Sage.

Panchamukhi, P.R. & Mehrotra, S. (2005) Assessing Public and Private Provision of Elementary Education in India, in S. Mehrotra, P. Panchmukhi, R. Srivastava & R. Srivastava (Eds) *Universalizing Elementary Education in India: uncaging the 'tiger' economy*. New Delhi: Oxford University Press.

Probe Team (1999) *Public Report on Basic Education in India*. New Delhi: Oxford University Press.

Rao, N. (2000) Education: quality with quantity, *Economic and Political Weekly*, 35(48), 25 November 2000, pp 4185-4187.

Rose, P. (2005) Privatisation and Decentralisation of Schooling in Malawi: default or design? *Compare*, 35(2), 153-165. http://dx.doi.org/10.1080/03057920500129890

Rose, P. & Adelabu, M. (2007) Private Sector Contributions to Education for All in Nigeria, in P. Srivastava & G. Walford (Eds) *Private Schooling in Less Economically Developed Countries: Asian and African perspectives*, 67-87. Oxford: Symposium Books.

Schneider, M. & Buckley, J. (2002) What Do Parents Want from Schools?: evidence from the Internet, *Educational Evaluation and Policy Analysis*, 24(2), 133-144. http://dx.doi.org/10.3102/01623737024002133

Schneider, M., Teske, P. & Marschall, M. (2000) *Choosing Schools: consumer choice and quality of American schools*. Princeton: Princeton University Press.

Singh, I. (1995) Restructuring School Education, in I. Singh (Ed.) *School Education: some reflections*, 139-149. New Delhi: S. Chand & Company.

Srivastava, P. (2006) Private Schooling and Mental Models about Girls' Schooling in India, *Compare*, 36(4), 497-514. http://dx.doi.org/10.1080/03057920601024958

Srivastava, P. (2007a) For Philanthropy or Profit: the management and operation of low-fee private schools in India, in P. Srivastava & G. Walford (Eds) *Private Schooling in Less Economically Developed Countries: Asian and African perspectives*, 153-186. Oxford: Symposium Books.

Srivastava, P. (2007b) Low-Fee Private Schooling: challenging an era of Education for All and quality provision? in G. Verma, C. Bagley & M. M. Jha (Eds) *International Perspectives on Educational Diversity and Inclusion: studies from America, Europe and India*. New York: Routledge.

Srivastava, P. (2008a) The Shadow Institutional Framework: towards a new institutional understanding of an emerging private school sector in India. *Research Papers in Education*. http://dx.doi.org/10.1080/02671520701809783

Srivastava, P. (2008b) From School to Secretariat: crossing organisational boundaries in fieldwork, in D. Sridhar (Ed.) *Anthropologists inside Organisations: South Asian case studies*. London: Sage.

Srivastava, R. (2006) The Impasse Broken: mapping change in elementary education in Uttar Pradesh, in S. Mehrotra (Ed.) *The Economics of Elementary Education in India: the challenge of public finance, private provision and household costs*, 54-105. New Delhi: Sage.

Stromquist, N.P. (1999) The Impact of Structural Adjustment Programmes in Africa and Latin America, in: C. Heward & S. Bunwaree (Eds) *Gender, Education and Development: beyond access to empowerment*, 17-32. London: Zed Books.

Tedin, K.L. & Weiher, G.R. (2004) Racial/Ethnic Diversity and Academic Quality as Components of School Choice, *Journal of Politics*, 66(4), 1109-1133. http://dx.doi.org/10.1111/j.0022-3816.2004.00292.x

Tilak, J.B.G. & Sudarshan, R. (2001) *Private Schooling in Rural India*. Working Paper Series, No. 76. New Delhi: NCERT.

Tooley, J. (1997) Choice and Diversity in Education: a defence, *Oxford Review of Education*, 23(1), 103-116. http://dx.doi.org/10.1080/0305498970230109

Tooley, J. & Dixon, P. (2005) An Inspector Calls: the regulation of 'budget' private schools in Hyderabad, Andhra Pradesh, India, *International Journal of Educational Development*, 25(3), 269-285. http://dx.doi.org/10.1016/j.ijedudev.2004.09.001

Tooley, J. & Dixon, P. (2007a) Private Education for Low-Income Families: results from a global research project, in P. Srivastava & G. Walford (Eds) *Private Schooling in Less Economically Developed Countries: Asian and African perspectives*, 15-39. Oxford: Symposium Books.

Tooley, J. & Dixon, P. (2007b) Private Schooling for Low-Income Families: a census and comparative survey in East Delhi, India, *International Journal of Educational Development*, 27, 205-219. http://dx.doi.org/10.1016/j.ijedudev.2006.08.002

Waslander, S. & Thrupp, M. (1997) Choice, Competition, and Segregation: an empirical analysis of a New Zealand secondary school market, 1990-93, in A.H. Halsey, H. Lauder, P. Brown & A.S. Wells (Eds) *Education, Culture, Economy, Society*, 439-459. Oxford: Oxford University Press.

Wells, A.S. & Serna, I. (1996) The Politics of Culture: understanding local political resistance to detracking in racially mixed schools, *Harvard Educational Review*, 6(1), 93-118.

Whitty, G., Power, S. & Halpin, D. (1998) *Devolution and Choice in Education: the school, the state and the market*. Buckingham: Open University Press.

Woolman, S. & Fleisch, B. (2006) South Africa's Unintended Experiment in School Choice: how the National Education Policy Act, the South Africa Schools Act and the Employment of Educators Act create the enabling conditions for quasi-markets in schools, *Education and the Law*, 18(1), 31-75. http://dx.doi.org/10.1080/09539960600787317

CHAPTER 11

Global–Local Dynamics in Expanding School Choice in Singapore

LESLEY VIDOVICH & YAP MEEN SHENG

SUMMARY This chapter examines the opening up of school choice in Singapore. The establishment of privately-funded international schools for the first time in Singapore in 2005 marked a significant and symbolic policy shift further away from highly centralised government control of education characteristic of Singapore. With this reform, families were able to choose these fully privately-funded schools (provided they could afford the fees) rather than the previous model of schools selecting students on the basis of 'merit'. This initiative potentially challenges the long-standing governing ideology of 'meritocracy' in Singapore. The chapter analyses the policy processes involved from the macro level of elite economic agencies, to the meso level of the Ministry of Education to the micro level of the new privately-funded international schools.

Introduction

The phenomenon of globalisation provides the broader context for this analysis of school choice in the Singapore setting. In an era of a 'global knowledge economy' education moves to centre stage in public policy making as it produces the human capital – in the form of the knowledge, skills and attitudes of students entering the workforce – to enhance national positioning in the global marketplace. Thus, international economic competition becomes a key driving force behind government-initiated education reform.

Globalisation has been defined in a multitude of ways, most of which point to the greater interconnectedness of the world. Bottery (2006) identifies many different forms of globalisation, including economic, cultural, political and environmental, but he maintains that it is economic globalisation which sets the framework; it 'captures the discourses' of the other forms of globalisation. The 'boom' in school choice policies, in all of their variants from forging quasi-markets within public education sectors to growing for-profit private education sectors, sits firmly within the ideological framework of neo-liberalism accompanying globalisation. Globalisation, however, is not necessarily an omnipotent, top-down pressure forcing standardised policy 'solutions' on passive nation-states. Green (1999), amongst others, has emphasised that while globalisation has facilitated a transfer of common policy discourses across many countries, there is less evidence of convergence of specific structures and processes, as revealed in his comparative study of education policies in Europe and East Asia. In the reporting of his study, he identified Singapore as a 'state developmentalist' model of education and training (along with Japan, South Korea, Taiwan) based on distinguishing contextual factors: 'the specific forms of East Asian capitalism; the nature and role of the "developmental state"; the historical evolution of traditional Confucian and "familiaristic" patterns in East Asian culture and society; and the effects of Japanese colonialism and occupation in the "Tigers"' (Green, 1999, p. 62). Thus, Green has brought to the fore the importance of localised, context-specific differences within an umbrella of globalisation, and such an approach is also the foundation of this current chapter. We argue here that in Singapore, the repositioning of education to serve the global knowledge economy has been a primary impetus for a symbolic shift in government policy on school choice through the mechanisms of simultaneous privatisation and internationalisation of secondary schooling.

The Singapore Context

Until 1956 there was no national system of education for Singapore, and education was conducted by private tutors, missionaries, clan associations and philanthropists. Schools were established along ethnic lines, fragmenting communities of Malays, Chinese and Indians. The 1956 Report of the All-Party Committee recommended a more integrative approach to education through parity of treatment for all and the provision of a common and nationally oriented curriculum for all schools. School registration was required under the 1957 Education Act.

After independence from Malaysia in 1965, there was a critical need for Singapore to achieve national survival, social cohesion and economic competitiveness. It was a new country with a small geographical size and population, and with no natural resources. Therefore, it would rely on its human resources to establish itself as a key player on the world scene. Education would be vital in this quest and the Government invested heavily in education, retaining tight control of a highly centralised system of public education (Low & Johnston, 2001). Promulgation of an ideology of meritocracy was a central plank in Singapore's survival strategy. Within this meritocracy, there was a social trust that academic merit is an acceptable criterion for educational and social selection. This approach to meritocracy is a legacy of Confucianism, and it contrasts with a stronger critique of the notion of meritocracy in the West. Cheng (1999, p. 2) maintained that 'in a culture of meritocracy, schools will legitimately choose students, rather than parents choosing schools as a matter of rights'.

In Singapore, formal education is divided into six years of primary (with streaming for the last two years) and four years of secondary schooling. Secondary schools offer three streams – Special, Express and Normal. Students from both Special and Express streams complete their secondary education by sitting for Singapore-Cambridge General Certificate of Education Ordinary Level (O level) examinations at the end of Secondary Four. By contrast, Normal stream students may take a fifth year to reach O levels or may divert into vocational education. Post-secondary education occurs in junior colleges and polytechnics, with junior colleges being the route to university entry through Singapore-Cambridge General Certificate of Education Advanced Level (A level) examinations.

The role of education in stimulating economic growth came into sharp focus in Singapore with the economic recession of 1985, and an Economic Committee was formed to make recommendations to stimulate economic growth. In recognition that education was the key to the development of the nation's human capital, the following year, the Ministry of Education (MOE) sent 12 selected principals on a mission to the USA and United Kingdom to study the management and operation of 25 high-quality schools. Their report, *Towards Excellence in Schools*, recommended the establishment of 'independent' schools in Singapore. These schools were given flexibility in staff deployment and salaries, finance, management, and the curriculum, and they were to serve as role models to improve Singapore's education system. In 1988, three well-established government-aided boys' secondary schools (Anglo-Chinese School, The Chinese High School, and St Joseph's Institution) became 'independent' schools. Another five schools gained 'independent' status over the next five years. Further, in 1992, several government schools were turned into 'autonomous' schools, with greater autonomy and resources to introduce curricular innovations along the lines of the 'independent' schools, while at the same time keeping the fees lower than 'independent' schools. 'Autonomous' schools would provide greater parental choice and also competition for the 'independent' schools (Fernandez, 1992).

It is important to note that 'independent' and 'autonomous' schools were still considered part of the public education sector, although arguably they signified a move towards privatisation with higher fees and greater institutional autonomy. However, the Government was careful to avoid using the term 'privatisation' with its connotations of profit-making (Tan et al, 1997), and it was never the Government's intention to deregulate the whole system, but to restrict the enhanced autonomy to 'top' schools with 'top' students, consistent with its meritocratic principles. It is also important to note that in the Singapore context, education is well resourced, and public schools are recognised as being of a high quality (Cheng, 1999).

In 2005, the public education sector consisted of government schools (often referred to as 'neighbourhood' schools) (254 in number), government-aided schools (65), 'autonomous' schools (25) and 'independent' schools (11). The private sector consisted of commercial schools (805), private kindergartens (500), foreign system (international) schools (36), special education schools (21), Islamic religious schools (9), private regular schools (2) and privately-funded schools (2). Regarding the latter, the opening of these first two privately-funded schools in 2005 represented a significant shift in policy on school choice. Until that point there were only two 'private regular schools' (Methodist and Adventist) and, further, Singaporean students were not permitted to enrol in international schools. With the two new schools, there was a transition to a more market-oriented model which features parent/student (customer) choice rather than the usual *modus operandus* in Singapore of schools selecting students on the basis of merit. Below we report a study of these reforms.

Singapore as a 'Global Schoolhouse': an analysis of the policy process

This was a study of the policy process involved in establishing the first two privately funded international schools in Singapore. After Ball (1994), Taylor et al (1997), Vidovich (2002, 2007), and a growing number of other policy sociologists, for the purposes of this study 'policy' is defined broadly as a process which incorporates the factors influencing the origin of the policy, the characteristics of the policy text itself, and the subsequent effects and consequences of the policy in practice. Policy is a messy process in which the original intent by central authorities is negotiated, resisted and transformed into a multitude of (often contradictory) practices as it progresses through a trajectory from macro, to meso (intermediate level) to micro levels of an entire policy process. The subsections below present an analysis of the macro, meso and micro levels of the policy processes involved in establishing the first two privately funded international schools in Singapore, progressively over the time period 2001 to 2006.

Sources of data were documents, interviews and surveys. Interviews were conducted with six members of the policy elite from economic agencies and the Ministry of Education (coded E1 to E6) and with school managers of the two new privately funded schools (coded SM1 and SM2). Surveys were then conducted with 12 teachers (coded T1 to T12) in the privately funded schools and with 240 parents whose children attend these schools. Quotations are used in presenting the data to provide greater insights using the voices of the respondents. The data from parent surveys is presented in tabulated form (see Appendix), given the significantly larger number of respondents in this category.

Macro Level: strategic economic organisations (2001-2003)

Economic discourses prevailed in macro-level policies on globalising school choice in Singapore in the period 2001-03, which was not surprising given the leading role played by the Ministry of Trade and Industry (MTI) and its agencies. The two key policy documents were the Economic Review Committee's *New Challenges, Fresh Goals – towards a dynamic, global city* (2003) and the *Report of the Junior College/Upper Secondary Education Review Committee* (Junior College/Upper Secondary Education Review Committee, 2002).

The Economic Review Committee (ERC), chaired by the Deputy Prime Minister and Minister of Finance, was set up in 2001, when Singapore was still recovering from recession, to propose strategies to enhance growth and development of Singapore's economy (ERC, 2003). The ERC report highlighted that the Singapore Government Agencies' Charter, which required the provision of services for local residents, and not for export for economic gain, had hindered the growth of 'exportable components' such as education. Therefore, it was recommended that the country should 'unlock the public sector expertise and allow the private sector to tap on them to develop new products and services' by 'pushing on with corporatization and privatization of government agencies so that they can build on their expertise and good reputations to go global' (ERC, 2003, p. 18). Thus, deregulation to bolster Singapore's global economic positioning was firmly on the national policy agenda.

The ERC's report particularly identified education as an area where Singapore could be internationally competitive, and urged moves to capture a bigger slice of the US$2.2 trillion world education market. Therefore, steps would be taken to make Singapore into a 'Global Schoolhouse that offers a diverse and distinctive mix of quality education services to the world' (ERC, 2003, p. 4). The Minister for Trade and Industry further explained the 'Global Schoolhouse' concept in terms of relocating 'choice' from a national to an international arena:

> Asians are on the move. Over 2 billion people want a better life for themselves and their children. ... Many are therefore prepared to pay large amounts to secure the best education for their children. ... Because of Singapore's position between the First and the Third World, our multi-lingual facility and our excellent public education infrastructure, this growing education market in Asia is a major economic opportunity for us. Building on the strengths of our public education sector, we will nurture the growth of the private education sector and make education an important contributor to our economy. ... Our objective is to make

> Singapore a 'Global Schoolhouse', providing educational programmes of all types and at all levels from pre-schools to post-graduate institutions, that attracts an interesting mix of students from all over the world. (Minister for Trade and Industry, 2003)

There was a high degree of synergy between the recommendations of the ERC's *New Challenges, Fresh Goals – towards a dynamic, global city* and the contemporaneous *Report of the Junior College/Upper Secondary Education Review*. The latter was established in 2002 (during the period of the ERC's review), was chaired by the Senior Minister of State for Trade and Industry and Education, and included broad representation from the political, education, private and public sectors. It maintained that in addition to attracting foreign students, privately funded international schools could contribute to Singapore's education system by providing greater diversity and choice for Singaporean students as well as adding sources of ideas and innovative practices in education. These schools could also 'cater to children of returning Singaporean expatriates who may prefer an alternative curriculum that they are more familiar with or prepared for. They could also cater to those whose parents otherwise send them overseas for secondary /Junior College education' (Junior College/Upper Secondary Education Review Committee, 2002, p. 29).

The Junior College/Upper Secondary Education Review Committee did acknowledge that privately funded schools could introduce less meritocratic practices since admission would partly depend on ability to pay, and therefore elitism and social segregation would be an inevitable development. Nonetheless, 'on balance, the Committee supports allowing 2-3 privately-funded schools. It is envisaged that they will be operating at the periphery of the education system, catering to about 1-2% of the cohort' (Junior College/Upper Secondary Education Review Committee, 2002, p. 29). Several conditions, however, were laid down by the Committee, including that the MOE's policies on bilingualism and National Education (citizenship education) must be adhered to, and that a minimum of 50% of Singaporean students must be enrolled in the privately funded schools.

Feedback on the Committee's recommendations was sought from a wide range of national and international stakeholders including teacher, business, parent and student groups, and visits were also undertaken to schools and systems in the USA, United Kingdom, China and Hong Kong. These consultations revealed broad support for privately-funded international schools as a source of innovation and diversity, and to promote Singapore as an 'education hub'. However, consistent with the anticipation of the Committee, some concerns of elitism and socially differentiated treatment of students were raised in feedback.

In parliament, the Minister for Education emphasised that 'changing our education system is a bit like changing the tyres on a car that is moving down the road. It is a hazardous business. It is a bumpy ride for the passengers, very dangerous for the driver, even more dangerous for the one trying to change the tyres' (*Parliamentary Debates*, 2002, p. 96). These comments reflect the anxieties about risks associated with changing education policies which have been recognised as producing quality educational outcomes in a global context (with, for example, Singapore's top international ranking in the Trends in International Mathematics and Science Study). In Parliament, the Senior Minister of State for Trade and Industry and Education reiterated that the Singapore Government would continue to maintain the two important principles of meritocracy and equal opportunity, and he assured parliamentarians that the privately funded schools would not receive funding from the Government and would not be offered scholarships as any capable students would always be able to secure a place in the best public schools. Overall, opposition to the privately funded schools policy was very limited, and the *Review of the Junior College/Upper Secondary Education Report* was endorsed by the Singapore Parliament in November 2002.

With the combination of the ERC's *New Challenges, Fresh Goals – towards a dynamic, global city* and the *Review of the Junior College/Upper Secondary Education Report*, the important role for education in securing Singapore's global economic positioning had been 'driven home', especially by the Ministry of Trade and Industry (MTI) and two of its key agencies – the Economic Development Board (EDB) and Singapore Tourism Board (STB).[1] The new role played by these agencies in championing the privatisation and internationalisation of education, over and above the role of the MOE, underlines the increasingly strong economic rationale underpinning education policies in Singapore. These agencies were also pushing for an expansion of the number of privately funded schools (beyond the two or three recommended by the MOE), largely out of concern that existing private education organisations were not regulated, whereas new privately funded schools would be registered by the MOE. Economic agencies envisaged the privately funded schools performing an important function of securing the confidence of international customers that Singapore could offer quality-controlled education.

Interviews with key policy players at the macro level offered further insights, in particular about the perceived problems with the long-standing meritocratic ideology in Singaporean education and the high standards in Singaporean schools. Given that only the most 'meritorious' students were selected for the prestigious 'independent' schools (albeit still seen as part of the public education system), many parents and students were unable to exercise choice, and a rapidly growing number of Singaporean students were turning to overseas education. Concerns about the subsequent loss to Singapore were raised by the policy elite during interviews. For example, it was observed that 'they [Singapore students] were all going away because they can't make it because we are so meritocractic ... So they were all going to Australia, England and America and they were all doing well. So I think that the EDB [Economic Development Board] felt we should do more in this area' (E6). At the same time it was increasingly difficult for international students to gain entrance to Singapore's public schools because of the strong academic focus, which was seen to act against prospective foreign students seeking admission. One member of the policy elite noted that 'if we are looking at privately funded schools that are offering programmes that are not hung up on *just* academic results, but looking at wider issues of strength in other areas, then we would be able to accept international students' (E5). Another respondent highlighted the benefits of diversity for Singapore: 'The way going forward for Singapore is to have different types of Singaporeans, experiencing different types of education, because we believe that as the world goes forward there is no single way that is the right education' (E6).

Overall, at the macro level, policy to establish privately funded schools was seen as 'a good compromise between taking steps towards privatisation, but also ensuring that national objectives for the education of Singaporeans were still met' (E4). Thus, the concept of a 'Global Schoolhouse' was emerging as a significant new policy agenda driven by a combination of global economic imperatives and local issues.

Meso Level: the Ministry of Education's registration role (2003-2004)

The selection and registration of the first privately funded schools during 2003 and 2004 was the role of the MOE at the meso level of the policy trajectory. In August 2003, the MOE invited proposals for registration of privately funded schools. The MOE website emphasised the importance of social cohesion: 'privately-funded schools should meet certain requirements to ensure that all Singaporean students continue to learn and interact with one another in an environment that nurtures a Singaporean spirit and character' (Ministry of Education, 2003). In January 2004, the MOE reported the receipt of five proposals for privately funded schools. According to the MOE:

> the proposals were evaluated based on the quality of the programmes, the credibility of the operators and whether they would be a valuable addition to the education landscape ... the strength of the management team, the coherence of their curriculum offerings, and the quality of education they can potentially offer to their students. (Ministry of Education, 2004)

Although the selection process for the privately funded schools was conducted by a wholly MOE review panel (without representation by the MTI or its key agencies of EDB or STB), the EDB did approach some of the top public secondary schools to encourage their application. Further, the EDB offered capital loans to such schools to support this venture, reflecting its 'engineering' role in the enactment of the policy.

In April 2004, the MOE announced the approval of the proposals for privately funded schools submitted by two of the original 'independent' (public sector) schools: the Anglo-Chinese School and Chinese High School (later amalgamated with a Junior College to form Hwa Chong Institution). Both institutions would develop separate privately funded international schools at 'arm's length' from the parent school. These privately funded schools would be clearly identified as international schools: Anglo-Chinese School International (ACSI) and Hwa Chong International School (HCIS). With this development, moves towards enhancing both privatisation and internationalisation were symbolically brought together, and 'piggybacked' on the established reputations of prestigious public (independent) schools with their rich histories, high academic standing and strong (international) alumni networks. This was a strategy of 'brand extension'. One notable proposal rejected by the MOE was that from another elite 'independent' school, Raffles Institution, which proposed a model of a privately funded school for a 100% foreign enrolment which would be much more clearly differentiated from the parent school and would operate on a franchise-like model, including paying the parent company over S$2 million for the use of its 'brand' and facilities. The idea of privatising the Raffles 'brand' of education was actively supported by the president of Singapore Education International, a new association for advancing education businesses venturing abroad: 'Raffles would be the ultimate brand name for Singapore education. It would be like Eton or Harrow of Britain going abroad' (Davie, 2003). However, the MOE preferred a more hybrid model where privately funded international schools remained connected to their 'parent' public schools and catered for Singaporeans as well as international students.

Interviews offered further insights, particularly into the tensions between MTI (macro level) and MOE (meso level) in terms of their different 'world views'. The limited role of the MOE in the multi-agencies approach to forging privatisation and internationalisation was explained by several respondents: 'the Ministry of Education had a role to play *only* in terms of giving the rubber stamp to the programmes' (E5), and 'the role of the MOE was to provide "light touch" regulations in the area of logistical needs, teachers and programmes' (E2). While politicians and corporate leaders were very optimistic about the new policy direction, the response from the MOE appeared to be less enthusiastic. A member of the policy elite was critical of the MOE's stance:

> The MOE has excess capacity in the public school system to admit the foreign students, but they are not there yet in setting the global perspective. MOE has not been encouraging. ... STB would prefer to have more of the privately-funded schools. (E2)

According to another respondent from an economic agency: 'they [MOE] are actually really not interested in the economic aspect because they think it is not in their charter' (E5). These views were contested by an MOE respondent, who highlighted three points. First, government schools in Singapore were never designed to increase the intake of foreign students, as their top priority was to serve Singapore citizens with quality education. Second, there was the issue of the MOE's efforts in trying to keep smaller class sizes and student–teacher ratios, and this would be difficult with an increased intake of international students. Third, the MOE was concerned about how to structure the school fees of international students. One MOE respondent particularly highlighted the clash of ideologies between MTI (and its economic agencies) and MOE:

> MTI is very much driven by the economic imperatives ... for MOE, not to say that we are not supportive, but MOE is driven by much larger considerations, some are not immediately obvious in terms of dollars and cents ... MTI agencies only look at the point 'We can earn money, come on, let's earn money'. (E5)

The restricted role of the MOE in the policy enactment underlines an increasing tension between preserving traditional educational values but in a climate of needing to embrace the economic and strategic pressures of globalisation.

Micro Level: privately funded international schools – perspectives of the school communities (2005-2006)

The first two privately funded international schools – Anglo Chinese School International (ACSI) and Hwa Chong International School (HCIS) – opened in January 2005. In early 2006, data was collected from managers (interviews), teachers (surveys) and parents (surveys) at each school to obtain perspectives from the micro level of the policy trajectory.

It is noteworthy that school fees for the privately funded schools were up to 10 times that charged by 'independent' schools, which in turn were up to 10 times that charged by government schools. Early enrolments in the newly established privately funded schools fell short of expectations – ACSI enrolled 150 students and HCIS enrolled 85 students – in 2005. Both schools received a higher proportion of local to international applicants than the intended 50/50 split, but anticipated that the latter would increase with more active marketing efforts. Despite the lower than expected numbers, one school manager pointed out that she had admitted students from 15 different countries during the course of the first two years, and the other claimed, 'it is like bringing globalisation to the doors of Singapore itself instead of sending students for exchange programmes' (SM2). These observations point to the beginnings of diversifying the student mix sought in the policy intent.

Both school managers highlighted the mounting demands from parents in Singapore for choice. One manager commented that 'for a long time the Singapore education system was very centralised; highly structured with a one-size-fits-all approach' (SM1). Then, with the introduction of the privately funded schools, suddenly there was enhanced diversity and choice:

> All your life you have been fed plain white rice, now I am offering you chicken rice, you can afford to pay for the chicken rice, would you like to try? ... So it is a matter of choice ... you have an alternative to the existing systems. (SM1)

School managers of both ACSI and HCIS believed that the main reasons for parents choosing privately funded schools were that they could provide alternative curricula (ACSI offers the International General Certificate of Secondary Education and International Baccalaureate, and HCIS offers the International General Certificate of Secondary Education and Advance Placement/Foundation Programme), a wider range of activities, and also an internationalised and innovative environment for the students (Lee, 2005). Interviews with school managers also revealed that another of the 'new freedoms' enjoyed by privately funded schools was flexibility to allow high-achieving students to 'fast track' through grade levels.

In addition to interviews with two privately funded school managers, a total of 12 teachers from the two schools (32% of teachers at HCI and 14% of teachers at ACSI) completed a survey about their perspectives on these new schools in which they worked. Teacher respondents expressed very similar views across the two schools. Their opinions about the factors that led to the introduction of the privately funded schools were also relatively consistent with the data from other levels of the policy trajectory. That is, the vast majority identified globalisation and the development of Singapore as an international 'education hub' as the primary influences. One teacher respondent succinctly summarised these factors:

> Globalisation and popularisation of the concept of global citizenship; Asia's rapid economic growth; trans-Pacific investment and local schools gaining international acclaim; government initiatives to provide globally-oriented education opportunities with economic goals; and private schools as a 'waterway' to private enterprise and consumer dollars. (T10)

As with the school managers, the vast majority of teachers maintained that diversity in the curriculum, teaching and learning, and assessment were the primary attractions of the new schools, and this set them apart from the public schools.

Several teachers identified concerns. While the privately funded schools enjoyed a high degree of flexibility to attract foreign students, they faced competition from the mainstream public schools, where the availability of school-based scholarships offered high-achieving foreign students an affordable alternative conduit to the Singapore education system. One teacher respondent summed up the feelings: 'with the high barrier [cost] of entry, the impact [of the privately-funded schools] will be minimal as most Singaporeans will still be studying in government schools' (T1). Another respondent raised concerns about corporate governance and the business orientation of the privately funded schools, as well as insecurity of employment which he associated with market-driven forces characteristic of globalisation.

On the question of the impact the teachers thought the privately funded schools would have on the educational development of Singapore, responses suggested that these schools could help overcome the rigidity of Singapore's centralised structures and high stress environment resulting from the overemphasis on academic competition and achievement. One respondent explained:

> [privately-funded schools] will create demand on schools to develop their own distinctive characteristics to attract and retain local and overseas students ... This will diversify the educational provisions found in Singapore ... equalise the qualification divide and bring upon a more laissez-faire approach to government legislation of education in Singapore. (T10)

Parents – the customers – at the two privately funded international schools responded to a survey about their initial views. The whole parent population of each school was sent the survey and the response rate was 71% at HCI and 68% at ACSI. That is, there were 132 respondents from HCI and 108 respondents from ACSI. The survey used a five-point Likert scale and contained a series of items distributed across two key themes: reasons for choosing the school and expectations of future developments in the school. Patterns of parental perspectives were relatively similar across the two schools (see tables in the Appendix). Parents at both schools identified key reasons for their choice as the broad education offered (beyond a purely academic education), smaller class sizes, the presence of international students, and a curriculum which was different from that of MOE schools (in particular the International Baccalaureate at ACSI was attractive to parents). At both schools parents had high expectations for future developments in the school to focus on more individual attention to their children, student self-discipline, academic rigour, additional subjects and more international teachers. Although the patterns were similar at the two schools the particular percentages in each response category varied. Overall satisfaction was high at both schools (85% at ACSI and 70% at HCI).

Altogether, then, at the micro level of the policy trajectory, within the two new privately funded schools, school manager, teacher and parent respondents might be described as 'cautiously optimistic' about this development in enhancing school choice in Singapore.

Discussion

In expanding school choice in Singapore in the early 2000s, internationalisation was conflated with privatisation – both relatively new policies in the historically highly centralised and government-controlled Singapore schooling sector – to bolster Singapore's position in the global economic marketplace. Opening up school choice in Singapore through the introduction of the first two privately funded international schools was both symbolic (signalling engagement with globalisation and its associated market ideology) and instrumental (an experimental reform of limited scale prior to potentially wider application).

Triangulation of the data along the policy trajectory, from macro, to meso, to micro levels of the policy process, shows a high degree of consistency in identifying: policy origins as a reaction to economic globalisation; policy texts as emphasising the need for 'differentiation' and 'customisation' of Singaporean education; and subsequent practices/effects as enhancing customer choice, especially in terms of curriculum diversity. There was only limited disquiet about potential elitism and social stratification, but the initial uptake of this choice option was lower than expected, with cost being identified as a key factor. It is important to emphasise that the policy trajectory data presented in this chapter was located at a particular point in time (2001-2006) and that policy dynamics will continue to evolve. In the meantime, some tentative meta-level themes to emerge from the current study may provide 'food for thought' in Singapore and possibly other contexts, as outlined below.

Navigating Ideological Tensions

From the literature (e.g. Bosetti, 2005), enhancing school choice is highly associated with an economic ideology in education which emphasises efficiency and effectiveness as well as innovation, purportedly to increase the quality of education for all, and hence national economic positioning in the global marketplace. In Singapore, an economic ideology has underpinned education policy in the struggle for 'survival' since independence in 1965. According to Tan et al (2001, p. 13) 'economic instrumentalism was a cornerstone of schooling provision in Singapore, and economic competitiveness was the major national project'. In 2005, with the establishment of two privately funded international schools, arguably, an economic ideology was further entrenched. Although generally there was a lack of strong contestation of the policy within Singapore, the hegemony of economic discourses was not complete, as other competing discourses were also evident; in particular, discourses around educational values, meritocracy, equity and social justice, creating a web of potential ideological tensions.

First, there was evidence from the data of tensions between education-centred ideologies prevailing within the MOE at the meso level of the policy trajectory, and the strong economic ideology of the MTI and its agencies at the macro level. The MTI was forging an international student market, but the MOE could be seen as a site of resistance to a pervading economic ideology as it focused on providing quality education to local students. Second, there was evidence of some level of public reluctance to relinquish the powerful meritocratic ideology embedded in Singaporean society in order to allow families to choose privately funded schools (if they were able to afford the fees). A meritocractic ideology had been a 'social cement' in Singapore, holding together the different ethnic groups since independence, and therefore, the Government found it necessary to reiterate that choice would operate only at the margins (2% of the cohort) to preserve meritocractic principles. Third, there was evidence of concerns about the privately funded international schools policy intensifying elitism and social stratification, with implications for the ideologies of equity and social justice. Less wealthy parents could not afford to choose such schools and therefore a combination of financial and cultural capital would operate to exclude certain 'customers', leading to a re-Balkanisation of society, along class rather than necessarily ethnic lines.

On the issue of equity and social justice, Paquette (2005) has highlighted the equity challenge of enhanced choice, especially the use of public funding to support private schools, which he asserts is immoral and unethical. While the privately funded schools in Singapore would not receive direct government financial support, they could receive loans and marketing assistance as well as the benefits of 'brand extension' from their parent public schools. It will be interesting to observe if in the future the Singapore Government decides that it needs to partially fund private schools to render choice more viable for a larger proportion of the Singaporean population, and to be more attractive in the international marketplace with lower fees. Also, Olssen et al (2004) juxtapose individual freedom to choose against social justice, and they argue that choice leads to 'covert social selection'. In Singapore *overt* social selection already occurs in the mainstream with 'top' public schools choosing 'top' students and teachers, as well as having access to extra resources from fees and sponsorship. Therefore, the introduction of privately funded international schools would add a 'covert social selection' dimension, exacerbating social stratification.

Thus, in Singapore's policy of enhancing school choice through privatisation and internationalisation, economic discourses clearly dominated, but there was also evidence of other ideologies (educational values, meritocracy, equity and social justice) in potential tension. One might argue that the Government was attempting to navigate these tensions by taking a hybrid approach to policy changes, thereby reducing the perceived risks – both economically and socially – as explored in the next section.

Hybridisation and Risk Management

Hybridisation has been a feature of contemporary 'global' education policy in many countries, although it takes different forms in different locales. For example, 'third way' policies (from the UK) purportedly marry neo-liberalism and social democracy, although critics argue that these ideologies are irreconcilable. Public–private partnerships in education are a manifestation of the 'third way', and the literature reveals a burgeoning series of arguments for and against such hybridisation, although they will not be rehearsed here. In Singapore, public–private partnerships were a significant feature of the school choice reforms. The new arrangements between the privately funded schools and their parent public school partners represented a formalised collaboration between the public and private sectors, with resources drawn from each school, alumni, private investors and government-linked agencies. The government was not prepared to give full autonomy to these new schools, but a partial or 'regulated autonomy' instead.

In addition to public–private partnerships, there was a hybridisation of global and local level foci around Singapore's privately funded international schools, in terms of student composition (international as well as national students) and curriculum (international curricula such as the International Baccalaureate and International General Certificate of Secondary Education as well as national policies on bilingualism and citizenship education). There is an irony, however, that the two privately funded schools have adopted curriculum 'packages' which originate elsewhere as they work to achieve curriculum innovation, such that local (Singapore) controls are reduced at the expense of being answerable to authorities outside of the country, as these schools search for international legitimacy or currency in the global marketplace.

Sharpe & Gopinathan (2002) draw on Brown and Lauder's (1997) two ideal-type national responses to meeting the 'crisis' of global competition when they describe reforms in Singapore towards the end of the last century as a hybrid between a 'neo-Fordist' emphasis on market competition, along with concerns to increase standards on the one hand, and a 'post-Fordist' emphasis on creativity, innovation and teamwork on the other. They argue that this hybridity is a distinct feature of the Singaporean education landscape. It is clear from this study that hybridisation continues to be a major national strategy, and we would suggest that the privately-funded schools initiative not only represents another example, but it takes hybridisation to a new level.

Such educational hybridisation in Singapore might be seen as a risk management strategy in terms of shoring up economic viability, social stability and quality reputation, simultaneously. Economically, a sudden marked swing towards privately funded schools could be very risky, especially given that they are relatively unfamiliar to local Singaporeans accustomed to a highly centralised education system, and also relatively unfamiliar to customers from other Asian countries where there is a strong history of centrally-controlled public schooling. Economic viability of the privately funded schools in terms of attracting Singaporean students is dependent on customers being prepared to accept the significant extra cost involved and to forgo deeply embedded meritocratic principles. Meritocracy is also highly relevant to social stability. Both providers and customers have been cautious in approaching the privately-funded schools option so that privatisation at the margins has been a litmus test for the broader social and emotional response from the community. Regarding quality reputation, preserving the high quality of Singapore's public education, which is recognised internationally, and transferring that reputation to the new privately funded schools by 'brand extension', has been an important risk management strategy.

Thus, in developing school choice through privatisation and internationalisation, the policy elite cautiously configured hybrids of new policies with existing policies so as not to 'throw the baby out with the bathwater', especially in terms of quality educational outcomes and social cohesion.

Global–Local Dynamics

We draw towards a conclusion by returning to the phenomenon of globalisation with which we began. Arguably this is a common stimulus for accelerating school choice policies across many countries, and increasingly there are both national and international dimensions to these choices. However, to suggest that Singapore's move to enhance school choice through privatisation and internationalisation is yet another example of a nation-state 'marching to the drum' of neo-liberal global trends would be to oversimplify. Olssen et al (2004) maintain that neo-liberal policies in Organisation for Economic Cooperation and Development (OECD) countries have involved reducing bureaucratic constraints on 'free' choice, and in the process reducing the state's responsibility for provision and maintenance of quality public education. However, Singapore continues to invest strongly in education and to showcase its high-quality public sector in the international arena. In fact, the privately funded schools have been identified as 'second chance' (or second choice) institutions for those Singaporean and international students who are not selected for the most elite public schools.

This study points to Singapore as a site of active engagement with globalisation, but it also points to the cautious negotiation of global–local dynamics. That is, Singapore has tailored its policy of enhancing school choice through privatisation and internationalisation to its localised context, which relates to a number of factors: first, its history of colonisation by Britain and Japan and then its separation from Malaysia, providing a strong impetus for nation building in terms of both economic survival and social cohesion; second, its strategic location between East and West and between First and Third Worlds; third, its high investment in education as an engine for economic growth; and fourth, its strong public education sector, which can offer customers superior quality assurance compared to existing private providers. Thus, in analysing Singapore's position within 'global' trends in school choice policies, we must examine closely localised contextual factors. As we focus on the dialectic between 'the global' and 'the local' (Marginson & Rhoades, 2002), we are able to examine the 'agency' that nation-states, organisations and individuals can exert in actively negotiating policies and practices appropriate to different settings. Global policy trends are clearly evident in Singapore, but with important localised variants adapted to the specifics of Singapore's context.

As we reflect on a variety of national/local approaches to school choice we have an opportunity for critical and active policy *learning* rather than uncritical and passive policy *borrowing* to subvert homogenising pressures towards policy convergence. We finish by referring to Bosetti (2005), editor of a special edition of the *American Journal of Education* on school choice, who urges us to examine more closely the 'particularities' of different school choice policies because 'at the heart of the matter is the larger question of what constitutes the good society to which we aspire. The answer to the question directs the goals and purpose of public education in society and the appropriate role of school choice in achieving these goals' (pp. 440-441).

Note

[1] In addition to the EDB and STB, there was a plethora of other economically oriented agencies also created to support the internationalisation of Singapore's education, such as International Enterprise (IE) Singapore; Standards, Productivity and Innovation Board (PSB); and Education Services Division (Singapore Education) within the STB.

References

Ball, S. (1994) *Education Reform: a critical and post-structural approach*. Buckingham: Open University Press.

Bosetti, L. (2005) School Choice: public education at a crossroad, *American Journal of Education*, 111(4), 435-442. http://dx.doi.org/10.1086/431179

Bottery, M. (2006) Education and Globalization: redefining the role of the educational professional, *Educational Review*, 58(1), 95-113. http://dx.doi.org/10.1080/00131910500352804

Cheng, K-M. (1999) Education and Market: how could it be different and what is new? http://www.tc.colombia.edu/CICE/articles/kc112.htm (accessed 6 September 2002).

Davie, S. (2003) Raffles, *The Straits Times*, 27 October.

Economic Review Committee (ERC) (2003) *New Challenges, Fresh Goals – towards a dynamic, global city*. Singapore: Ministry of Trade & Industry.

Fernandez, W. (1992) *The Sunday Times*, 19 July.

Green, A. (1999) Education and Globalization in Europe and East Asia: convergent and divergent trends, *Journal of Education Policy*, 14(1), 55-71. http://dx.doi.org/10.1080/026809399286495

Junior College/Upper Secondary Education Review Committee (2002) *Report of the Junior College/Upper Secondary Education Review Committee*, Ministry of Education, Singapore.

Lee, L. (2005) Going International, *The Straits Times*, 3 January.

Low, L. & Johnston, D. (2001) *Singapore Inc: public policy options in the third millennium*. Singapore: Asia Pacific Press.

Marginson, S. & Rhoades, G. (2002) Beyond National States, Markets and Systems of Higher Education: a glonacal agency heuristic, *Higher Education*, 43(3), 281-309. http://dx.doi.org/10.1023/A:1014699605875

Minister for Trade and Industry (2003) Speech. http://www.sedb.com/edb/sg/en_uk/index/news_room

Ministry of Education (2003) http://moehqap64/project

Ministry of Education (2004) http://www.moe.gov.sg/press/2004/pr20040412

Olssen, M., Codd, J. & O'Neil, A. (2004) *Education Policy*. London: Sage.

Paquette. J. (2005) Democratic Education and School Choice Revisited, *American Journal of Education*, 111(4), 609-616. http://dx.doi.org/10.1086/431186

Parliamentary Debates (2002) *Singapore Official Report*, November 2002. http://www.moe.gov.sg/icreview/parliament.htm

Sharpe, L. & Gopinathan, S. (2002) After Effectiveness: new directions in the Singaporean system? *Journal of Education Policy*, 17(2), 51-166. http://dx.doi.org/10.1080/02680930110116507

Tan, J., Gopinathan, S. & Ho, W-K. (1997) *Education in Singapore*. Singapore: Simon & Schuster.

Tan, J., Gopinathan, S. & Ho, W-K. (2001) *Challenges Facing the Singapore Education System Today*. Singapore: Pearson Education.

Taylor, S., Rizvi, F, Lingard, B. & Henry, M. (1997) *Educational Policy and the Politics of Change*. London: Routledge.

Vidovich, L. (2002) *Expanding the Toolbox for Policy Analysis: some conceptual and practical approaches*. Hong Kong: Comparative Education Policy Research Unit, Department of Public and Social Administration, City University of Hong Kong.

Vidovich, L. (2007) Removing Policy from Its Pedestal: some theoretical framings and practical possibilities, *Educational Review*, 59(3), 285-298. http://dx.doi.org/10.1080/00131910701427231.

APPENDIX
Parent Surveys

Hwa Chong International School (HCIS): parent survey

	Strongly agree %	Agree %	Undecided %	Disagree %	Strongly disagree %
Reasons for choosing					
Studying with international students	26.00	48.10	13.70	12.20	0.00
Broad education	31.30	39.80	21.10	6.25	1.56
IGCSE Programme	16.90	33.10	30.80	10.00	9.20
Foundation Programme	18.80	46.10	22.70	7.80	4.70
Flexibility of subject combinations	21.50	43.10	23.80	8.46	3.08
Smaller class sizes	38.50	33.80	16.90	8.46	2.31
Selected teachers	25.40	28.50	33.10	9.23	3.85
Lower fees than other international schools	14.00	18.60	24.00	24.80	18.60
Co-education	13.80	33.10	26.20	19.20	7.69
Boarding accommodation	15.20	9.85	26.50	23.50	25.00
Recommendation of other parents	12.90	24.20	19.70	27.30	15.90
Location within Singapore	16.80	19.10	19.80	29.00	15.30
Affiliation with Hwa Chong/Chinese High	31.30	31.30	22.10	10.70	4.58
Asian tradition and culture	24.60	30.20	26.20	7.69	5.38
Expectations					
Individual attention	38.60	40.90	14.40	2.27	3.79
Self-discipline	36.60	33.60	33.60	5.34	2.29
Academic rigour	29.20	45.40	45.50	1.54	0.77
Additional subjects	32.80	40.50	40.50	6.87	3.82
More international teachers	26.00	35.90	35.90	15.00	3.05
Wider co-curricular programme	25.20	33.60	33.60	14.50	2.29
More performing arts	18.30	25.20	25.20	20.60	6.11
More sports	22.10	24.80	24.80	14.70	5.50
More information to parents	20.00	28.00	33.00	16.00	3.00
Further facilities	21.00	27.00	38.00	11.00	3.00

Overall satisfaction	17.40	53.70	16.50	9.10	3.31

IGCSE: International General Certificate of Secondary Education (both schools).

Anglo-Chinese School International (ACSI): parent survey

	Strongly agree %	Agree %	Undecided %	Disagree %	Strongly disagree %
Reasons for choosing					
Studying with international students	32.40	40.00	9.50	8.60	9.50
Broad education	67.30	29.80	1.90	1.00	0.00
IGCSE Programme	35.50	36.40	18.70	5.70	3.70
IB Programme	59.50	25.30	12.20	1.00	2.00
Flexibility of subject combinations	51.40	39.00	8.60	1.00	0.00
Smaller class sizes	91.50	7.40	1.10	0.00	0.00
Selected teachers	63.00	25.90	9.30	1.80	0.00
Lower fees than other international schools	15.20	19.20	21.00	29.40	15.20
Co-education	7.40	37.00	12.00	34.30	9.30
Boarding accommodation	5.60	9.40	16.80	34.60	33.60
Recommendation of other parents	6.50	17.80	16.80	28.00	30.90
Location within Singapore	12.10	18.70	12.10	27.10	30.00
Christian institution	41.70	25.90	14.00	12.00	7.40
ACS tradition	45.30	22.70	21.60	7.30	3.10
Expectations					
Individual attention	71.60	26.60	1.80	0.00	0.00
Self-discipline	66.00	25.50	5.50	2.00	1.00
Academic rigour	52.30	34.90	9.20	2.80	0.80
Additional subjects	24.80	39.00	22.80	10.50	2.90
More international teachers	50.00	27.80	13.00	4.60	4.60
Wider co-curricular programme	40.00	33.30	17.20	8.10	1.00
More performing arts	37.80	27.80	26.70	6.70	1.00
More sports	41.65	30.30	18.00	7.90	2.20
More information to parents	47.90	35.10	9.60	5.30	2.10
Further facilities	46.60	17.20	29.30	5.20	1.70

Overall satisfaction	27.50	57.80	11.00	28.00	0.90

IGCSE: International General Certificate of Secondary Education (both schools)
IB: International Baccalaureate (ACSI only)

CHAPTER 12

Japanese Shadow Education: the consequences of school choice

JULIAN DIERKES

SUMMARY Deregulation has been a prominent aspect of Japanese educational reform discussions for the past 25 years. These discussions often refer explicitly to global discourses on school choice in general, and to British and North American debates in particular. National policy has enabled local education boards to establish school choice for primary and secondary schools. Some municipalities have implemented various forms of school choice. Although choice is being introduced into parents' and students' decision making at the primary and secondary level, it has been an important aspect of Japanese educational experiences for over 30 years in the form of supplementary, or 'shadow' education. The experience with shadow education suggests that school choice is more conducive to producing a variety of organizational forms within an education market than to producing curricular diversity.

Two Aspects of School Choice in Contemporary Japanese Education

School choice has been on Japanese academics' and policy makers' minds for about a decade. In this chapter, I will focus on two aspects of the implementation of school choice in Japan. First, I will give an overview of the introduction of school choice in public primary and secondary education. Secondly, I will discuss the Japanese 'shadow education' system as a long-standing implementation of an educational market, i.e. of significant choice for students and parents.

Arguments for the introduction or expansion of parental and students' choice among public schools have mainly been built on two observations and claims: First, the economic stagnation following the burst of the Japanese economic bubble in the early 1990s brought about much hand-wringing about the causes of stagnation. Particularly in the late 1990s the apparent success of the US-based 'new economy' led many Japanese commentators to flag a lack of creativity and entrepreneurialism as one of the causes of stagnation. School choice, and the presumed competition that would result, was seen as one possible remedy for the lack of a diversity of offerings within Japanese education.

Secondly, the 1990s saw the culmination of a long-term trend of a prestige reversal between public and private primary and secondary schools in metropolitan Japan. While this trend is largely limited to central Tokyo, it has led to a significant decline in the trust and confidence in public education. Placing public schools in a competitive relationship with one another through the introduction of school choice is often presented as one possible remedy for this perceived decline in the quality of public education. The introduction of 'school choice' in this context has been an element in an overall effort aimed at the liberalization of education.

While school choice in the public education system has only been introduced in the early years of the millennium, parents and students have had a significant level of choice for some time. Private schools are a particularly common option at the upper secondary level where approximately 30% of all students attend private institutions. Further choice is available in the for-profit 'shadow education' system.

My examination of school choice and the shadow education system in Japan illustrates two aspects of the globalization of school choice. Public discussions of educational policy make it clear that 'choice' is a relevant term of reference and Japanese policies are thus responding to a policy paradigm that has been well institutionalized at the global level. The implementation of school choice shows, on the other hand, that references to 'school choice' are primarily metaphorical and do not imply very specific policies. The policy discourse is clearly substantially decoupled from any specific policies. Even more striking is the fact that one possible implementation of school choice, namely an entirely voluntary, for-profit shadow education system has existed in Japan for some time, yet it has only begun to be discussed in the context of school choice.

School Choice in Japanese Public Education

Japanese educational reforms since the mid-1980s have revolved around the themes of individualism, diversification, and flexibility, as well as marketization and liberalization (Fujita, 1997, p. 40). Fujita compares the recent trends in Japanese education reform with US and British trends and concludes that the rationale for reforms varies widely across contexts. In fact, the ultimate motivations for reform would seem to be diametrically opposed, although similar ideologies support arguments for reform (1997, p. 28). Fujita traces these opposite motivations to different histories of education (p. 41). While some of the aims of recent reforms in the USA and Britain have been to improve students' overall academic attainments, Japanese reforms have focused on the diversification of the education system (Fujita, 1997, p. 41). Underlying some of these reforms is the overarching goal of 'catching up' with 'the West' (Fujita, 1997, p. 71). There is a general belief in Japan that since the country has long caught up with Western nations economically, what is now required is the creation of individualistic and creative personalities to lead the world (Fujita, 1997, p. 73).

The School Choice Discourse in Japan

The introduction of 'school choice' is one example of the muddled nature of recent educational reforms. It was in the 1980s that 'school choice' emerged as a reform trope in Japan. As Yasui (2003, p. 2) writes, 'In March 1984, the Kyoto Group for the Study of Global Issues published a policy proposal for education reform; this became the first systematic attempt to propose school choice that had a substantial impact on policy arguments'. The report recommended introducing school choice in order to stimulate competition in education, and drew at least in part on Milton Friedman's proposal of school vouchers (Yasui, 2003, p. 28). The discussion of school choice was continued by the 'Ad Hoc Council on Education' established by then-Prime Minister Yasuhiro Nakasone. Yet, partly due to the Ministry of Education's opposition, the idea was not realized at the time (Yasui, 2003, pp. 32-33), as was the case with many of Nakasone's reform proposals (Schoppa, 1991). However, by the mid 1990s, the situation changed. After the Ministry of Education's discussion of the 'flexible use of the school attendance catchment area system' in 1997, Kiho town in Mie Prefecture introduced school choice at the lower secondary level in 1998 and Shinagawa ward in Tokyo did so in 2000 (Fujita, 2005, p. 140).

Varieties of School Choice

The Japanese education system consists of six years of primary school, three years of junior high school, three years of senior high school, and four years of university. Primary and junior high school education is compulsory. Based on the School Education Law, these schools are 'administered and financed by local school boards and municipalities' (Yasui, 2003, p. 20). Students are assigned to a public school based on catchment area, which is established by local school boards.

The school choice system consists of five types: free choice, block choice, neighbouring-area choice, specially approved schools, and a specific area choice system (Ministry of Science and Education [MEXT], 2006, p. 3). The free choice system allows students to choose any school within their municipality. The block choice system divides a municipality into blocks, and students can attend any schools within the block in which they live. The final three varieties all maintain regular school catchment areas. The neighbouring-area choice system permits students to go to schools within neighbouring wards. The specially approved school system allows students to attend certain schools within the municipality. The specific area choice system gives permission only to those students who live in a particular area to choose their school. Schools are granted various level of authority over selection of students, typically based on entrance examination scores.

As of 2004, 8.8% of municipalities with more than one school have introduced a school choice system at the primary school level, and 11.1% of them have introduced it for lower secondary schools (MEXT, 2006, pp. 1, 10). Some 95 municipalities for primary school and 89 for junior high school have actually implemented these changes (Fujita, 2005, pp. 140-141).

Aims of the Japanese School Choice System

Proponents echo various discontents towards public education, and use them as the basis for supporting the school choice system (Fujita, 2005, p. 148). First, there is a general anxiety about the worsening school environment due to problems such as bullying, violence, and classroom disruption, and parents do not want their children to go to the schools where these issues are apparent. Second, parents and the public are not satisfied with the quality of teachers and with educational leadership. Third, there are many complaints about schools and teachers for not listening to students and parents. Fourth, there is widespread dissatisfaction with standardization. Fifth, people are discontent with public schools that lack the ability to reform themselves. Finally, since the 1980s, criticism by government, educational institutions, and the media has exacerbated the general decline in confidence in public education without offering much specific evidence. The last three reasons question the very function of uniform compulsory education. Critics thus seem to favour the notion of 'freedom of choice' as a supreme value grounded in neo-liberal thoughts and philosophies (Fujita, 2005, p. 151). Importantly, the competitive market mechanism implied by school choice is intended to encourage those schools that are unpopular to reform themselves, and thus improve the overall quality of schools (Fujita, 2005, p. 80).

Shinagawa Ward and the Unfolding of the Japanese School Choice System

To examine the unfolding of the school choice system, Shinagawa ward may serve as a useful example. Shinagawa ward is one of the 23 wards of the city of Tokyo. It is just to the south-south-east of the central downtown business and government areas in Tokyo. It is well-known for Shinagawa Station, one of the Shinkansen stations in Tokyo. Surrounding the station are commercial developments and, further to the South, *Shitamachi* ('downtown') residential areas.

Shinagawa was one of the first to introduce school choice as a part of its 'Plan 21'. This plan aims at current discontents and criticisms by taking into account issues such as 'teaching approaches that meet individual needs', 'creation of schools with special characteristics' and 'improvement of educational quality' (MEXT, 2006, p. 13). In 2000, Shinagawa implemented the block choice system at the primary level, which separated the school districts into four blocks. Within these blocks, students and their parents are free to choose any school. In 2001, school choice was introduced at the junior high school level, allowing students to attend any of the 18 schools within the ward. Parents in Shinagawa ward who availed themselves of free choice at the primary school level increased from 12.9% to 22.9% between 2000 and 2006 (MEXT, 2006, p. 14). At the junior high school level, the number increased from 22% to 29% between 2001 and 2006.

While it may be still too early to evaluate the impact of school choice as mediated by schools' efforts to distinguish themselves among ward schools, some observers have suggested that the school choice system does not do what its advocates claim that it would. One argument that supporters make is that the school choice system would promote schools to have diverse characteristics in order to attract students. However, parents do not seem to put schools' unique features as a top priority when choosing a school. Fujita proposes three criteria for choosing a school: excellence, safety, and distinctiveness of schools (2005, p. 157). He claims that what matters the most is excellence and safety, while distinctiveness becomes important only when the other two standards are met (pp. 157-158). The case of Yashio Minami junior high school in Shinagawa ward provides evidence to support Fujita's claim. The junior high school did not have any newly enrolled students in spring 2006 (the beginning of the Japanese school year) despite the fact that it became a six-year secondary school by combining it with a high school to attract students last year (Asahi Shimbun, 2006a). The loss of new students was caused by a vicious cycle; the fewer students a school has, the fewer parents tend to choose the school (Asahi Shimbun, 2006a).

This point was also supported by the research conducted by Junichiro Yasui and by Arakawa ward in Tokyo. Yasui examined the school choices of Shinagawa parents whose children entered elementary schools in 2000 (2003, p. 57). According to Yasui, parents were most concerned with the number of students and their advancement to prestigious high schools, followed by factors such as 'proximity to school and length of commute', 'students' and/or parents' friends', and 'impression at school visits' (Yasui, 2003, p. 72). On the other hand, parents did not see curricular characteristics as an important criterion for selecting a school, despite the contrary expectation of the Shinagawa school board (Yasui, 2003, p. 73). Similarly, Arakawa ward school board found that parents emphasized the number of students, 'distance to school' and 'same as friends' the most, while 'distinctive features of education' was the fourth criterion (Asahi Shimbun, 2006b). Therefore, although proponents of choice emphasize the importance of school choice in relation to the diversification of schools as a way to meet individual students' needs, parents do not see this as the most important feature when choosing a school.

The school choice system seems to have created a gap between popular and unpopular primary schools in Tokyo. The ratio of applicants to places is 25 in Itabashi ward, 14 in Arakawa ward, and 6 in Eto ward (Asahi Shimbun, 2006b). This means that not all students can enter the school they want to attend, and thus free school choice cannot be realized (Fujita, 2005, p. 164). Furthermore, Fujita claims that the gap between popular schools and unpopular schools will eventually lead to a ranking of schools (p. 155) as is already happening in Adachi ward in Tokyo. The ranking of schools could generate various unintended secondary influences such as the extension of academic competition to enter primary school, unequal educational opportunities resulting from institutional discrimination, and access differences in relation to socio-economic status (Fujita, 2005, p. 155).

Although 'school choice' and its broader policy discourse cousin, 'liberalization', remain dominant in politicians' discussions of education reform, the implementation of these aims remains somewhat incomplete. Initial evaluations of the attempts at implementation that have been undertaken suggest that the desired outcomes are difficult to evaluate and perhaps even more difficult to achieve. Additionally, unintended consequences may well overwhelm any benefits that result from the introduction of school choice.

Shadow Education: the ultimate school choice

In contrast to the formal education system, 'shadow education' (Stevenson & Baker, 1992) has offered a much more developed model of school choice to Japanese parents and students on a large scale at least since the 1970s. The for-profit afternoon and evening *juku* that constitute this shadow education system offer a particularly fruitful environment for testing some of the supposed beneficial effects that school choice has on education according to its advocates.

Visitors to Japan frequently comment on seeing school-age children emerge from juku late in the evening. Such observations are often coupled with outrage at the perceived need for children to attend such schools. But in a recent survey of satisfaction with education, over 70% of Japanese parents indicated that 'cram schools' were doing a better job educating their children than public schools (Asahi Shimbun, 2005). Is there a connection between the fully marketized nature of the shadow education system and parents' satisfaction with or confidence in juku?

Education Markets and their Impact on Varieties of Learning

Policy makers advocating the introduction of market mechanisms in education generally welcome the rise of options for parents and students in selecting educational 'service providers' (Davies & Quirke, 2005). This advocacy is based on a presumed logical sequence of choice leading to competition between educational institutions, leading in turn to innovation, and finally to a more responsive and generally better education system.

After tallying the results of studies that examined innovation in charter schools in Canada and the United States, Lubienski (2003, and in this volume) concluded that although charter schools were characterized by significant administrative innovation, their curricular practices remained somewhat traditional, replicating existing models. Lubienski qualified this finding by pointing out that the decision to send a student to a charter school is far removed from a decision made within a perfect market. He focused on 'push' as well as 'pull' factors in creating imperfect education markets. On the consumers' side, he saw obstacles to diversity in conservative parental preferences, the lack of consumer information, and in market failures (2003, pp. 419-421). For producers, he highlighted the mimicry of competitors' practices, corporate organizational forms, and market differentiation.

However, the examination of charter schools only constitutes a weak test of the claim that market mechanisms will lead to more variegated educational offerings. Similar limitations apply to policy contexts where more radical voucher systems have gone further than North American charter schools in approximating markets. A primary limitation to marketization is the need for education markets to establish themselves over extended periods of time. These limitations and caveats do not apply to the shadow education system in Japan. One might go as far as to claim that shadow education systems in densely populated metropolitan areas may constitute the closest empirical approximation to an education *market* that we might observe at the primary and secondary level. Aside from Japanese cities, Hong Kong and metropolitan areas in Taiwan and South Korea might provide parallel examples.

Geographical dispersion within Tokyo is not much of a concern for parents and students selecting a cram school, since the very well-developed transportation system and its frequent usage by children and youth put almost all parts of metropolitan centres within a student's reach for the juku, which are usually not held every day. From my visits to suburban juku it has emerged that a distance of over 90 minutes from the circular Yamanote train line demarcates central Tokyo for commuters. The shadow education system also allows for greater mobility among schools as students are free to leave particular schools and enter new schools in the course of the academic year. The for-profit nature of cram schools includes an immediate feedback between a perceived decline of quality and sanctions in the form of students voting with their feet. Students' decisions can then quickly question the economic viability of a particular school. The long-standing and well-entrenched for-profit shadow education market in Japan thus offers a strong test of the impact of market mechanisms on the variety of educational offerings.

While parental preferences might be as conservative in Japan as elsewhere, shadow education has flourished for more than 30 years, providing opportunities for shifts in parental preferences. Japanese shadow education institutions compete in a public market that offers detailed comparisons of the success of schools in placing students in higher education institutions. The concentration of the Japanese population in cities coupled with increasing disposable income since the mid-1970s have created conditions approximating very active consumer markets, with some clear market failures, but few obvious obstacles. While the copying of competitors' practices is widespread among shadow education institutions, truly innovative practices should have had opportunities to overcome such copying as well as the obstacles represented by 'corporate capture'. Finally, Japanese shadow education institutions have differentiated their offerings to an amazing degree, but such differentiation should have created opportunities for innovation given the extent to which it has occurred. In sum, the obstacles to the implementation of a market logic perceived by researchers to exist in North America do not exist in the Japanese shadow education system; schools operating in this system thus offer a unique opportunity to test the applicability of a market-logic in a mature education market.

A Brief Overview of the Japanese Shadow Education System

Juku have always been acknowledged as a prominent component of the postwar Japanese education system. Rooted in pre-modern *terakoya* (temple schools), juku grew in importance and prominence during the so-called 'juku-boom' of the 1970s to become a common element in Japanese trajectories of educational attainment, reaching more than half of all students by the time they complete secondary education by some estimates (Yuki et al, 1987; Amano, 1990). The recent liberalization of Japanese curricula under the slogan of *yutori kyoiku* (variously translated as 'education for life', 'free education' and 'quality education') seems to be prompting another juku-boom based on parental fears that curricula have been watered down.

Any scholarly discussion of the Japanese education system includes statements about the importance of shadow education and the impact of 'examination hell' in structuring students' education (for example, Rohlen, 1983; Takeuchi, 1995). Yet, little empirical research on juku has been published in English (for the main exception, see Tsukada, 1991). The Japanese literature on juku is also sparse. The Japanese Ministry of Education and the Japan Broadcasting Corporation conducted superficial surveys in the 1980s and 90s that yield little more than summary statistics of juku attendance, but do not differentiate between types of juku attended and offer no information on prevalent teaching styles. Given the importance attributed to juku as a locus of exam preparation, a large how-to literature on juku exists. Recently, these manuals have been joined by polemics by juku teachers, journalists, and policy makers.

Although observers point to shadow education as a very important element of education, the Japanese Ministry of Education does not regulate juku as educational institutions. Instead, juku fall under the purview of the Ministry of Economy, Trade and Industry (METI) as a service industry. The lack of official regulation of juku as educational institutions has meant that very little statistical information on these schools is available. The lack of regulation and of focused academic attention also indicates a lack of legitimacy that shadow education carries in the eyes of the public, of academics, and of policy makers. Ironically, juku operators claim that the children of teachers and education bureaucrats almost universally attend shadow education institutions.

Some Observations on Diversity in the Shadow Education Market

Juku can be classified broadly into *gakushujuku* (academic juku) and those directed at various artistic endeavours, technical training, or English conversation skills. The finest distinctions between various academic types can be made in metropolitan regions where the plethora of juku offerings has led to a high degree of specialization. Urban juku typically stratify their students by ability and are themselves stratified similarly. Remedial instruction (*hoshu*) is distinguished from accelerated instruction and exam preparation (*juken* or *shingaku*).

Roesgaard (2006) classifies juku along eight different dimensions: competitive vs. nurturing environments; focus on entrance examinations vs. concentration on current schoolwork; connection to regular schooling; academic grouping of students; teaching materials used; size of the school in terms of students attending and number of branches, if any; admission procedures; and the nature of advertising. For Roesgaard these variables add up to a continuum of juku types clustered around four distinct varieties: 1. *shingaku* juku with their focus on exam preparation; 2. *hoshu* juku concentrating on remedial work; 3. *kyosai* juku that cater to students in danger of falling between the cracks of educational institutions for academic or social reasons; and 4. *doriru* juku that offer little instruction, but instead focus on the practising of basic skills.

Juku are organized in a number of regionally fragmented associations, making a national inventory of juku impossible. A representative of the National Juku Federation suggested to me that there are currently approximately 50,000 juku in operation, enrolling 500,000 students; these estimates were echoed by a METI official.

During 2006 and 2007 I visited 12 juku in metropolitan Tokyo. Visits to the juku included interviews with their operators as well as classroom observations. In classroom observation I focused on classes directed at elementary and middle (lower secondary) school. Classes were offered in all academic subjects commonly taught at these levels: Japanese, Arithmetic/Mathematics, English, Science, and Social Studies. When given a choice I mostly observed instruction in Japanese and mathematics. While I visited most juku once for an entire 'school day', I have made repeat visits to three juku and have spent a total of five days at a further school.

Contact with juku was generated through a network of juku operators associated with one of the national juku associations. The observed juku constitute a somewhat particular set within the metropolitan juku market. They ranged in student numbers from 30 to 1300, although most of them had fewer than 100 students enrolled. All but one of the juku have been operating for over 25 years and were thus founded during the first juku-boom of the 1970s. Having remained in operation for this long, they are clearly successful in attracting students, yet they have also not grown into the corporate giants that have come to be concentrated near major train stations. Almost all of these schools are in locations somewhat removed from transportation hubs and they thus largely draw on students in their immediate neighbourhood. Most of the schools are located in central Tokyo, although three of them are in outlying suburbs. All operators interviewed could be portrayed as charismatic educators. Their thoughtful and eloquent responses to my interview questions as well as their participation in various juku and general education study groups suggest that they are engaged in debates about educational policy as well as teaching practices.

My selection of small and medium-sized academic juku excludes franchises and chains of schools, schools focused exclusively on university entrance examination preparation for high school graduates (*yobiko*), and schools offering instruction through various media and technologies (online, satellite lectures, *kumon* and other supervised self-study). While corporate and franchise juku are playing an increasingly important role in the Japanese education system, the lack of an existing understanding of what actually occurs within juku as well as difficulties in accessing corporate juku have prompted my focus on smaller and medium-sized schools.

This project explores whether the increasing integration of educational institutions in market relations promotes a variety of learning environments and thus educational choices as the outcomes of education are seen to be increasingly commensurable with quantifiable standards. The overwhelming conclusion so far is that while the shadow education market is highly differentiated in terms of the use of different delivery techniques and in terms of targeting minutely specified customer groups (e.g. remedial mathematics instruction for fourth-year elementary school students in Tokyo aiming for a mid-level prestigious private middle school), there are no fundamentally different conceptions of education or of learning in evidence in this differentiation. To put it in other terms, while juku operators have pointed me to several 'unique' schools, none of these are, for example, based on a fundamentally different conceptualization of pedagogy. To put it more succinctly, there are no Waldorf juku. Instead, differentiation only occurs on the assumption of a common conceptualization of teaching and learning, as well as on the basis of the public school curriculum and its attendant implementations in textbooks and entrance examinations.

While the Japanese shadow education system is rife with choice of different delivery techniques and formats, it appears not to have produced much variety in terms of a fundamentally different educational philosophy. Surprisingly, some diversity of offerings that is present in schools is not replicated among juku. While a subset of Japanese parents and students continue to prefer single-sex education, my question to juku operators about single-sex juku was met with puzzlement. Most juku operators interpret a preference for single-sex education to be rooted in a traditional attitude toward gender relations or in alumni (especially alumnae) loyalty, in contrast to some views in North America and parts of Europe where a single-sex classroom is seen as offering advantages particularly to girls in mathematics and the sciences.

The marketization of juku has led to a very high degree of differentiation of offerings in the market and of significant innovation of teaching techniques and delivery methods, but it has done so in lockstep with the official school curriculum and in replicating the evaluation criteria specified by the conventional system of education.

Shadow Education Classroom Settings

Classroom observations have given a sense of the pedagogy presented in shadow education institutions. It should be noted that my research only focuses on schools where there is a live teacher present in front of a group of students, not on individual tutoring or various worksheet methods.

Individually-operated juku (*kojinjuku*) generally are of a fairly uniform appearance and many of them could be described as somewhat dingy. Frequently found on the ground floor of private residences, juku are often divided in a fairly haphazard fashion into classrooms that are stuffed to the ceiling with informational materials about education. Classroom furniture is identical to the ubiquitous Kokuyo line of classroom furniture in schools and is generally arranged in a conventional form of rows of students facing a teacher standing by a blackboard. The crammed quarters coupled with aging furniture and the generally bad lighting make these classrooms appear as if juku operators are not especially concerned about the appearance of their classrooms or about the conduciveness of furnishings to learning. Some of the juku I have visited boasted dedicated instruction facilities that were purpose-built, however. The largest of these even offered students the use of a small library and a school bus system that picked children up and delivered them back home after instruction.

As students stream into these juku in the mid afternoon (the first class for elementary school students generally starts at 16.00 or 16:30 in line with the hours of Japanese schools and the club activities that students often engage in after school), the atmosphere in the schools is transformed quickly, however, and contrasts with conventional schooling become apparent. The overwhelming impression of the atmosphere in juku classrooms, especially in contrast to other learning settings in Japan, is one of informality. While juku operators and teachers are generally addressed as '*sensei*' (teacher, with some elements of an honorific address) or '*jukucho*' (juku principal), this is not consistently the case. The polite and honorific terms that are often demanded by school teachers are generally dropped in juku.

While this is not the case for all teachers I have observed, juku teachers engage students in a fair bit of banter before classes begin and often even during classes. Students share stories from their schools (most juku enrol students from multiple schools) and include the juku teachers in this conversation. Such stories often include jokes and are accompanied by laughter among the students. Juku teachers walk through the classroom and engage in conversations of this sort with individual students before, during and after instruction.

Conversations between students and teachers are generally not limited to banter, but also include reports of progress in learning by students and of their results in various tests. These reports are characterized by a frankness that certainly surprised me. As the most extreme form of such self-disclosure of academic success in a learning setting, I observed a frequently recurring pattern of juku teachers seeking volunteers who were unable to answer specific questions or solve particular problems, and then asking these volunteers subsequently to find the answer. While stereotypes as well as some social scientists see Japanese students generally as reticent participants in classroom activities (McVeigh, 2002), students in this extramural education setting readily self-identify themselves as being unable to complete a task in front of the teachers and their fellow students, full knowing that this will lead to them being called upon to perform the required task in front of everyone. However, it is also clear that as class size grows across different juku and different classes, larger classes are more like conventional schooling with lectures to a largely passive student body, than the more interactive format I saw in smaller groups.

This example of a classroom atmosphere of marked difference to formal Japanese classrooms also illustrates another feature of most juku teaching, namely the reliance on textbooks and worksheets in class for all subjects. While some juku devise their own teaching materials and others purchase materials made available by corporate juku and large publishing houses dedicated to the publication of teaching materials, all juku rely on textbooks and problem sets in some fashion. Very frequently, these materials replicate the structure of problems posed in school textbooks, which are also in and of themselves relatively uniform (Dierkes, 2005). Materials used in the juku classroom draw on the curriculum and school textbooks in that they replicate identical problems in their structure and, often, multiply the same kind of exercise several times for practice purposes. While these repetitions do offer an opportunity for students in the juku classroom to ask questions of the teacher (which they do with great frequency), they do not approach a similar topic from an entirely different direction. English instruction that is focused on grammatical patterns, vocabulary and English-to-Japanese translation/understanding retains this focus in juku classrooms.

Just as juku shadow 'official' education, so does the teaching materials publishing industry shadow Ministry of Education-approved textbooks. Publishing houses like Ikushinsha as well as juku-spin-offs like Yotsuya Otsuka thus offer collections of problem sets that follow the structure and content of the curriculum and of official textbooks closely. Private schools have even begun to substitute the official textbooks with alternatives published by teaching materials publishers. Juku as well as these publishers seem to exist in the 'cracks' of the education system. For example, publishers do not show an imprint on the spine of alternative textbooks and they do not include a copyright or library cataloguing block that is otherwise universal in published materials. At the same time, these textbooks do not seem to depart significantly from official textbooks with the one exception that they often include material that harks bark to older curricula and goes beyond the current curriculum with its reduced content as of 2002 (leading juku operators to speak of a '2002-problem' as one of the causes of the current growth in student enrolment).

Possible Explanations for Substantive Overlap between Schools and Juku

Some researchers have turned to neo-institutional theory to explain the lack of diversity in education markets. Neo-institutional theory in sociology was initiated by John W. Meyer's work on educational organizations (Meyer, 1977). Meyer concluded that schools are focused on seeking legitimacy rather than on optimal educational outcomes. A somewhat similar argument is used by advocates of choice, who point to supposedly ossified administrative structures as the culprit for the lack of innovation and excellence in public schools (Chubb & Moe, 1990). Through DiMaggio & Powell's (1983) analysis of isomorphism in organizational structures and Granovetter's (1985) discussion of structural embeddedness as a key feature of market actors, institutional analysis has thrived as a theoretical paradigm in economic sociology for the past 20 years. These theoretical foundations have stressed legitimacy and the uncertainty of economic actors in producing homogeneity in organizational behaviour across entire organizational fields. Leaving direct regulation aside, isomorphism is thus posited to arise from normative and mimetic pressures on economic actors.

Davies et al (2006) argue that Canadian teachers and parents are socialized to value traditional curricula, precluding the emergence of innovative niches in elite private education. For 'third sector' private education, where little legitimacy is conferred by the institutional environment, they find great variety in curricula. In elaboration of this finding, I hypothesize that education markets that are organized around collectively agreed-upon outcomes (i.e. standardized tests) force for-profit education businesses into highly isomorphic offerings, rather than opening the door for an increased variety of teaching content and methodologies. This would hold especially under circumstances of a general lack of legitimacy of the shadow education system, which is reflected by the lack of attention paid to this element of education by Japanese policy makers and researchers. This assertion echoes Lubienski's (2005) contention that marketized environments push schools toward an increased focus on marketing, rather than curricular innovation.

In the context of the Japanese shadow education system, it should be noted that this entire sector is generally seen as somewhat illegitimate. In the current near-panic about 'the decline of academic abilities' (*gakuryoku teika*, akin to the German 'PISA-Shock' of 2002) various forms of privatization and liberalization are back on the educational policy-making agenda. Surveys of students and parents like the one cited above attribute great pedagogical value to juku instruction. Anecdotal accounts also suggest that many teachers and educational policy makers send their children to juku. Juku operators as well as some journalists suggest that the shadow education system should be increasingly integrated into the conventional system of schooling. Yet, despite all these factors lending some legitimacy to shadow education, this business is still portrayed as an 'insecurity industry' (*fuan sangyo*). Rather than providing a true alternative to conventional school, juku thus continue to shadow conventional education and to follow the dictate of the standardized testing that dominates Japanese primary and secondary education. When the overarching goals and their measurement in an educational system are standardized and legitimate, even vibrant education markets may – in the end – not lead to much diversity of a fundamental kind.

The Interaction between School Choice and Shadow Education

Of course, the fully marketized shadow education system and marketizing of public education are intimately intertwined, particularly in the metropolitan education market of the greater Tokyo region. Here especially, juku serve as a buffer between increasingly concerned parents and the highly differentiated market of public and private primary and secondary education. School choice at the senior secondary (grades 10-12) level had preceded the introduction of choice at the primary and lower secondary level on the basis of its status as non-compulsory education. Until the early years of this decade, the Tokyo metropolitan region was thus divided into educational districts spanning up to four wards. Controversial governor Shintaro Ishihara removed this last constraint on school choice in 2003 and Tokyo residents thus face a choice of approximately 500 public and private high schools. Just as the shadow education market has become highly differentiated by serving smaller and smaller niches of target populations, so have the profiles of senior secondary schools become more differentiated.

Obviously, perceived academic prowess remains the dominant criterion of structuration of this highly differentiated senior secondary school market. Thick manuals are published regularly by the large publishers that constitute another facet of *jukensangyo* (examination industry), detailing the number of applicants to particular schools as well as their success in placing their graduates in employment or universities. This latter criterion especially leads to a collectively agreed-upon hierarchy of schools stretching from Japan's most famous and highly regarded Hibiya High School to the technical high schools of outlying or more blue-collar dominated wards.

While the examination industry provides some technical assistance in slotting aspiring middle school graduates into the 'appropriate' rank of high school that they might apply for on the basis of standardized tests, even within the group of schools that might be attainable for a particular students, a bewildering number of schools are offering their services.

Despite the overall loss of confidence in (public) education and its ability to secure lifelong careers for graduates of particular schools, parents in metropolitan regions clearly attach an inordinate amount of importance to minute differences between particular schools. It is this insecurity about making important choices for their (typically single) child that has opened up a vast demand for educational advising that is served by juku. According to some juku operators, parents and students are not satisfied with merely targeting a particular class of schools that seems to be a good match for a students' abilities and achievements, but they are lining up an increasingly extensive and specific list of criteria in selecting particular schools. From such formal markers as co-educational or parochial (Christian or Buddhist) education to such more detailed information as a school's ambitions for its baseball team (perhaps not championship materials – too much pressure and distraction from schooling – but ambitious nevertheless) and the perceived fashionableness of a school's uniform, juku operators draw on their long-term knowledge of this educational market in advising parents and students on their choice.

Some Conclusions: standardization or diversity?

I have tried to show that school choice has become a prominent feature of debates about educational policy in Japan. While implementation remains somewhat hesitant and incomplete, it seems clear that for the foreseeable future, marketization and choice will be one of the organizing principles of the Japanese education system. I have also tried to point to the lack of a clear basis for the introduction of these policies in the reality of Japanese education. Yet, the overall disenchantment with public education has left policy makers grappling for radical solutions that may or may not be related to some of the perceived problems being faced by education.

One of the main goals of the introduction of school choice in Japan – as elsewhere – is the fostering of competition and the presumably attendant diversity in educational offerings this competition will breed. By examining the for-profit shadow education market, I have tried to point to some indications that it is not diversity in teaching approaches that the education market produces, but rather a minute differentiation of educational offerings to target populations that remains wedded to the overall educational philosophy represented by Japanese curricula and entrance examinations.

My discussion of school choice in Japan, its implementation in the official education system as well as its continuing prominence in the form of the shadow education system, shows that Japan is clearly participating in a global rhetorical rush towards choice as framing education systems. My analysis also shows, however, that the global school choice policy paradigm can be and is interpreted in highly localized fashion and that the implementation of this paradigm at the national level is highly dependent upon the selective adaptation of associated educational philosophies, concepts and policies.

Acknowledgement

The research reported here was made possible by a Standard Research Grant from the Social Sciences and Humanities Research Council of Canada. Research assistance by Michiyo Hayase, especially on recent educational policies aimed at school choice in Japan, is gratefully acknowledged. I am also heavily indebted to Kazuyuki Hirabayashi for introducing me to an entire universe of Tokyo juku and to many juku operators for their ready willingness to be interviewed and to be observed in their classrooms.

References

Amano, Ikuo (1990) *Education and Examination in Modern Japan.* Tokyo: University of Tokyo Press.

Asahi Shimbun (2005) *'Gakko yori juku ya yobiko ga yushu' Oya no 7wari Naikakufu ga Shochosa* [In a first-time survey by the Cabinet Office, 70 per cent of parents declare *juku* and *yobiko* superior to schools]. October 7, 2005. http://www.asahi.com/edu/news/TKY200510060270.html

Asahi Shimbun (2006a) *Kyoiku 'sentaku' nosue nyugakusha zero* [Zero new students as a result of 'choice'], September 27, 2006. http://mytown.asahi.com/tokyo/news.php?k_id=13000270609270001

Asahi Shimbun (2006b) *Koritsukosentakusei niyoru ninkido: Shokiboko, Toshibu de Sakibosori* [Popularity based on the school choice system in public primary schools: tapering off among small scale schools and schools in urban areas], July, 31, 2006. http://www.asahi.com/edu/news/TKY200607310206.html

Chubb, John & Moe, Terry (1990) *Politics, Markets and American Schools.* Washington, DC: Brookings Institution.

Davies, Scott & Quirke, Linda (2005) Providing for the Priceless Student: ideologies of choice in an emerging educational market, *American Journal of Education*, 111(4), 523-547. http://dx.doi.org/10.1086/431182

Davies, Scott, Quirke, Linda & Aurini, Janice (2006) The New Institutionalism Goes to Market: the challenge of rapid growth in private K-12 education, in H.-D. Meyer & B. Rowan (Eds) *The New Institutionalism in Education.* Albany: SUNY Press.

DiMaggio, Paul & Powell, Walter (1983) The Iron Cage Revisited: institutional isomorphism and collective rationality in organizational fields, *American Sociological Review*, 48(2), 147-160. http://dx.doi.org/10.2307/2095101

Dierkes, Julian (2005) The Stability of Postwar Japanese History Education amid Global Changes, in E. Vickers & A. Jones (Eds) *History Education and National Identity in East Asia.* London: Routledge.

Fujita, Hidenori (1997) *Kyoikukaikaku: Kyoseijidai no gakko zukuri* [Education reform]. Tokyo: Iwanami Shoten.

Fujita, Hidenori (2005) *Gimu Kyoiku o Toi Naosu* [Reassessing compulsory education]. Tokyo: Chikuma Shinsho.

Granovetter, Mark (1985) Economic Action and Social Structure: the problem of embeddedness, *American Journal of Sociology*, 91(3), 481-510. http://dx.doi.org/10.1086/228311

Lubienski, Christopher (2003) Innovation in Education Markets: theory and evidence on the impact of competition and choice in charter schools, *American Educational Research Journal*, 40(2), 394-443. http://dx.doi.org/10.3102/00028312040002395

Lubienski, Christopher (2005) Public Schools in Marketized Environments: shifting incentives and unintended consequences of competition-based educational reforms, *American Journal of Education*, 111, 464-486. http://dx.doi.org/10.1086/431180

McVeigh, Brian (2002) *Japanese Higher Education as Myth.* Armonk: M.E. Sharpe.

Meyer, John W. (1977) The Effects of Education as an Institution, *American Journal of Sociology*, 83(1), 55-77. http://dx.doi.org/10.1086/226506

Ministry of Science and Education (MEXT) (2006) *Shogakko/Chugakko ni okeru gakko sentaku seido nitsuite Jireishu* [Case studies of the school choice system in primary school and junior high school]. http://www.mext.go.jp/a_menu/shotou/gakko-sentaku/06041014/001.pdf

Roesgaard, Marie Højlund (2006) *Japanese Education and the Cram School Business – functions, challenges and perspectives of the* juku. Copenhagen: Nordic Institute of Asian Studies Press.

Rohlen, Thomas (1980) The *Juku* Phenomenon: an exploratory essay, *Journal of Japanese Studies*, 6(2), 207-242.

Rohlen, Thomas (1983) *Japan's High Schools*. Berkeley: University of California Press. http://dx.doi.org/10.2307/132321

Schoppa, Leonard (1991) *Education Reform in Japan – a case of immobilist politics*. London: Routledge.

Stevenson, David & Baker, David (1992) Shadow Education and Allocation in Formal Schooling: transition to university in Japan, *American Journal of Sociology*, 97(6), 1639-1657. http://dx.doi.org/10.1086/229942

Takeuchi, Yo (1995) *Nihon no meritokurashii: Kozo to Shinsei* [Japan's meritocracy: structure and mentality]. Tokyo: Tokyo University Press.

Tsukada, Mamoru (1991) *Yobiko Life: a study of the legitimation process of social stratification in Japan*. Berkeley: Institute of East Asian Studies.

Yasui, Junichiro (2003) *School Choice in Japanese Education Reform (1980-2002): implication for educational equity*. MA dissertation, Stanford University School of Education.

Yuki, Makoto, Sato, Akira & Hashisako, Kazuyuki (Eds) (1987) *Gakushujuku* [Academic *juku*]. Tokyo: Gyosei.

Notes on Contributors

Janice Aurini received her PhD from McMaster University in 2006, and was a Postdoctoral Fellow at Harvard University in 2006-07. She is currently an Assistant Professor in the Department of Sociology at the University of Waterloo, Canada. Her interests include sociology of education, organisations, qualitative methods and sociology of culture. She has published studies of new educational businesses in *Sociological Forum*, *Canadian Journal of Sociology* and *Canadian Review of Sociology and Anthropology*. Her current research compares changing parenting cultures among urban upper middle-class families in Canada and the United States.

Scott Davies is Professor of Sociology and Ontario Research Chair in Educational Achievement and At-Risk Children at McMaster University, Canada. He is also an associate editor of *Canadian Public Policy*, and sat on the editorial boards of *Sociology of Education*, *American Journal of Education* and *Sociological Inquiry*. His research interests include studies of markets, social movements, organisations, and stratification in education. His current projects are on school choice, comparisons of Canadian and American higher education, and the use of school organisations in other societal sectors. He has won awards from the American Educational Research Association and the Canadian Society for Studies in Education.

Julian Dierkes received his PhD in sociology from Princeton University, USA and is an assistant professor and the Keidanren Chair in Japanese Research at the Institute of Asian Research of the University of British Columbia, Canada where he also is the associate director of the Centre for Japanese Research. He has examined portrayals of the nation in history education in Japan and East and West Germany and has completed a manuscript on this topic, entitled 'Guilty Lessons? Postwar History Education in Japan and the Germanys'. He has also done research on the integration of the teaching of formal mechanisms of conflict resolution in graduate legal education in Japan. Julian's current research focuses on Japanese education reform and the for-profit nature of 'shadow education' (juku) within Japanese education.

Martin Forsey lectures in Anthropology at the University of Western Australia. He teaches introductory anthropology, as well as Australian culture and society and the anthropology of organisational enterprises. Martin's research interests include the organisational culture of schools, school choice and educational reform and he has written about ethnographic method, neo-liberal reform of schooling and organisational change. His monograph, *Challenging the System? A Dramatic Tale of Neo-liberal Reform in an Australian Government High School*, was recently published by Information Age Publishing.

Andrew Kipnis is a Senior Fellow in the Contemporary China Centre and the Department of Anthropology, Research School of Pacific and Asian Studies, The Australian National University, Canberra. He is author of *Producing Guanxi: sentiment, self and subculture in a North China village* (Duke University Press, 1997), *China and Postsocialist Anthropology: theorizing power and society after communism* (Eastbridge Books, 2008) and is co-editor of *The China Journal.* He is currently working on a book on 'education fever' in the People's Republic of China and often travels to China for both research and pleasure.

Christopher Lubienski is an Associate Professor of Education Policy in the Department of Educational Organisation and Leadership at the University of Illinois, Urbana-Champaign, USA where he studies the political economy of education. He received his PhD in education policy from Michigan State University, and completed post-doctoral training at Brown University and with the National Academy of Education. His research focuses on the intersections of public and private interests in education policy in areas such as school choice, charter schools, voucher programmes, and home schooling. His work has appeared in journals such as the *American Educational Research Journal*, the *American Journal of Education*, and *Educational Policy*.

Mariano Narodowski is a professor at Universidad Torcuato Di Tella in Buenos Aires, Argentina and currently the Minister of Education for Buenos Aires City. He was a John Simon Guggenheim Fellow 2002 and a Visiting Scholar at Harvard University, USA in 2006.

Izhar Oplatka is a senior lecturer in the Programme of Educational Administration and Policy in the Department of Education, Ben Gurion University, Beer Sheva, Israel. His current areas of interest are school marketing and school choice, career and career development of teachers/principals, and the foundations of educational administration as a field of study. He has published in a wide variety of journals in education, among them *Educational Administration Quarterly*, *Comparative Education Review*, *Journal of Education Policy*, *British Journal of Educational Studies*, and *Journal of Educational Administration*. He is the co-editor of *Women Principals in a Multicultural Society: new insights into feminist educational leadership* (with R. Hertz-Lazarowitz, Sense Publishers, 2006).

Kristin D. Phillips is a joint PhD. candidate at the University of Wisconsin-Madison, USA in the departments of Anthropology and Educational Policy Studies. Her research interests include rural political culture, the politics of poverty, educational development in East Africa, and the anthropology of food and hunger. She is currently (2007-09) a pre-doctoral fellow at the University of Virginia's Carter G. Woodson Center for Afro-American and African Studies where she is writing her doctoral thesis on educational development and the production of rural citizenship in central Tanzania. Her article, 'The Gendered Regime of Women's Work: a view from Tanzanian Internet cafés', appeared in *Women's Studies Quarterly* in 2003.

Prachi Srivastava is Assistant Professor at the new School of International Development and Global Studies, University of Ottawa, and Visiting Research Fellow with the Centre for International Education, University of Sussex. She received her doctorate from the University of Oxford, and has previously held posts as Lecturer in Education at the University of Sussex, and as Economic and Social Research Council Post-doctoral Research Fellow at the Department of Educational Studies, University of Oxford. Dr Srivastava has worked for international NGOs in the Balkans, and has also served with the United Nations Interim Administration Mission in Kosovo. She continues to provide expertise to a number of international NGOs in the area of education sector reform in developing and conflict-affected countries. Her research interests include: the marketization and privatisation of schooling in South Asia; school choice and access in economically developing countries; and applications of new institutional theory to educational governance. Dr Srivastava has published nearly a dozen journal articles and book chapters on the privatisation of schooling in India and international research methodology. Her work on low-fee private schooling in India led to an invited report for the Government of India, and to UNESCO as invited expert for the 2009 Education for All Global Monitoring Report. Her co-edited book, *Private Schooling in Less Economically Developed Countries: Asian and African perspectives,* was published in 2007 by Symposium Books.

Amy Stambach is Associate Professor of Educational Policy Studies and Anthropology at the University of Wisconsin-Madison, USA. Her work examines the intersections of religious belief, educational practices, policy and politics in East Africa and the United States. She is currently working on a study of non-denominational church networks across East Africa and North America. Among her publications are 'Revising a Four-Square Model of a Complicated Whole: on the cultural politics of religion and education' (*Social Analysis*, 2006), 'Rallying the Armies, Bridging the Gulf: questioning the significance of faith-based educational initiatives in a global age' (*Indiana Journal of Global Legal Studies*, 2005) and 'Feminist Theory and Education Policy: how gender is "involved" in family–school choice debates' (with Miriam David, *Signs*, 2005).

Lesley Vidovich is an Associate Professor of Education at the University of Western Australia. Her professional career has spanned both schooling (where she was a science teacher, curriculum developer and tertiary entrance examiner) and higher education sectors. Her primary research focus is the field of education policy and practices – both in the schooling and higher education sectors – with a special interest in education policy development in a context of globalisation and internationalisation. While she has published research on a wide range of policy domains, her largest volume of work has been on quality/accountability policy and curriculum policy. She has conducted research in a number of different countries, and papers stemming from her research have been published in international journals based in the United Kingdom, continental Europe, North America, Asia and Australia. She has recently completed an Australian Research Council Grant project on higher education policies and practices in mainland China, Hong Kong Special Administrative Region and Singapore.

Geoffrey Walford is Professor of Education Policy and a Fellow of Green College at the University of Oxford, United Kingdom. He is the author of more than 100 academic articles and book chapters. His books include: *Life in Public Schools* (Methuen, 1986), *Privatization and Privilege in Education* (Routledge, 1990), *City Technology College* (Open University Press, 1991, with Henry Miller), *Doing Educational Research* (Routledge, editor, 1991), *Choice and Equity in Education* (Cassell, 1994), *Policy, Politics and Education – sponsored grant-maintained schools and religious diversity* (Ashgate, 2000), *Doing Qualitative Educational Research* (Continuum, 2001), *Private Schooling: tradition and diversity* (Continuum, 2005) and *Markets and Equity in Education* (Continuum, 2006). Within the Department of Education at the University of Oxford he teaches on the MSc in Educational Research Methodology course, and supervises doctoral research students. He is Editor of the annual volume, *Studies in Educational Ethnography*, and has been Editor of the *Oxford Review of Education* since January 2004. His research foci are the relationships between central government policy and local processes of implementation, private schools, choice of schools, religiously-based schools and ethnographic research methodology.

Yap Meen Sheng is an Assistant Director at the Ministry of Education, Singapore. He has held teaching and senior management positions in various junior colleges, government schools and independent schools. He then ventured into the private sector in mid career as director of a multinational consortium before rejoining the Education Service. Meen Sheng's interest is in school change and education policy. He has spoken in various international conferences in Korea, China, Hong Kong, the United Kingdom and Australia.

Oxford Studies in Comparative Education

Series Editor: David Phillips

Lessons of Cross-national Comparison in Education, ed. David Phillips, 1991

Education and Economic Change in Eastern Europe and the Former Soviet Union, ed. David Phillips & Michael Kaser, 1992

Something Borrowed, Something Blue? A Study of the Thatcher Government's Appropriation of American Education and Training Policy, Parts 1 & 2, ed. David Finegold, Laurel McFarland & William Richardson, 1992

Key Issues in Educational Development, ed. Terry Allsop & Colin Brock, 1993

The University and the Teachers: France, the United States, England, Harry Judge, Michel Lemosse, Lynn Paine & Michael Sedlak, 1994

Developing Schools for Democracy in Europe, ed. John Sayer (with others), 1995

Aspects of Education and the European Union, ed. David Phillips, 1995

School Choice and the Quasi-market, ed. Geoffrey Walford, 1996

Global Perspectives on Teacher Education, ed. Colin Brock, 1996

Education and Change in the Pacific Rim, ed. Keith Sullivan, 1998

Education and Privatisation in Eastern Europe and the Baltic Republics, ed. Paul Beresford-Hill, 1998

Education for Reconstruction: the regeneration of educational capacity following national upheaval, Nina Arnhold, Julia Bekker, Natasha Kersh, Elizabeth McLeish & David Phillips, 1998

Processes of Transition in Education Systems, ed. Elizabeth A. McLeish & David Phillips, 1998

Comparing Standards Internationally, ed. Barbara Jaworski & David Phillips

The Education Systems of the United Kingdom, ed. David Phillips, 1999

Education in Eastern Germany Since Unification, ed. David Phillips, 2000

Opening Windows to Change: a case study of sustained international development, ed. John Sayer, 2002

Faith-Based Schools and the State: Catholics in America, France and England, Harry Judge, 2002

Can the Japanese Change Their Education System? ed. Roger Goodman & David Phillips, 2003

The InstitutionS of Education, William K. Cummings, 2003

The Challenges of Education in Brazil, ed. Colin Brock & Simon Schwartzman, 2004

Educational Policy Borrowing: historical perspectives, ed. David Phillips & Kimberly Ochs, 2004

New Approaches to Vocational Education in Europe, ed. Regina H. Mulder & Peter F.E. Sloane, 2004

Political and Citizenship Education, ed. Stephanie Wilde, 2005

Partnerships in Educational Development, ed. Iffat Farah & Barbara Jaworski, 2006

School History Textbooks Across Cultures, ed. Jason Nicholls, 2006

Education's Abiding Moral Dilemma, Sheldon Rothblatt, 2007

Reforming Teaching Globally, ed. Maria Teresa Tatto, 2007

Private Schooling in Less Economically Developed Countries, ed. Prachi Srivastava & Geoffrey Walford, 2007

Exploring Cross-national Attraction in Education, Jeremy Rappleye, 2007

Aspects of Education in the Middle East and North Africa, ed. Colin Brock & Lila Zia Levers, 2007

The Changing Landscape of Education in Africa, ed. David Johnson, 2008